HENRY HODGES

ARTIFACTS

AN INTRODUCTION
TO EARLY MATERIALS
AND TECHNOLOGY

HUMANITIES PRESS • NEW JERSEY
JOHN BAKER • LONDON

First published 1964 by
John Baker Publishers Ltd
35 Bedford Row   London WC1R 4JH

Reprinted 1965, 1968, 1971, 1976 (with corrections), 1981

© 1964, 1976 John Baker Publishers Ltd

ISBN 0-212-35918-5 (England)
ISBN 0-391-02246-6 (U.S.A.)

Printed in the United States of America

For

H. M. J. and **E. M. J.**

Strew'd above and around,
On the hearth, on the table, the shelves and the ground,
All sorts of instruments, all sorts of tools,
To name which, and their uses, would puzzle the Schools,
And make very wise people look very like fools.

— Ingoldsby, *Legends*

PREFACE

When this book first appeared in print some twelve years ago it had been written because there seemed to be a need for an annotated glossary of technological terms for the archaeologist and the ethnographer, especially of those terms used by the vanishing and erstwhile craftsman. At the same time it was felt that both archaeologists and anthropologists might gain a great deal by exploring in greater detail the materials used by man, and the means he employed to fashion them. The book therefore examined the methodology of analysing the materials and techniques of the past. Unfortunately space did not allow a description of anything beyond what might be called the primary technologies, and the more elaborate applications of man's handiwork, such as agriculture, building and transport, could barely be touched upon.

The choice of a suitable terminology proved to be more difficult than might have been anticipated. Not only was the number of tools and processes to be defined enormous, and hence had to be reduced to a manageable number, but also it was found that various craftsmen were habitually using the same term to describe rather different things, while in some cases the identical tool or operation had acquired a large number of names. Under these circumstances it seemed prudent to list only those terms in most common use and to define all terms as they are most normally used by the craftsmen. A further difficulty lay in the fact that some misnomers, never used by the appropriate craftsmen, were so deeply ingrained in the archaeological and ethnographic literature that it was felt advisable to include them in the text, although not to encourage their continued use.

Clearly a book of this nature had to concern itself primarily with pre-industrial, or more correctly non-industrial, materials and techniques. However, since I have never been able to discern, nor ever found the need to define, the interfaces between archaeology, ethnography and folk-life studies, the book was written with a deliberate disregard for either time or place. Not being clairvoyant, I was at the time unable to foresee the new direction towards historical and early industrial archaeology that my colleagues were to take. That the book proved to be of some use in both these fields was, therefore, no more than a happy accident.

In previous printings of the first edition a number of minor changes had already been made in the text so that it was felt that no further alterations needed to be made in the present edition. The bibliography, however, could not be left as it stood and has been revised and updated to include those books which seem best to amplify the text. Here again, sadly, I have had to be selective, and have included, where possible, only those books which are reasonably available.

In the Introduction to the first edition I acknowledged the help given to me by Miss Mavis Bimson, Miss Joan Sheldon, Dr. Ian Cornwall and Mr. Robert Organ in preparing this book. I would like to renew those thanks and add my gratitude for their continued help and friendship over the years. At the same time I also thanked Miss Bernadette Davies for typing my manuscript. Today, as my wife, she has far more to contend with than my poor handwriting, and I find it impossible adequately to thank her.

H. W. M. Hodges

Queen's University
Kingston, Ontario
1st December 1975

CONTENTS

ILLUSTRATIONS

TABLES

FLOW DIAGRAMS

INTRODUCTION

As THIS BOOK has been written mainly for those interested in archaeology, something must first be said about the bearing that the study of early technology has on archaeological theory, for the connection between the two subjects is not immediately apparent. Admittedly a great deal of archaeological classification depends entirely upon technological considerations: indeed, the Three Age system, in which the whole prehistoric period of the Old World is divided into Stone, Bronze and Iron Ages, is an example of a classification derived initially to a very large degree from material and technological studies.

It would be true to say that archaeologists are on the whole more con-concerned with technique than with technology: their methods are classically those of the art historian in which stylistic detail is observed and recorded, and in which stylistic change over the years is accepted as a phenomenon to be expected without necessarily examining the precise cause. The study of styles and their changes is, of course, essential to archaeological theory, and without it there could be no working hypothesis. Equally, the study of technology must always be, to the archaeologist at least, of secondary importance, for a history of technology, no matter how complete, cannot pretend to describe more than a single aspect of the past of mankind. Nevertheless, the contribution that technological studies make, or could make, to our understanding of the past is enormous.

Perhaps the most obvious field in which technological studies can supplement the more normal archaelogical methods is the examination of raw materials and their sources, for through them we can often get unexpected information about early trade. The systematic study of the petrology of neolithic stone axes in the British Isles is a single example of this line of enquiry; and it has shown not only how widely stone axes were traded in antiquity but has also provided valuable evidence of their chronology.

Less obvious, but just as important, is the information that can be derived from the study of the spread of a technique of manufacture. Occasionally it can be shown that people who shared little or nothing in common, to judge by normal archaeological criteria, were in fact using similar methods of manufacture, although applying them to quite different classes of objects. This can probably be seen nowhere better than in the techniques of bronze casting in the Old World, in which ideas were borrowed, adapted, elaborated and transmitted steadily over a long period, but were, even so, as often as not applied to peculiarly local types of bronze implement.

By contradistinction it not infrequently happens that in the past attempts were made to copy artifacts by craftsmen who were not conversant with the essential techniques. The copies may in fact be so close to the prototypes that without proper examination the originals and the copies may, on stylistic grounds, become classified as a single type,

13

thereby giving the erroneous impression that there was a far greater degree of interdependence between one people and another than actually existed.

What is true of the study of methods of manufacture is equally true of the study of the formulation of compounded materials, such as alloys and glasses. These substances were often made from a number of different raw materials, the complexity and proportions of which might vary considerably. Detailed examination of compounded substances of this kind have often shown quite unsuspected changes of formulation. The addition of lead to the copper-tin alloy, bronze, is typical of this kind of change, a modification which in fact spread to become virtually ubiquitous throughout the Old World in the Bronze Age.

At times technological studies may be necessary to correct impressions gained by an uncritical examination of the styles of artifacts alone. It is unfortunate that pottery, on which so much archaeological theory must of necessity depend, is of all things the most dependent in style on the materials that go into its making. One cannot make superlative pottery in a region in which the only available clays are of a poor quality: a technique of manufacture although perfectly satisfactory when applied to one type of clay may be quite fruitless when applied to another. In making comparisons between pottery from different regions it is thus essential to consider first the nature of the local clays. Differences of technique may result not from different traditions, but only from expediency dictated by the raw material itself. It is also unfortunate that any one clay, as a result of relatively small alterations in its preparation, application and firing, can be made to produce a wide variety of textures and colours. It is only after the material has been given thorough examination that one can decide whether variations of this kind were the intention of the potter or due to the vagaries of his methods of production.

This book, however, is not concerned directly with the application of technological findings to archaeological theory but with the more limited problem of showing how useful technological data is gathered. The examination of an artifact with this end in mind is not a simple haphazard affair but a painstaking study, often quite unrewarding, based upon a knowledge that a raw material, when treated in a particular way, will behave in a characteristic manner. This is fundamental to the study and because of it the larger part of the book is devoted simply to a description of the materials available to early man and the methods he commonly used to fashion them.

The reason why technological studies have not already played a greater role in archaeology becomes apparent when one surveys the methods of examination that must be applied to the artifacts. As a general rule it would be true to say that, because systematic examination of the kind required demands a specialized education, the work that has been done so far in this field has been carried out not by those whose initial training was that of an archaeologist but by those whose living depends upon the application of the necessary techniques of examination to other fields of study—biologists, chemists, petrologists and metallurgists. It is obviously impossible to review fully all the methods that may be employed in a book that aims only at furnishing an introduction to the study: and those that are considered have had to be dealt with summarily. The objective of the second part of this book is primarily to show the kind of evidence for which one must look, and the limits within which any selected method of examination must be confined.

To the reader of this book whose interest may be solely that of an amateur, it should perhaps be pointed out that a survey of the fashioning and uses of materials reaching back into the early history of man is an essential—and even a fascinating and absorbing—part of the process of coming to understand our ancestors. In many fields of interest—in geology and geography, in industry, in social organization, in an appreciation of the intellectual and artistic ability of early man—this book aims to show this type of archaeological investigation as it bears on history extended into the distant past. Although many books have been written on the subject of more orthodox methods of archaeological examination—most particularly excavation—in very few indeed has the process of technological investigation been discussed. It is hoped that this book will go some way towards making good this omission.

PART I

MATERIALS AND METHODS OF WORKING

Chapter One

POTTERY

SYNOPSIS

General: Weathering · Wedging · Elutriation · Plasticity · Fillers · Clay wares · Biscuit · Glost · Flat and hollow wares. *Clay:* Kaolinite · Water of Plasticity · Sinter point · Fluxes · Maturing temperature. *Clays:* Primary and secondary · China clays · Ball clays · Red clays · Infusible and fusible clays. *Bodies:* Permeable and impermeable · Terracotta · Earthenware · Stoneware · China · Porcelain. *Fillers. Forming:* Pinching · Coiling · Slab-forming · Moulding · Jiggering · Casting · Throwing · Drawing-up · Piece-forming · Applied parts · Fettling · Shaving and turning · Burnishing · Luting. *Decoration:* Impressed · Incised · Applied · Slurry · Slip · Gloss · Encaustic · Mineral surfacing · Roughened surfaces · Smoking. *Drying.* *Kilns:* Bonfires · Updraught kilns · Pit-kilns · Downdraught kilns · Muffle-kilns · Draught-kiln fittings. *Firing Sequence:* Water smoking · Annealing · Pyrometric cones. *Firing Conditions:* Oxidizing and reducing atmospheres. *Treatment after Firing. Firing Mishaps.*

GENERAL

EVEN IN ITS most primitive form the making of pottery demands five distinct processes: digging the clay, preparing it, forming the pottery, drying and firing it.

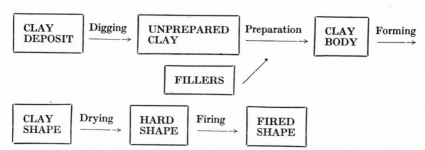

No clay immediately after digging is suitable for making pottery, for it has first to be worked into a homogeneous mass and any lumps of extraneous matter must be removed. Clay that has been quite simply dredged from the banks of rivers, lakes or ponds may be prepared for forming straight away, but clay dug from deeper deposits is not uncommonly spread out on the ground or in shallow troughs and exposed to the weather. This *weathering* has the effect of breaking down any small

19

lumps, the process normally being helped by regular turning, pommelling or treading under foot. Even finer clay may result from a prolonged period of damp storage in tubs or vats after weathering, when the clay acquires a sour smell, the process being known as *souring* or *stinking*. The final preparation of the clay before forming, *wedging*, is generally done by hand, and involves beating, thumping and rolling the clay until it is judged to be evenly mixed and all the air is expelled. Not infrequently the potter will cut the clay in half during wedging to examine its texture. Today this work is done industrially by a device, the *pug mill*, which cuts and mixes the clay, but more primitive machines rather like butter-churns with fixed projecting blades inside are of considerable antiquity.

Clay may be further refined by *elutriation*, sometimes less correctly termed *flotation* or *levigation*. The principle of this process is that the clay is mixed with water until the heavier particles have subsided. The remaining fluid is then decanted and the finer clay allowed to settle out of this. The process may be carried out in a small way using tubs or on a large scale employing settling tanks.

Pottery need not be, and today seldom is, made only from a clay prepared in this way, for generally other ingredients are added. The reason for this may be simply to produce a different colour, but far more commonly solid materials are added because the clay is found to be too *plastic*. Such clays are sticky or greasy to handle and shrink seriously on drying, being referred to by potters as *long*, *rich*, or *fat*. Equally a clay may be too *aplastic* to work, the material being crumbly, also known as *short*, *mealy*, *lean*, or *open*. A clay that is too plastic may be modified by adding a fine material such as sand which will not shrink on drying. Flint may also be added, often being calcined and ground first to break it down, or some of the clay itself may be fired and ground down to serve the purpose. Broken or spoilt pottery is commonly used, and while the term *grog* is general amongst all potters to denote the addition of fired clay, some potters also use the terms *pitchers* and *sherds* (or *shards*) to mean the same thing. Any material added to a clay to reduce plasticity may be referred to as a *filler*. Some potters use the term grog in this wider sense or refer to *opening materials;* some archaeologists use the term *backing*, and others *temper*. Both these latter terms are alien to the potter's terminology, and on the whole seem redundant. A clay that is too aplastic, on the other hand, can be improved by souring or by mixing with a plastic clay.

This mixture of clay or clays with other mineral materials used for forming pottery is called a *body*. Some archaeologists have used the word *paste* in this sense, but this is unfortunate since by most potters the term is applied only to the particular white clay bodies from which European porcelains are made.

Once pottery has been shaped, but before it has been fired, it is said to be in the *clay state* and may be referred to as *clay ware*. After a period of drying, clay wares change their colour and become tough and aplastic; they are then said to be *green-hard* or *leather-hard*.

Most commonly in antiquity pottery only needed to be fired once, the glazes on most wares being stable at the temperature and under the kiln conditions in which the body was fired. But this was not always the case, the glazes sometimes demanding a lower temperature or different kiln atmosphere to those of the body. In such cases, the first firing in which the body is cooked is called the *biscuit* (or *bisque*) firing and the pottery after firing *biscuit ware*. The second firing, in which the glaze is fired, is referred to as the *glost* firing, and sometimes where a very low-temperature glaze is being applied an oven, the *glost-oven*, is used instead of a kiln.

In discussing the shapes of wares, potters generally distinguish between two major types, flat and hollow wares. *Flat wares* include such things as saucers, plates, dishes and bowls—any form, in fact, in which the opening represents the widest part of the vessel. *Hollow wares* are those pots that are narrower at the mouth than at their maximum girth.

CLAY

Clay is a deposit of the smallest particles produced by the weathering of certain rocks, few particles being larger than 0·01 mm. in diameter. The chief constituent of most clays is a hydrated silicate of aluminium, kaolinite* ($Al_2O_3 . 2SiO_2 . 2H_2O$) which is derived from the physical or chemical breakdown of felspathic rocks, the potassium or sodium oxides of the felspars being attacked and made soluble by naturally occurring acids in the soil. Because of its mode of origin this *clay substance*, or *kaolinite*, is never found in a pure state in nature; at the best it is found with other minerals deriving from felspathic rocks, such as mica and quartz and, of course, unweathered felspar particles; but more commonly there are many other impurities as, for example, calcareous matter or compounds containing iron.

Kaolinite exists as very small, plate-like crystals. When damp, water penetrates between these crystals, each crystal being separated from its neighbours by a thin layer of water, and it is this that gives clay its plasticity. A simple mechanical analogy can be made between the behaviour of kaolinite crystals and sheets of glass. When dry, sheets of glass piled one upon another are not easily moved by a sideways thrust. The same sheets of glass when wet will move readily and remain in the position into which they have been pushed. In any clay, of course, the groups of kaolinite crystals are randomly orientated to give a material that can be thrust from any direction and that will retain the newly produced shape.

The same analogy is useful when considering the shrinkage of clay during drying. The spaces between the kaolinite crystals are occupied by water, and the smaller the crystals the greater their surface area per unit volume, and hence the greater the volume of water that separates them. Thus, in a clay containing little else but finely divided kaolinite the volume of water contained may be very great, and a total shrinkage on drying of up to 10% in volume is not uncommon. Clearly, the more finely divided the kaolinite particles, the greater the plasticity, and *vice versa*. It is for this reason that weathering, which breaks down the particle size, is important in making a clay more plastic.

---

* Other clay minerals, resulting from the weathering of non-granitic rocks, behave physically in a very similar manner to kaolinite.

This *water of plasticity*, which is not chemically combined with the clay in any way, must not be confused with the *water of chemical combination* which is an integral part of the molecules making up the kaolinite crystals. This is not lost during air-drying, but only after the clay has been brought to very much higher temperatures.

Other materials may be added to clay, or be naturally present in it, which, while they may reduce the tendency to shrink on drying, also

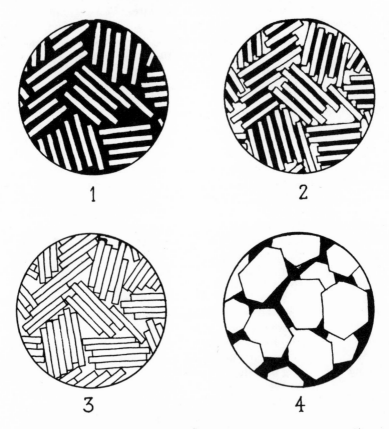

FIG. 1   SCHEMATIC DIAGRAM OF SECTION THROUGH KAOLINITE CRYS-
TALS (1, 2 AND 3) SHOWING HOW LOSS OF WATER (BLACK) CAUSES SHRINK-
AGE AND REDUCES PLASTICITY. HEXAGONAL KAOLINITE CRYSTALS (4)
AS REVEALED BY THE ELECTRON MICROSCOPE.

have a modifying effect on its behaviour during firing. As the tempera-ture is raised, clay goes through a number of physical changes, and a point will be reached at which the outer surfaces of the particles only will become soft or molten. If firing is not carried beyond this point, the resulting fabric will be one in which the surfaces of the particles are fused together on cooling. This is generally known as *sintering*, and the tem-perature at which this takes place as the *sinter point*. If heating is carried beyond this, the particles melt and coalesce completely, and the material is said to be *vitrified*. Pottery cannot, of course, be completely vitrified since in so doing it will collapse in the kiln. Pure kaolinite has a relatively high melting point, 1,770°C., but many substances, especially chemical bases, when added to it have the effect of lowering the melting point. These are known as *fluxes*, and those most commonly occurring are soda, potash, lime, mica, magnesia and various compounds of iron.

Naturally occurring clays have, thus, a very wide range of melting points, depending upon the fluxes they contain. In some cases, because of these fluxes, the temperature difference between the sinter point and melting point is so slight that it is virtually impossible to fire to the sinter point without actually arriving at the melting point and so ruining the pottery. For this reason potters frequently refer to a *maturing temperature* for clays, or bodies, by which is meant the temperature at which any clay or body may be fired to produce the densest structure without the pottery changing shape—the highest temperature, in fact, at which it is practical to fire the clay or body.

CLAYS

Different naturally occurring clays may be defined by a number of different criteria: (1) by the manner in which they were deposited; (2) by the nature of the impurities contained in them; or (3) by their behaviour during firing.

1. Clays may be found on the site of their parent felspathic rock. These *primary* or *residual clays* thus contain as impurities only those minerals derived from the mother rock—felspar, quartz and mica when derived from a granite, for example.

Far more commonly clays have been transported from the site of their formation. Very often these *secondary clays* have been deposited in the lower reaches of rivers that have invaded the primary beds and carried the clay downstream, or in the relatively static water of lakes as *lacustrine clays*. During this process impurities such as lime, magnesia, alkalis and iron oxides may have become mixed with the clay particles. These clays are thus not only less pure than primary clays but also generally more finely divided and hence more plastic. In areas that were at some time glaciated, clays may have been carried and deposited by ice sheets. These *boulder clays* are never as well sorted as water-deposited clays and generally contain a large proportion of very coarse material. To the modern potter these clays are usually of little value, but to the primitive potter in some areas they represented the only readily available source of clay.

2. *China-clays* or *kaolins* are relatively pure primary clays, but even so they seldom contain less than 5% felspar or other impurities derived from the parent rock. Due to this absence of other impurities they are white or very pale yellow and without additional fluxes have a high sinter and melting point. Because they are not well-weathered they tend to be aplastic.

Ball clays are relatively pure secondary clays. They are far more plastic than china clays, and because of this their shrinkage is frequently very high, sometimes up to 20%. They are relatively free from iron and are white or blue when unfired; off-white, grey or buff when fired. Again, because of the absence of fluxes, they have high sinter and melting points.

Red clays, earthenware clays or *canes* are secondary clays containing, amongst other things, iron oxides. Their composition is extremely varied, but they usually have a low melting point, with a maturing temperature between 1,000°C. and 1,200°C. When fired their colour may vary from yellow to deep red. Normally they are very plastic.

Marls or *calcareous clays* are secondary clays containing a considerable proportion of sand and lime, and often other fluxes as well. They are thus aplastic and have a wide range of maturing temperatures depending upon their composition.

Sandy clays or *siliceous clays* are secondary clays containing a high proportion of sand and are often deposits laid down in the middle reaches of rivers. Their composition is again extremely varied, but because of the high content of sand they are somewhat aplastic.

3. *Fire clays, refractory clays* or *infusible clays* are those clays with a high melting point and which will thus withstand high temperatures without suffering distortion, that is to say temperatures in the region of 1,500°C. Needless to say, such clays are virtually free from any fluxes. Fire clays are normally only found underlying coal measures.

Stoneware clays are those that mature between 1,200°C. and 1,300°C. While they may contain many impurities and are usually plastic, they contain a low proportion of fluxes.

Fusible clays are those which not only sinter but melt at low temperatures—below 1,200°C. They naturally contain a high proportion of fluxes and are very plastic.

BODIES

Broadly speaking one may distinguish two major types of body: (1) those that either by accident or by design are fired below the sinter point to produce a porous or permeable fabric, and (2) those that are to be fired until sintered to give an impermeable material.

1. The great majority of early pottery was never fired anywhere near the maturing point of the clays either because the rather crude kilns could not attain a high enough temperature or because they were too difficult to control. Any additions made to such clays must therefore be seen as fillers intended to alter the plasticity rather than as fluxes. Such bodies, fired well below 1,000°C., should, according to most modern potters, be described as *terracotta*. On the other hand, the same bodies when fired to their maturing point, which may lie anywhere between 1,000°C. and 1,200°C. are generally referred to as *earthenware*, although a few potters reserve this term to describe any low-fired, coloured body covered with a glaze. Bricks and tiles are normally made of unmodified clays maturing at the same temperatures as earthenware and are called *heavy clay bodies*. The lining and fittings of kilns are made of *refractory bodies*, and many naturally occurring marls may be used for this purpose, although silica in some form may be added to finer clays with low flux content to produce the same type of material.

2. *Stoneware bodies* sinter between 1,200°C. and 1,300°C. Since they normally lack iron, these bodies fire buff, grey or light brown. Naturally occurring clays may be used, but very commonly they are made of a mixture of siliceous and china clays. The terms *china* and *porcelain* are synonymous and cover such a wide range of bodies that it is absolutely essential to qualify them to avoid confusion. Any impermeable body that fires white, that is to say any *paste*, may be called china. It is normal to distinguish between *soft paste* porcelains, those that sinter at a low temperature, and *hard paste* porcelains which are fired at much higher temperatures. The essential ingredients of all china pastes are kaolin, quartz and felspar, to which may be added ball clay, or other materials, principally fluxes. *Vitreous china*, unlike the others, is dense and not translucent, while *bone china*, because of its content of calcined ox-bones which act as a flux, is a soft paste that fires very white and translucent. In China and Japan semi-decomposed beds of felspar may be worked to produce hard paste porcelain without additions, but in Europe hard pastes are almost invariably composite bodies, their differences lying chiefly in the proportions and nature of the china clay, silica and felspar they contain.

FILLERS

As has already been pointed out, a filler may be any material that does not become plastic in water and can stand the temperature at which it is intended to fire the wares without undergoing violent changes. Amongst primitive potters quartz sand and calcined flint seem to have been the most commonly used, although any pulverized rock may have served as well as some organic materials such as chaff, or materials of organic origin such as shell.

To the archaeologist the examination and determination of the nature of the fillers used may be most important since these may betray a source of origin far from the finding place of the pottery. Particles of grog may be derived from completely different wares, and even quartz grains will show different degrees of smoothing depending upon whether derived from ice-laid, water-laid or wind-laid deposits.

FORMING: PRIMARY PROCESSES

Hand-modelled, Pinch pottery, Squeeze pottery

A ball of clay is formed and this is held in the palm of one hand, the thumb of the other hand being dug into the clay ball. The ball is then rotated slowly while the clay is gently squeezed between the thumb and fingers of the shaping hand. The process is continued until a pot is formed.

Essentially this method produces round-based pots, although if the clay is soft and plastic enough the partly-formed pot may be transferred to a flat surface and work continued, so producing a flat-based form.

Although theoretically the simplest way of forming pottery, and the starting point of nearly all art-school classes, it is doubtful that the method was ever used much in antiquity, save perhaps by children. The

size of pot that can be built in this way is strictly limited by the length
of the worker's fingers; only one hand can be used in the forming process;
and the supporting hand rapidly becomes fatigued. The method appears
seldom amongst modern primitives.

Coil-building and Ring-building

In both these methods the walls of the vessel are formed by the addition
of sausage-shaped rolls of clay of various lengths. These rolls may be

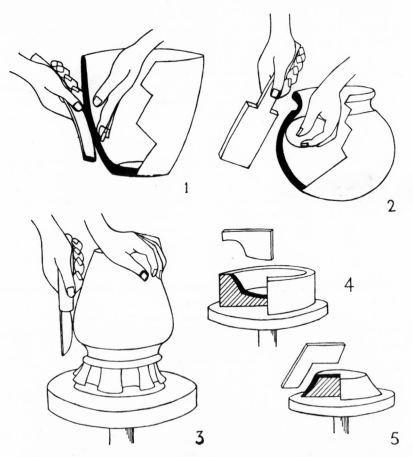

FIG. 2 FORMING AND FINISHING OF POTTERY. DRAWING UP WITH A
RIB (1). EXTENDING WITH BEATER AND ANVIL (2). SHAVING (TURNING)
ON WHEEL-HEAD (3). JIGGER-MOULDS AND TEMPLETS (4 AND 5).

formed either by rolling lumps of clay on a horizontal slab or by rubbing
backwards and forwards between the palms of the hands held vertically.
The base may be made of a coil prepared in this way or more simply of a
flattened lump of clay. It is general to smooth down each ring or each
turn of the coil as the work progresses, although some workers add

several rings or turns of the coil before smoothing. This may be done by hand, but more commonly a curved piece of wood or bone, called a *rib*, is used. Rib-bones are, in fact, ideal for this purpose. In coil-building the whole coil may be wound round the forearm of the worker before he begins. Although unquestionably a matter of expertise, and not strictly speaking essential, this does prevent the coil picking up extraneous matter during building.

Ring or coil-built pots are generally flat-bottomed since they are frequently formed on a turn-table, or *tournette*. This may be no more than a suitably shaped stone or it may be an elaborate device with a bearing of some kind. Equally the pots may be built on matting which can be turned, and the impression of the mat may be seen on the base of the fired pottery.

In poorly finished wares there is a tendency to lumpiness, and the profile may even be wavy, the hollows corresponding to the joins of the rings; but these features far more often than not are obscured by later work. If the clay used is particularly aplastic, or if the surface of the rolls has picked up too much dirt during the forming process, the join between the rings may be imperfect, and in fragmentary vessels these junctions may be clearly visible. This failure of some clays to bond is of concern to many industrial potters today, but it should never be taken for granted that absence of visible joins in the fracture means that a pot must, therefore, have been formed by some other process; a clean, plastic clay will often bond leaving little or no trace of the junction.

Slab-forming

In this process the clay is rolled out flat like pastry and slabs of the required shape are cut from it. The vessel is then assembled by pressing together the edges of the slabs.

The method is ideally suitable for the making of box-like vessels, more common in the Far East than elsewhere. On the whole the method is unusual but within this century more than one African tribe is recorded as having made round bottomed pots by joining a number of triangular slabs with their apices all at the centre of the base.

Moulding

Pots may be formed in open or piece-moulds. The moulds may be of wood, stone or even metal. More commonly, however, the moulds are made of a sand-filled clay, themselves moulded off a solid model. The clay from which the vessel is to be made is normally rolled out fairly evenly and pressed into the mould and the work cleaned up by hand.

Shallow, open forms may be produced in this way in a single piece, but more complex shapes, for example the figure-pots of the New World, were moulded as two or more pieces which were then joined. Amongst primitives it is quite common to find an existing pot used as an inner or outer mould to produce flat wares.

Jiggering or Jollying

This process is really nothing more than mechanical moulding. The mould is placed on a turn-table or wheel and roughly lined with clay. A templet is gradually brought down into the mould as it revolves, so removing any surplus clay, to produce a vessel of the required thickness.

This method is only really suitable for the production of flat forms, and one would normally expect to find it associated with the semi-industrialized production of pottery. It was possibly a method of forming Samian wares and remains the usual way of manufacturing domestic pottery today.

Slip-casting

This is a fairly sophisticated process demanding the use of a mould capable of absorbing a large proportion of water, as for example lime plaster, plaster of Paris and porous ceramic material. The mould may be either an open or a piece-mould. A clay slip is poured into the mould and allowed to stand. The absorption of water by the mould results in the formation of a layer of thicker clay over the matrix of the mould. The excess slip is then poured off and the clay allowed to dry out until it can be handled.

This process is most suitable for the making of fairly complex hollow shapes such as porcelain figures, and is again nearly always to be associated with the semi-industrialized production of pottery.

Throwing (Wheel-throwing)

This is the making of pottery from a single lump of clay on a turn-table that can be made to rotate continuously over a fairly long period of time, the centrifugal force acting on the clay being utilized by the potter to form the vessel.

Any attempt to distinguish sharply between the tournette and the wheel is liable to be somewhat arbitrary, for obviously a large and heavy tournette can be given sufficient momentum, by hand-pushing or kicking, to act as a wheel; but the essential structural distinction would seem to be that the wheel is made up of two functional parts, the *wheel-head* on which the pottery is formed and the wheel itself which acts as a fly-wheel, while the tournette is a single entity. The wheel-head may be only just above the level of the wheel, in which case impetus is given to the wheel either by pushing directly with the hand or with a pole, the potter squatting down to his work. Alternatively, a second person (generally the unhappy apprentice) provided the power by pushing or kicking the wheel. Where the wheel-head was well above the wheel, joined to it by a shaft, the potter could either sit or stand one-legged and kick directly on the wheel. A final refinement of this principle was the introduction of a cranked shaft and pedal bar, to which system the term *kick-wheel* is most commonly applied. This is an established potters' term and is unfortunately somewhat misleading since it is in reality a pedal-driven wheel. Many archaeologists are in the habit of distinguishing between a *slow wheel*, that is to say a device in which the movement of the wheel-head is either intermittent or relatively slow, and a *fast wheel* in which the movement is continuous and relatively rapid. These terms have no direct bearing on the means by which the wheel was made to rotate. Where any confusion is liable to be caused, the terms hand-rotated, direct kick-wheel and pedal kick-wheel should be used.

Pottery may also be thrown without the use of a wheel in the sense in which it has just been defined. Thus, the Mexican *molde* consists of two saucer-shaped ceramic objects. A ball of clay is placed in the upper saucer and this is balanced on the other inverted saucer. The potter spins the upper saucer and the clay it contains with his foot, using both hands to throw the vessel. The process demands a great deal of skill, and it should be noted that the clay itself provides the major part of the weight, and hence of the momentum. Pottery made in this way, apart from being round based, bears all the indications of being wheel-thrown.

Since most people are both right-handed and right-footed, it is traditional that the wheel should be made to rotate anti-clockwise, in which case it is most comfortable for the left hand to form the outside of the pot while the right hand forms the inside. For the larger part of the process, therefore, the left hand can be looked upon as an adaptable templet into which the clay is formed by the right hand.

The possible number of forms that can be thrown on the wheel is endless, which probably accounts for its popularity amongst artist-potters today and possibly even its survival after the introduction of the jigger into industry. Because of this it is difficult to say anything critical about forms except to point out that it is an inconvenient way of producing extremely flat shapes such as plates and meat-dishes.

Bases are usually flat, but not necessarily so. By leaving some clay on the wheel-head and undercutting the shape, rounded and conical bases are easily produced. Furthermore, bases may be pushed inwards or outwards after removal from the wheel-head while the clay is still plastic. Shapes may be removed from the wheel-head either by undercutting with a knife or by using a 'cheese-wire' made of horse hair, gut, or any other suitable material which leaves a characteristic marking of concentric circles of fine grooves and ridges on the base. Alternatively, a removable wheel-head of clay or plaster, called a *bat*, may be used, from which the pot will shrink on drying.

The presence on the inner and outer surfaces of pottery of fine horizontal grooves and ridges, called *rilling*, caused by the coarser particles in the clay body and irregularities of the potter's hands, is commonly held to be a certain indication that pottery was wheel-thrown. This is far from true. The same effect can be produced in the final tidying of, for example, ring-built pottery, where a substantial tournette has been used. Much early pottery that has been described as wheel-thrown was probably initially ring-built and only finally given its form on a rotating wheel.

A rather deeper and more pronounced ridge and groove running in a corkscrew spiral up the inside of some pottery results from using a poorly wedged clay and bringing up the sides of the pot too quickly. This effect could mistakenly be interpreted as evidence of coil-building, but it is quite indicative of rather inferior wheel-throwing.

It is, of course, perfectly possible to make drastic changes in the form of a pot after it has been thrown but while it is still on the wheel-head. Grooves and flanges can be produced either with the fingers or with tools, while by *collaring*, that is to say squeezing in gently with the thumb and forefinger of both hands, vessels with narrow necks can be produced. It is perhaps in the final treatment of the rim that the characteristics of the individual potter or school are most apparent, and ideally it is in terms of the probable placing of the thumbs and fingers of both hands that rims should be considered. Quite minor changes of positioning can often produce exaggerated differences in rim-form; equally, quite similar rim shapes may result from utterly different manipulation.

Drawing up

The sides of pottery built by hand-modelling, coil- or ring-building, or slab-forming may be considerably heightened during the forming process by the use of the rib so long as the clay is adequately plastic. During the work the sides of the pot are supported on the inside by the fingers of one hand while the rib is scraped upwards over the outer surface. If no later work is done on the outer surface to obscure them, a number of broad vertical facets are generally visible as a result of this process.

Pottery built of less plastic clays can be heightened by beating the outer surface with a flat tool while supporting the inside with the hand, or a smooth stone. To this process anthropologists have given the term *paddle and anvil* or *beater and anvil* technique. The beater may be quite smooth or the whole working surface may be covered with a carved pattern which becomes impressed upon the surface of the pot; and in some cases considerable care is needed before deciding whether a decorated surface results from this use of a beater or from later impression.

FORMING: SECONDARY PROCESSES

Piece-forming

As already said, moulded pottery is often made in several pieces that are later joined. This joining is usually carried out after the clay has dried sufficiently to allow it to be handled gently without distortion but before it is so dry that it will not bond properly. It is not uncommon to find that more than one method has been used in producing the various parts of a vessel. Thus a large storage jar may be found to have a moulded base, ring-built sides and a hand-modelled neck.

Applied parts

These may all be added while the clay is in the same state as mentioned above, and it is often in the details of the manner in which these additions were made that one can distinguish individual characteristics. Pouring lips are commonly simply pinched out of the rim, but sometimes a triangular or semi-circular piece of clay is applied. Medieval 'parrot-beaked' jugs, for example, were made by poking the forefinger of one hand through the neck below the rim and applying a triangular piece of clay over it, the characteristic shape of the lip being no more than the reflection of the crooked forefinger. Spouts were generally pre-formed on a forefinger or a stick which was then poked through the wall of the vessel and the spout smoothed in on the outside. Alternatively a hole may have been cut in the vessel through which the spout was passed and then smoothed in inside and outside. Equally, handles may have been applied directly to the wall of the vessel or carried through a hole in its side. Foot-rings and feet were generally applied directly to the base, although feet are sometimes passed through a hole in the base and smoothed in.

Fettling

This is a more or less general term applied to the tidying up of pottery, usually with a knife. It applies to such things as the removal of casting flashes, where they exist, and cleaning away the inevitable unevenness around the bases of thrown pots. Sometimes, where the base and lower part of the vessel were initially too thick or uneven, large knife scars can be seen, usually indicative of poor workmanship or an intractable clay.

Shaving and Turning

Once the clay is green-hard the looks of a rough pot can be greatly improved by shaving down the surface, the process often having the additional advantage of thinning down the vessel. Although specially designed tools are normally used today, the job can be done with any suitable knife, or even a flint blade. Symmetrical pottery, as for example wheel-thrown shapes, may be put on a lathe, or more commonly upside-down on a conical projection, the *chuck* or *chum*, or even on a lump of clay on the wheel-head, and turned down with a knife or broad, chisel-shaped tool. At the same time, if the base is thick, the centre may be turned out leaving only a ring at the perimeter of the base.

When exceptionally well executed, turning leaves no discernible trace. This is uncommon, for usually, because the craftsman is using a straight-edged tool against a curved face, slight, even, horizontal facetting can be seen. Added to this, unless the body is unusually well-graded, there is a tendency for the turning-tool to pick up from time to time a large grit and to carry it over the face of the pot until it works free. This has the effect of producing a number of horizontal scored lines on the otherwise smooth surface.

Burnishing

Burnishing, as applied to pottery, means rubbing down the surface of a green-hard shape with a smooth, hard, round-faced tool. Water-worn pebbles and bones have both been used for this purpose. The effect is quite simply to compact the surface of the clay, and tools used for this purpose acquire a characteristic shine. When burnishing is carried out freehand, the surface of the vessel acquires a multitude of short, smooth facets, each one corresponding to a separate stroke of the tool. Pottery may be set up on a tournette or wheel as in turning, and burnished by holding the tool against the rotating shape. Vessels that have been treated in this way are often very difficult to distinguish from turned wares if the work has been well carried out.

If the body has become too dry before burnishing, the tool may ride over irregularities in the body to produce a series of shallow ridges and depressions over the surface at right angles to the direction of burnishing. The effect of this *ripple burnish* can be highly decorative, and at times it was clearly deliberately produced. Even so, one must appreciate that it is a discovery—or defect—likely to have been repeated many times in antiquity.

To distinguish exceptionally well-burnished pottery from wares of inferior workmanship, some archaeologists have used the term 'polished'. This is unfortunate since the word has a distinct meaning amongst potters, referring to treatment *after firing*, and it is to be hoped this special application amongst archaeologists will not become widespread.

Luting

When green-hard, handles, spouts, knobs and so on may be stuck on using a little slip as adhesive. Parts applied in this way cannot, of course, be worked down or smoothed into the body of the pot, the junction is always clearly visible even beneath a heavy glaze, and the parts themselves no matter how well designed tend to have a somewhat detached look. The method is not really suitable for low-fired ceramics. Domestic cups and teapots are nearly always produced in this way, the handles or spouts being cast or moulded; on the cheaper wares at least the unfettled casting flashes are clearly visible.

The distinction between parts luted into position and those applied and smoothed in is not always clearly adhered to in archaeological writing, but as far as potters are concerned the term luting has only one meaning.

PLASTIC DECORATION

Apart from colouring and glazing, pottery may be decorated by impressing patterns into the plastic shape, by removing areas of the surface when the shape is either soft or hard, or by applying further clay to the surface.

Impressed patterns

A bewildering variety of objects has been used over the ages to impress the surface of still plastic pottery—shells, string, bird-bones, flint blades wrapped in string, and fingernails, to mention only a few. More sophisticated people might cut small stamps expressly for the purpose, as did the early Saxons. Because the continued use of one type of impression shows a cultural continuum, the objects used have been studied in considerable detail. Technically there is nothing much to be said about the process, so simple is it. A very rough and badly formed pot can be made to look much better by breaking up the surface with a mass of impressed pattern.

Incised and Excised patterns

Here, too, there is little to say. When the clay is still plastic designs based on curved lines are possible, but when green-hard it is really only practicable to cut straight lines.

A distinction is sometimes made by archaeologists between *incised* decoration (in which no clay is, theoretically, removed) and *excised* (in which some clay is removed). In some instances this distinction can quite legitimately be made, but in many cases it cannot without taking

into account the type of tool used for the purpose and the working qualities of the clay—both usually unknown. Practical experience will show
that identical effects can be produced in plastic and green-hard clay
simply by changing from, say, bone to flint tools.

Applied decoration

In its simplest form applied decoration need be no more than pellets
or bands of clay stuck directly on to the wet surface of the vessel and
these may be further tooled while still plastic to produce rosettes, rope-
patterns and so on.

The clay may be applied in a fairly fluid form using for the purpose a
container with a nozzle, much as a cake is iced by bakers. This method is
called *slip-trailing*, and most commonly the applied clay is of a different
colour from the body of the pot. By changing the shapes and sizes of the
nozzle, and by varying the pressure, a multitude of different patterns and
line thicknesses can be produced. In a process known as *pâte-sur-pâte*,
clay made to the consistency of a thin paste may be painted on, layer by
layer, to produce low relief modelling.

Applied decoration may also be moulded in small open moulds, called
sprig-moulds, and these mouldings are either applied directly to the pot
while still plastic, or luted on when green-hard.

Two or more of these techniques may be used in conjunction. Thus,
for example, on the Roman Castor pottery the heads, necks and bodies
of animals were applied quite simply by hand, while the finer details—
legs, ears and tails—were slip-trailed.

SURFACE DECORATION

Slurry or Wet-hand surface

After a pot has been formed and allowed to stand for a short time the
look of the surface can be greatly improved by working it over with a
damp cloth or sponge, or simply with damp hands. This has the effect of
bringing to the surface some of the finer particles of the drying clay. A
slurry or *slub* is generally defined by potters as any rough mixture of clay
and water, and the term *slurried surface* would seem appropriate to
describe this form of treatment.

Slip (Fr. Engobe)

Clay may be mixed with water to an even, pea-soup consistency and
applied to the surface of pottery either by dipping the partly dried pot
into the slip, or by pouring the slip over the pot. Generally the clay is
of a different colour from the body of the pot and may be used to disguise the body. When used in this way some potters refer to the slip as
engobe, but to others the terms slip and engobe are merely synonyms.

Slip may be applied over the inner or outer surface only, or over part
of either surface only, or even applied only locally with a brush, a technique called *slip painting.* One particularly elaborate form of slip painting,
feather combing, involves the use of a brush with multiple points (the
flight feathers of some birds naturally produce such a brush). Differently
coloured slips are used, often being applied as festoons or ogee curves.

Areas may be blocked out with materials that will burn away during firing—wax, grease, paper, leaves and so on—before slipping, a process known as *resist* or *reserved slip* decoration, to provide a colour contrast between body and slip. Equally, after slipping, areas may be scored away with tools, a method referred to as *sgraffito* (sgraffiato).

It is often very difficult to distinguish between a slurried and a slipped surface, particularly under some firing conditions, and this problem will be discussed later.

Some archaeologists, particularly in the New World, use the term *wash* to describe a very thin slip. The word is not used in this sense by potters, and on the whole seems redundant.

Gloss

Certain classes of ware, typified by Samian wares, have a surface that appears at first sight to be glazed. In fact these wares have been shown to have been slipped in a very fine clay containing an unusually high proportion of the clay mineral Illite, and bear no relationship to true glazed wares. Since this type of surface treatment stands in such strong contrast to the normal slip, the use of the term *gloss* seems perfectly justifiable in this specialized sense.

The preparation of slips and glosses depends upon being able to separate from the clay the finer particles only. This is normally done by elutriation, but many acidic clays do not easily form a suspension in water, but instead flocculate. In general terms this is because the clay particles normally carry a number of free negative electric charges (hydroxyl ions) which in an acid solution combine with free positive charges (hydrogen ions) so causing the particles to cohere. By adding small quantities of alkaline *deflocculents*, such as potash, the balance of positive and negative charges is altered and the clay particles repel one another, and so remain in suspension, provided they are very small. On a purely empirical basis this phenomenon was used to separate very fine clay particles from the coarser ones in naturally occurring clays.

Encaustic Decoration

This method of decoration is virtually the inlaying of a body with a clay of another colour, a process far more commonly applied to tiles than to pottery. The most practical way of carrying out this form of decoration is to use a mould in which those areas to be filled are initially impressed in the surface of the tile or pot, although examples are to be found in which the body has been tooled away when green-hard and then filled.

Mineral Surfacing

Powdered minerals such as graphite and haematite may be rubbed into the surface of green-hard pottery, so giving the wares a distinctive colour. Although these minerals are sometimes applied gently with the fingers or a rag, they do not then remain very fast after firing, and it is far more common to find them put on with a burnishing technique. Equally such minerals may be painted on as a suspension in water or even mixed with varying proportions of clay and applied as an artificially coloured slip. It is often impossible to say which method of application has been employed without resort to thin-sectioning.

Needless to say, the minerals used for this purpose must be such as are unaffected by the firing conditions and kiln temperature. In the proper recording of such wares the identification of the minerals should correctly be guided by criteria other than colour and inspired guesswork.

Roughened surfaces

Sometimes either for decorative or functional purposes, as in the case of mortaria (grain-crushing bowls) coarse particles of grit such as flint or quartz sand may be worked into the inner surface of the still plastic shape. At the same stage the surface may be covered with chopped vegetable matter or chaff which on burning out will leave a roughened, if rather crude, surface effect.

Smoking

Some primitive black terracotta pottery is given a long period of smoking over a dirtily burning fire before firing. The intention of this treatment is quite simply to fill all the pores of the pottery with soot particles. Care is needed during the firing to ensure conditions which will not burn out this soot.

DRYING

Before pottery can be fired it must be dried, otherwise during firing steam will be formed within the walls of the pot, which will cause it to burst.

In hot climates it may be possible to dry pottery perfectly adequately in the open air, indeed freshly-made shapes may even have to be set in the shade to dry initially, for too rapid drying may mean that the thinner parts may dry out completely, and in so doing shrink, while the thicker parts may remain relatively damp, with the result that the vessel will crack.

In temperate climates, on the other hand, it may be impossible to dry pottery adequately without heating, especially in the winter. Under primitive conditions pots may have been set by the domestic hearth to dry, but under semi-industrialized circumstances some form of drying oven often had to be provided. This could be built either alongside the kiln, from which it drew its heat, or as a free-standing structure. Otherwise the kiln may have been set, and a small fire kept burning in the firepit over a rather long period before firing proper began, the kiln itself thus acting as an oven, but this may be a quite false impression. Kilns, on the whole, exercise a strong lure for the excavator, while workshops are more often than not ignored. One need only work clay for a short period in mid-winter in an unheated workshop to appreciate the great benefit of even a very small fire; the logical place for the drying oven is in the potter's workshop.

KILNS

The design and use of kilns has varied so widely in place and time that generalizations are difficult to make. The following remarks refer principally to wood-fired structures, those fired by coke and coal being mainly of relatively recent introduction. The firing-pattern of any kiln must depend to some degree on the nature of the fuel being used, and even wood fires vary enormously according to the type of wood, its size, and how well seasoned it may be. There are, too, other vegetable fuels such as grasses, heathers and even dried dung that have been used for firing. These factors must be taken into account when considering kiln design, especially when dealing with the proportions of kiln capacity to fire area.

Domestic Fires

It is not generally appreciated that very primitive pottery can be fired in almost any open hearth. The modern potter, used to handling relatively clean clays, will shudder at the thought, but a clay that is well-weathered and full of organic and mineral fillers can be treated in the most cavalier fashion without breakage. A pot made of such a body may be rotated in the fire by degrees until all parts of it have been fired. Primitive as it may be, this method of firing was still being used in the Hebrides and other parts of Europe at the end of the last century.

Bonfires

The stacking together of a number of pots and their firing under a bonfire is, of course, only one stage removed from the domestic hearth, and this style of firing may suggest either a communal approach to pottery production or may result from a dearth of suitable firing materials.

A bonfire, once a light has been set to it, will normally rise fairly rapidly to its maximum temperature and thereafter the temperature will fall slowly. A domestic fire, on the other hand, is normally kept at a fairly even temperature. These are, of course, generalizations, but it will be seen later that the two types of firing tend to produce rather distinctive wares.

Updraught Kilns

Basically an updraught kiln is any structure in which the fire is set in a fire-pit below the pottery which is itself enclosed in a dome, or similar structure, provided with a vent or blow-hole to allow the smoke and gases of combustion to escape. Such kilns are generally round or oval and may be provided with one or more stoke-holes. The pottery may be set on shelves or on *fire-bars* of clay that may traverse the whole kiln or radiate from a central support.

In small kilns only the footings of the dome may have been permanent, since the dome needed to be broken away after each firing to gain access. In larger structures only a part of the dome or kiln wall may have been removed after firing. After re-setting, of course, this gap had to be made good. In either event the potter could normally be expected to keep a stock of clay nearby for the purpose of rebuilding the damaged dome or clamming the semi-permanent entrance. Contrary to what some excavators would have us believe, such stocks need not be seen as the store of potting clay, for it would certainly be an act of insanity to keep this within a few feet of a kiln, where all the debris of firing might fall into it.

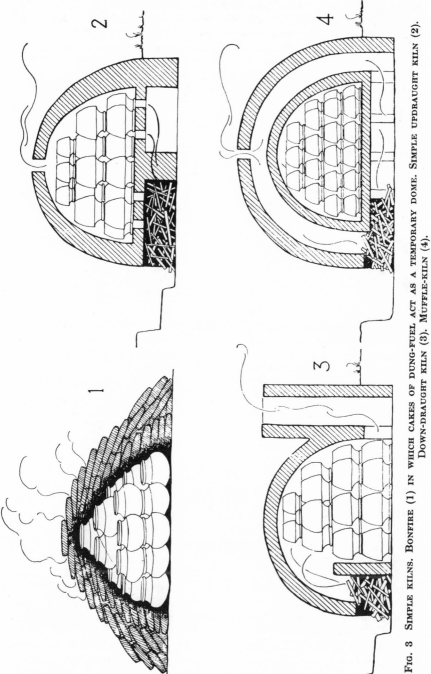

FIG. 3 SIMPLE KILNS. BONFIRE (1) IN WHICH CAKES OF DUNG-FUEL ACT AS A TEMPORARY DOME. SIMPLE UPDRAUGHT KILN (2). DOWN-DRAUGHT KILN (3). MUFFLE-KILN (4).

Updraught kilns naturally vary considerably in design, and are not infrequently given a multitude of more-or-less descriptive names. Thus, tall kilns with a chimney-shaped vent are often called *bottle-kilns*, while those built into an excavated hillside are generally known as *bank-kilns*.

Pit-kilns

Pit-kilns are generally seen as a development of the bonfire, and thus as a transitional type of structure in the development of the updraught kiln. As the name implies, the fire is set in a pit often with fire-bars above, or with columns standing up in the pit, upon which the pottery is set. The pit may or may not be surrounded with a wall with one or more gaps acting as stoke-holes. Equally, shelves for the setting of the pottery may protrude from this surrounding wall.

Downdraught kilns

Downdraught kilns are those in which the fire, instead of being set below the pottery as in the updraught kilns, is deflected from the roof of the kiln downwards on to the pottery, the smoke and gases being carried away by a vent below the fire-bars which normally opens into a chimney. The flames from the fire are prevented from coming in contact with the pottery before being deflected from the roof by a wall called the *bag-wall* or *baffle-wall*.

Fuel for fuel, it is always possible to achieve higher temperatures in a downdraught than in an updraught kiln, and as a generalization it may be said that temperatures above 1,100°C. are more easily obtained in a downdraught kiln when firing with wood.

Muffle-kilns

A muffle-kiln is a structure in which the flames of the fire are prevented from coming in contact with the pottery by an internal wall, floor and roof. The kilns may be either updraught or downdraught, and are, of course, primarily used for the firing of glazed and similar wares where the direct contact of the fire would spoil the appearance of the pottery.

Draught

The use of any form of bellows to increase the draught through pottery kilns is most uncommon, if only because of the long periods of firing required by any but the simplest of kilns. Generally kilns are so sited that the stoke-holes face into the prevailing winds. Thus, in southern Britain, for example, it is normal to find a single stoke-hole facing south-west, or two stoke-holes one facing south-west and the other north-east. In many cases, one supposes, the potter must have waited for a suitable wind before kindling the kiln; a damp day without wind would have resulted in a sulky fire; a gale would have resulted in a fast-burning fire incapable of being controlled.

Kiln fittings

Apart from fire-bars, shelves and bats, there are other kiln-fittings made of refractory clays. Some glazed wares need to be protected from the direct flame, and if a muffle-kiln is not being used, this may be done by

placing them in lidded boxes called *saggars* (*saggers* or *seggers*)—a cor-
ruption of the word safeguard. As it is obviously economically necessary
to pack as much pottery into a kiln for each firing as possible, and since
glazed wares will stick to one another should they touch, a number of
small refractory supports, generically known as *setters*, are used to
keep wares separated from one another or from the bats or shelves on
which they stand. These setters vary considerably in shape, and their
names are usually adequately descriptive—saddle, stilt, spur, thimble,
pin—but all share in common the same feature of design in that the
actual surface area of the setters that comes in contact with the wares
is kept as small as possible, for after firing they must be detached from
the glazed wares leaving as small a blemish as possible.

FIRING SEQUENCE

After the wares have been placed in the kiln—a process also known as
charging or setting—and the entry has been made good and clammed, a
small fire is kindled in the fire-pit. In the early stages the fire is kept
small, and the kiln temperature allowed to rise very slowly to the
boiling point of water, at which temperature the kiln is maintained for
a considerable time. During this period of firing, known as *water smoking*,
the remaining water of plasticity is driven out of the wares. If carried
out too rapidly steam may be generated in sufficient quantities in the
bodies of the wares to make them burst. The more porous the body, the
less risk there is of this happening, and it may well have been partly for
this reason that so many of the early terracotta bodies contained such a
high proportion of fillers.

When all the water of plasticity has evaporated, the size of the fire
is increased and the temperature again allowed to rise slowly. Above
400°C. the water of chemical combination contained in the kaolinite is
given off and too rapid a climb of temperature may cause the same kind
of generation of steam with the same fatal results. A new danger point is
reached at a temperature of 573°C., especially in the firing of thin-
walled wares with bodies containing much quartz, for at this point
quartz changes its molecular structure, and in so doing expands slightly
—about 2% by volume. Here again, if the temperature is approached
too rapidly, this expansion may damage the pottery.

All in all, the early stages of firing are thus slow, the potter judging the
next move by careful examination of the smoke and gases escaping
through the vent, or by noting colour changes inside the kiln through a
spy-hole in the wall; the temperature is allowed to rise slowly by stages,
each rise being followed by a period at which a steady temperature is
maintained for a time, a process known as *soaking*.

Finally the temperature is raised to the maturing point of the wares,
and here again a steady temperature is maintained to ensure an even distribution of heat throughout the kiln—the annealing fire—after which
the fire is drawn and the fire-pit banked down to prevent too rapid
cooling of the wares. Amongst primitive potters the judgment as to when
the maturing point had been reached was presumably always a matter
of experience in which colour change must have been the determining

factor. Today potters use small cones of clay—*pyrometric cones*—which melt below the maturing point of the wares being fired to give warning as to when to stop raising the kiln temperature. There are several series of pyrometric cones of which the Seger cones are, perhaps, the most commonly used; and most potters will refer to a cone number when speaking of firing temperatures. This practice saves the time and effort of converting backwards and forwards between degrees Celsius and the numbers of the cones actually being used, but from the point of view of general intelligibility the Celsius system is obviously to be preferred.

FIRING CONDITIONS

Apart from variations in rate of temperature climb, the differences of the maximum temperature attained, the nature of the atmosphere within the kiln can vary greatly. On the one hand the fuel may burn brightly with a clean flame when it is dry and there is a good draught. Chemically, under such conditions all the carbon in the fuel is being burnt, or converted to carbon dioxide, while there remains a surplus of oxygen in the kiln atmosphere. Such a state is known as an *oxidizing atmosphere* since any carbon derived from organic matter in the bodies of the wares will also be converted into carbon dioxide and so burnt out of the pottery.

On the other hand, when the fuel is damp, or the air supply to the kiln is restricted, the fire will burn with a sooty flame. In fact, all the fuel is not being burnt and some of it is being carried into the kiln as carbon particles (the soot) while the gases contain carbon monoxide and little or no oxygen. This will produce a double effect in the wares. The organic matter will not burn out since there is no oxygen present to convert it to a gas, and the wares may even acquire more carbon from the soot. At the same time some of the metallic oxides in the wares may lose part or all of the oxygen they contain. Under such conditions the oxides are said to be reduced, and the kiln atmosphere a *reducing atmosphere*. Above 825°C. ferric oxide, the colouring matter in red clays, may be reduced to magnetite which is black, and under extreme conditions its presence can be demonstrated with a simple magnet.

These are the two extremes, but in much primitive firing one cannot say that the conditions were constantly either one or the other. In bonfires and pit-firing, parts of pots may have become buried in ash, or a large piece of unburnt wood may have come to rest on the surface of the pot, so cutting down the supply of oxygen to those areas. The result will be a surface partly oxidized red and partly reduced black, and at times deliberate use was made of this knowledge to produce decorative effects. Much terracotta ware, while having a generally red surface, will be found to have a dark core in the fracture, and this is commonly an indication of a fairly brief firing in which inadequate time has been allowed to burn out all the carbon derived from the organic matter in the body.

While it is generally safe to assume that red unglazed surfaces result from oxidizing conditions, it is not always as safe to ascribe all black surfaces to reducing conditions. Some black minerals are stable at low temperatures, including the black oxide of iron, magnetite, and this may be added to the body or applied as a coloured slip to produce a ware that may appear to have been reduced.

Treatment after Firing

Treatments carried out after firing are usually designed either to improve the looks of the wares or, in the case of permeable bodies, to fill the pores and so make them more serviceable.

Glazed wares may have a light *polishing* on either a leather or rag buffing wheel. A little polishing alumina may be used. The aim is simply to remove any minor blemishes and to increase the shine of the surface.

Permeable wares are sometimes coloured at this stage using vegetable dyes, and these may be applied either by dipping or painting while the wares are still warm from the firing. Vegetable resins may also be applied while the wares are still warm with the intention of filling the pores; indeed any resins, fat or oil may be used for this purpose, and the choice can usually be shown to depend upon the availability of suitable materials.

Defects in the wares may also be made good by using the same materials; while in some regions plaster or bitumen may be used to fill cracks and other small flaws, but these are expedients that suggest not only poor workmanship but also, in some degree, dishonesty.

Firing Mishaps

Over the years any potter will produce a mass of *wasters*—broken, misshapen and defective pottery—which being of no commercial value accumulates around his kiln and workshop. Any intending excavator should at least be able to recognize this kind of material; for it could easily happen that an archaeologist while examining one kind of structure might fail to recognize this detritus of a nearby potter's workshop and in so doing fail to examine a valuable site.

The shattering or *blowing* of a pot during firing may be due either to the use of badly wedged clay or to the generation of steam in the body resulting either from inadequately dried wares or too rapid a raising of the kiln temperature. If many pots blow early on in the firing the potter will in all probability draw the kiln to save fuel and effort. The result will be a lot of under-fired, broken pots to be discarded. Equally, if the kiln is allowed to cool too rapidly, or if a draught is allowed to enter it, the pottery may *dunt* (or *stunt*), that is to say it may split or crack, or a piece may flake out of the surface. These roughly circular flakes are a very common feature of kiln-wasters.

Misshapen wares may result from *warping* which is generally due to uneven distribution of heat within the kiln causing, for example, one side of a pot to contract more than the other on cooling. On the other hand, *sagging* or *squatting* is due to firing above the maturing point and so allowing wares partially to melt.

Chapter Two

GLAZES

SYNOPSIS

General: Glaze formers · Glaze modifiers · Glaze colourants. *Glaze Formers:* Silica · Boron oxide. *Glaze Modifiers:* Sodium oxide · Potassium oxide · Lead oxide · Calcium oxide · Barium oxide · Magnesium oxide · Zinc oxide · Alumina. *Glaze Colourants:* Iron oxides · Copper oxides · Cobalt oxide · Manganese oxide · Chromium oxide · Nickel oxide · Gold oxide · Tin oxide. *Preparation of Glazes:* Raw glazes · Frits · Glaze fit · Crazing · Scaling. *Applying Glazes:* Dry footing · Maturing. *Colour Decoration:* Underglaze · Overglaze · Majolica · Enamelling. *Classification of Glazes:* Soft and hard glazes · Lead glazes · Alkaline glazes · Soda-lime and potash-lime glazes · Ash glazes · Salt glazes · Felspathic glazes · Slip glazes · Crackle glazes · Matt glazes · Crystalline glazes · Lustres. *Glaze defects.*

GENERAL

GLAZES ARE VITREOUS coatings applied to the surfaces of wares either to make them impermeable or for decorative effect, and are, in fact, one aspect of a wider group of vitreous materials including glasses and enamels. Physically, these vitreous substances are super-cooled liquids; that is to say, they are liquids of very high viscosity at normal temperatures, and thus in the solid state are not crystalline.

A number of inorganic oxides have the ability to form vitreous materials, including silica (silicon oxide) and boric oxide. Of these, silica is far the more important to the archaeologist, although boric oxide, introduced as borax (sodium borate), probably familiar to many readers as the 'borax bead' of analytical chemistry, was infrequently used in antiquity.

Silica appears naturally in the form of a glass as obsidian, a mineral laid down under the high temperatures of volcanic conditions. Silica melts at 1,710°C., and since this temperature is far in excess of the melting point of any ceramic body silica must be modified with a flux to be of use as a glaze. A number of other metallic oxides have the ability to act as fluxes to produce stable glasses; the oxides of sodium, potassium lead, calcium, barium, magnesium, zinc and aluminium.

One particular difficulty in discussing glasses is the fact that no exact chemical formula can be devised to describe them. In the case of crystalline substances the elements of which they are composed are arranged in a definite pattern, the units of which repeat one another at regular intervals. Thus, in the case of rock crystal (a crystalline form of silica) the silicon and oxygen atoms are arranged in a regular lattice pattern, and this is reflected in the regular shape of the crystals. In glasses, on the other hand, the silicon and oxygen atoms are believed to be arranged in a random network pattern so that there is no repetition of units, hence their non-crystalline appearance. The metallic atoms of the modifiers or fluxes are believed to occupy the interstices of this network in an equally random manner.

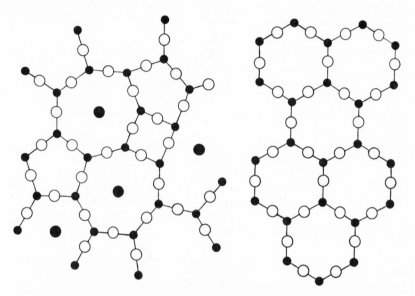

FIG. 4 DIAGRAM TO SHOW THE MOLECULAR STRUCTURE OF A GLASS (*left*) AND QUARTZ (*right*). OXYGEN ATOMS, WHITE; SILICON ATOMS, SMALL BLACK. LARGE BLACK CIRCLES REPRESENT THE POSITION OCCUPIED BY GLASS MODIFIERS.

Because of this the formulae of glasses are often expressed as complex oxides, the percentage proportion in which the oxides are known to be present being stated. The modifiers are given first, and then the glass formers. A simple lead glaze might thus be written as: 60·6% PbO: 39·4% SiO_2, meaning it contains 60·6% lead oxide by weight, the remainder being silica.

A second group of metallic oxides act as colourants in glasses. These include iron, copper, cobalt, chromium, manganese and nickel. While some also act as modifiers, others may most conveniently be looked upon as being in suspension in the glass rather than as part of its chemical structure.

GLAZE FORMERS

Since *silica* is present in nearly all ceramic bodies, the silica of many glazes is derived from this source. In other words, the modifier only may be applied to the surface of the pottery and this reacts with the silica and clay at the surface to form the glaze. Apart from this, silica may be derived from a wide variety of sources, for example flint, usually calcined and ground to a powder, or quartz sand (silver sand or Lynn sand). The yellow and red sands contain iron oxides which are glaze colourants, and hence these sands cannot be used for preparing white or colourless glazes. Rock crystal may equally be pulverized and used as a source of silica.

Apart from these relatively pure forms, silicon may find its way into glazes combined with other materials. It is, of course, a constituent of kaolinite, and may also be introduced in mica or felspars, or any pulverized rocks containing these.

Boron oxide is usually derived from sodium borate (borax or tincal) either hydrated ($Na_2O . 2B_2O_3 . 10H_2O$) or in the anhydrous form. Since borax has a very low melting point (741°C.) it has the effect of acting not only as a glaze former but also as a flux in combination with silica.

GLAZE MODIFIERS

Sodium oxide is quite commonly derived from sodium carbonate either as soda crystals ($Na_2CO_3 . 10H_2O$) or in the anhydrous form, soda ash (Na_2CO_3). Sodium nitrate is a less common source. It is, of course, introduced into any glaze in which borax is a constituent, but apart from this it may be derived from some rocks such as those containing albite (soda spar). In the process known as salt glazing it is derived from sodium chloride, generally in the form of rock salt, which is decomposed in the kiln atmosphere.

Potassium oxide is most commonly introduced either as potassium carbonate (pearl ash) or as the nitrate (nitre or saltpetre). Potassium carbonate is one of the important constituents of wood or vegetable ash, and potassium oxide may find its way into a glaze from this source. Some rocks used in glaze preparation, such as those containing orthoclase felspar, may be a source of potassium oxide.

Lead oxide may be introduced directly as either of the two oxides litharge (PbO) or red lead (Pb_3O_4). Equally the basic lead carbonate, white lead ($PbCO_3 . Pb(OH)_2$) may be used or even the sulphide ore, galena (PbS).

The commonest source of *calcium oxide* is from calcium carbonate added as whiting, chalk, limestone or marble; or calcium magnesium carbonate, dolomite. Other sources are from hydrated calcium sulphate (gypsum), calcium fluoride (fluorspar) and bone ash, which contains both calcium phosphate and calcium carbonate. Wood ash also contains the carbonate.

The usual source of *barium oxide* is the mineral sulphate, barytes or heavy spar.

Magnesium oxide is generally derived either from magnesium carbonate (magnesia, magnesite) or from the hydrated silicate as talc or steatite.

Zinc oxide is normally derived either from calamine ($ZnCO_3$) or zinc blende (ZnS). It seems not to have been used deliberately in antiquity, although today it is an ingredient of commercial 'Bristol glazes' used on domestic wares.

Alumina most commonly finds its way into glazes in kaolinite, felspar or mica, and is one of the constituents of wood ash. Apart from these very common sources it may be added as the hydrated mineral, bauxite, or in the calcined form.

GLAZE COLOURANTS

Since most secondary clays contain iron in one form or another, it is seldom necessary to look beyond these for a source of *iron oxide*. When fired under oxidizing conditions iron oxide colours glazes yellow, red or brown, depending upon the quantity present. Under reducing conditions it gives greens. When too much iron oxide is present, 10 % of the glaze or more, it will be coloured deep purple-brown or red-black. Any of the ores from which iron may be smelted (p. 81) may be ground and added to the glaze. When the ore is poorly ground, or when a red clay contains small nodules of iron ores, these will produce local patches of excess iron oxide in the glaze appearing as dark brown or black spots in the surface.

Copper oxides may be introduced as any of the common copper ores (p. 65) although the oxide and carbonate ores are the most common sources. Under oxidizing conditions copper oxide colours glazes blue or green depending partly upon what glaze modifiers are present. Thus, with lead oxide, copper oxide will give greens, with sodium or potassium oxide the colour will be turquoise blue. Under reducing conditions copper oxide gives a red colour. Copper oxide is normally present in the proportion of 2-5 %. Above this, the glaze darkens and may be black.

The commonest source of *cobalt oxide* is the mineral ashbolite, an impure oxide of manganese. Less common is the sulphide, linnaeite. By itself cobalt oxide gives a clear blue, as typified in early blue-and-white china (as, for example, Willow-pattern) but may be used with other colourants to give blue-greens (with iron, copper or chromium oxides) or violet-blues (with manganese oxide). A very strong colourant, cobalt oxide is normally only used in the range of $\frac{1}{2}$-1 %.

Manganese oxide may be introduced either as the dioxide or carbonate of manganese, and will give purple-brown or violets depending upon what other modifiers are present. With iron it gives a black. It is generally used as about 2-6 % of the glaze material but its colour fades if fired above 1,200°C.

Chromium oxide is generally added directly as the oxide chromite, which also contains iron, or as a chromate or bichromite. It is a difficult colourant to use since its colour so often depends not only on the other modifiers present but also on the temperature to which it is fired. Thus with lead it will produce reds at low temperatures and brown or green at higher temperatures. With tin it will give reds or pinks. It is normally used as 2-5 % of the glaze.

Nickel Oxide may be introduced from a number of sources, chiefly the mineral millerite (NiS). Alone it produces drab greens, but with iron gives browns, and in greater concentrations black.

Gold has only been used as a colourant in comparatively recent times, since in antiquity the metal could not be dissolved. It forms a colloidal mixture with tin oxide which is a deep purple, purple of Cassius, and is thus technically not a true colourant.

Tin oxide was normally introduced as cassiterite (SnO_2) although it could also have been added accidentally, as when pewter (p. 95) was calcined to provide lead oxide. Tin oxide is not strictly speaking a colourant, but gives glazes a white opacity since it exists in the glaze material as a mass of minute crystals, that is to say as a colloid.

PREPARATION OF GLAZES

Although some glazes may be formed simply by applying dry materials from which the glaze modifier is to be derived directly to the surface of the vessel, it is far more common to apply glazes as a suspension of fine particles in water, with or without an adhesive. Any glaze in which the raw materials are simply ground up and applied in this way is called a *raw glaze*. For a number of reasons many raw materials cannot be applied in this way. All the sodium and potassium compounds mentioned above, with the exception of the felspars, are highly soluble in water, and if applied directly to the biscuit would be absorbed by the body rather than remain on the surface. To overcome this difficulty the raw materials that make up the glaze are fused (fritted) in a crucible to form an insoluble glass, or *frit*. This material is then pulverized, suspended in water, and applied to the biscuit. Other raw materials such as calcium carbonate or sulphate give off gases, carbon dioxide or sulphur dioxide, at high temperatures and these may cause blisters in the glaze. This difficulty can again be overcome by getting rid of these gases while fritting. When lead glazes are applied raw there is a danger that some of the lead salts may remain uncombined and so become a potential source of poisoning. Although it was never done in antiquity, lead glazes are usually fritted today to avoid this risk.

The first essential in the making of a good glaze is to reduce all the ingredients to a sufficiently fine particle size. Many crushing machines were used for this purpose in antiquity, varying from simple querns or pestles and mortars to roller mills, and the material was often either elutriated or passed through fine-mesh screens to remove any large particles.

Today the potter can, by applying a few very simple chemical concepts, foretell the characteristics of any glaze he may concoct within fairly narrow limits. This, of course, was not the case in antiquity and the formulation of any glaze had to be arrived at by trial and error; and when one considers the probable cost of such experimentation to the potter it is hardly surprising that once a satisfactory glaze had been devised it remained in use, unaltered, over a long period. Even today the greatest single difficulty is for the potter to devise a glaze that will contract on cooling to the same degree as the body to which it is applied, and when this is achieved the glaze is said to *fit*. If the glaze contracts more than the body, it will part to produce a mesh of cracks over the surface, a defect known as *crazing*, while if the glaze does not contract sufficiently it will lift from the body, or *scale*. Glazes containing a high proportion of sodium or potassium oxide, for example, have a high coefficient of contraction, and are thus particularly prone to crazing, while glazes containing much calcium or lead oxide have a far lower coefficient of contraction and hence are less likely to suffer from this defect.

APPLYING GLAZES

When glaze materials are not applied dry, the liquid glaze may be sprayed on to the wares or the wares may be dipped in the fluid; while applying all-over glaze with a brush, although practised, resulted in a very uneven coating. After the wares have been allowed to dry they may either be placed on setters or, if these are not being used, the glaze material has to be removed from the bases of the wares, a process known as *dry footing*, to prevent their sticking to the bats or shelves during firing.

As has already been said, glazed wares may be fired in a conventional kiln only when the result of direct contact with the fire is not likely to affect the finished product. Otherwise the wares are set in saggers, or a muffle-kiln or glost oven is used. During firing the glaze should not only melt but, ideally, run evenly over the surface of the wares. The temperature at which this takes place is known as the *maturing point* of the glaze, and it should be noticed that the maturing point of a glaze is slightly above its melting point, in contrast to the maturing point of a body, which must be lower than the melting point.

COLOUR DECORATION

When glazed wares are to be decorated in colour, the colouring materials may be applied directly to the green-hard or biscuit wares before glazing. These *underglaze colours* must be such as will stand the temperature at which the glaze is to be fired. In general the colours are painted on, either as a suspension in water or mixed with gums or oils. In the latter instance it is essential to burn out the gum or oil in a low temperature oven before applying the glaze, a process known as *hardening-on firing*.

By contrast *on-glaze* or *overglaze decoration* may be applied either to biscuit wares that have been glazed but are, as yet, unfired or to glazed wares that have had a glost firing. Unfortunately, there seem to be no universally accepted terms to describe these rather different processes. The application of glaze colouring materials to an unfired glazed surface is called *majolica* by some potters; but to other potters the term may mean any glaze of low maturing point with overglaze colouring. The process of applying colours to an already fired glazed surface is called *enamelling* by some potters, while to others the term is synonymous with over-glaze colouring no matter how or when applied. Strictly speaking, the term enamelling is applicable only to a particular type of glass generally fired to a metal backing (p. 63).

The colouring materials used in the majolica type of overglaze decoration must, like those used in underglaze decoration, be able to stand the temperature of the glaze maturing point, and there is naturally a tendency for the colours to run into the glaze when it is molten to produce a fuzzy edge to the coloured areas. Colours of the enamel type may be applied alone or mixed with a flux. In the former case the temperature of the wares is raised until the glaze softens sufficiently to allow the colours to be absorbed by it, but not sufficiently to melt the glaze fully. Where a flux is used the temperature is raised only enough to produce a softening of the glaze in the painted areas.

Overglaze colours were most commonly applied in antiquity by brush. *Transfer printing* is of comparatively modern date (from the eighteenth century in Europe). In this process the frit was mixed with oils or resins and the mixture applied to a printing plate. The pattern was thus transferred to unsized paper and by applying the paper to the pottery the frit and oil or resin binders were again transferred, the oil and resin burning out on firing. Transfers of this kind are, of course, extensively used today and are sometimes erroneously called *decalcomania*. This term, however, should be reserved to describe unfired transfers in vogue in the middle of the nineteenth century. In *bat printing* oil only was applied to the printing plate, and this was transferred by means of a sheet of gelatine to the surface of the pottery. The pottery was then dusted with dry frit which adhered to those areas in which there was oil, and the pottery was fired.

Classification of Glazes

Glazes may be classified by a number of quite different criteria: (1) by their maturing temperatures; (2) by the nature of their contents, principally the main modifier; (3) by the visual effect they produce; and (4) by reference to the wares to which they are normally applied.

1. It is general to speak of soft and hard glazes, *soft glazes* being those that mature at low temperatures and *hard glazes* being those that mature at high temperatures. The terms have no precise meaning and are used in a relative sense to describe not only glazes in general, but differences within a specific group of glazes; thus one may say that lead glazes are soft and felspathic glazes are hard, and equally one may speak of hard and soft lead glazes or hard and soft felspathic glazes.

In industrial potteries today the following classification depending upon maturing temperature is commonly used, and it should be noticed that the terminology depends upon the wares to which the glazes are commonly applied:

$$900°-1,050°C. \quad \text{Majolica glazes}$$
$$1,000°-1,150°C. \quad \text{Earthenware glazes}$$
$$1,200°-1,300°C. \quad \text{Stoneware and sanitary ware glazes}$$
$$1,300°-1,450°C. \quad \text{Porcelain glazes}$$

The difficulty of using this type of classification when speaking of archaeological material is that it refers to only one feature of the glaze, ignores the chemical composition of the material and is too broad a classification to have much meaning.

2. A classification of glazes based upon the principal modifiers or their source of origin thus seems the most practicable for the present purpose.

1. Lead glazes
2. Alkaline glazes
   a. Soda-lime glazes
   b. Potash-lime glazes
   c. Salt glazes
   d. Felspathic glazes
3. Slip glazes

Lead Glazes are exceptionally easy to produce since the damp clay shapes need only be powdered with lead oxide, white lead or galena and fired until the glaze matures to produce perfectly serviceable wares. But the use of lead for glazing is restricted by the fact that it volatilizes at about 1,150°C., and bodies that mature near or above this temperature must first be fired as biscuit and then be glazed and glost fired. A better quality of glaze nearly always results after applying the lead compound as a suspension in water, and a very common feature of lead glaze applied as a powder is not only its generally blotchy nature but also a tendency for larger lumps of the material to etch small pits into the body of the wares, leaving, on cooling, a small number of small glaze-filled craters.

Soda-lime and *potash-lime glazes*, because of the solubility of sodium and potassium salts, cannot easily be applied raw as are lead glazes, but are normally fritted first. In theory it is possible to produce a wide range of glazes with different maturing points by altering the proportions of alkali, lime and silica, but in practice too much alkali will produce a glaze prone to crazing while too much silica may result in a glaze with a maturing point either too high for the primitive kiln or for the body to which it is to be applied. It is for this reason that this type of glaze was, for example, used in early Egypt only on objects of quartz, steatite or Egyptian faience (itself a soda-lime-quartz composite material) but never on pottery. Suitable deposits of sodium minerals are not common, and potash derived from wood or vegetable materials was often used instead. Such ashes vary considerably in their content, but the usual constituents are: alumina (10-15 %), silica (30-70 %), potash (up to 15 %), lime (up to 30 %), with variable small quantities of iron oxide, magnesia and phosphates.

Wood ashes, in fact, contain all the essential ingredients for producing a glaze, and in *ash glazing* the wood ash is simply dusted on to the surface of the wares before firing. Because of the rather low potash content, the maturing point of this kind of glaze is never much below 1,200°C., and this restricts its use to the less primitive kilns and bodies with relatively high maturing points.

Salt glazing works on a rather different principle since the salt is thrown into the fire, where it vaporizes and reacts with steam from the fuel to produce sodium oxide, which forms a glaze with the silica of the body of the wares, and hydrochloric acid which escapes through the vent. This chemical reaction will not take place below 1,100°C. and has an optimum rate at about 1,250°C. so restricting its use to the glazing of bodies that mature around this temperature. The glaze tends to be rather thin with an uneven surface somewhat like orange-peel, although a thicker glaze results if the body contains some lime. All the inner surfaces of the kiln, of course, also become glazed during the process.

Felspars may be pulverized and used alone or as the main constituents of a glaze. Although a flux such as lime may be used to lower the melting point slightly, because of their relatively high alkali content it is also necessary to add some silica to prevent crazing. On balance, therefore, *felspathic glazes* tend to be hard glazes, and are normally to be found on porcelain bodies.

Glazes that are composed principally of clay are called *slip glazes*. Thus a fusible, iron-bearing clay may be used over a more refractory body that has been already biscuit fired. Few red clays melt below 1,200°C. and most mature (in the sense of a glaze) rather above this. Care must be taken to distinguish slip glazes, which have vitrified, from glosses, which are fine, unvitrified slips (p. 34).

Briefly, it will be seen that unless a fritted glaze is being used, the choice of glaze is very much dictated by the nature of the body being glazed; lead glazes for earthenware bodies; salt or ash glazes for stoneware bodies; felspathic glazes for porcelain bodies. When all is said and done, frits are time-consuming to produce and, unless the contents are carefully controlled, erratic in their behaviour, since small changes in their balance may result in quite large variations in their maturing points and alter their fit. Seen in this light the apparently extreme conservatism of the potters of antiquity may not seem so extraordinary.

3. Apart from the normal clear, unbroken vitreous glaze a number of more or less decorative effects may be produced by what, under other circumstances, might be looked upon as defects; matt glazes, crystalline glazes, aventurine glazes, lustres and crackle glazes.

Crackle is nothing more than a polite name for crazing, and is often simpler to produce than to avoid. It is generally produced by raising the proportion of alkali to silica in the glaze, either accidentally or deliberately. On an impermeable body which would hold water anyway without glazing, it is an excusable decorative effect, but on a permeable body crazing must be regarded as a sign of inferior workmanship.

Matt glazes are those which are dull in appearance, the effect resulting from non-vitreous inclusions in the glaze, such as particles of bone, pitchers, felspar or talc that have not been dissolved. In such cases the glaze has, in fact, not been matured and remains under-fired.

On the other hand, too much zinc or calcium oxide in the glaze will form zinc or calcium silicate crystals if the glaze is allowed to cool very slowly. Since most early kilns cooled, if anything, rather too quickly, matt glazes in antiquity are generally a sign of under-firing.

Crystalline glazes may be substantially no more than matt glazes in which the cooling has been so delayed that large crystals of zinc or calcium silicate have been given time to form. Because of the difficulty of producing slow cooling conditions, this type of glaze is virtually unknown in antiquity. On the other hand, glazes may be overloaded with some colourant, such as iron or manganese oxide, to such an extent that on cooling flecks may appear in the glaze. These *aventurine glazes* are not true crystalline glazes, and should not be described as such.

After long burial, glazes sometimes devitrify, becoming crystalline, and it is important to distinguish those that have devitrified with age from deliberately produced crystalline glazes. On the whole this is not difficult since glazes that have devitrified with age have usually also decayed.

Lustres are essentially glazes that have been so reduced that some of the metallic oxides added as modifiers or colourants have been converted to the metal. There are two fundamental types: in-glaze and on-glaze lustres. Most lustres depend upon the reduction of silver or copper salts, or a mixture of the two. In-glaze lustres are fired in the normal way, but at some stage during cooling (usually about 650°-750°C.) a great deal of damp organic matter is fed into the kiln fire to produce heavily reducing conditions. On-glaze lustres are applied directly to the surface of glazed wares which are then re-fired and, again, reduced heavily on cooling.

4. It would not be possible to list here all the names of wares that have been used to specify different glazes or glazing techniques. A few examples will be sufficient to show the difficulty of this type of classification, a difficulty born initially from the fact that few potters agree as to how widely any one term may legitimately be applied.

Today the terms faience, majolica and tin-enamel glaze are all variously applied to mean wares with a red body covered with a tin-opacified lead glaze which has been coloured with over-glaze designs. The terms faience and majolica initially referred only to wares made under Moorish influence at Faenza and Majorca, but in the wide sense in which they are now used by many potters they would include not only the original Moorish wares but also the Dutch Delft wares which were made in imitation of Chinese porcelain.

This is itself sufficiently confusing, but the term faience is often used by archaeologists to describe the turquoise-blue alkaline glazed objects of early Egyptian origin, with a core of quartz, steatite or a soda-lime and quartz composition. In view of this, it is always advisable to qualify terms such as faience, where any confusion might result from a failure so to do. Such phrases as Egyptian faience, true faience and faience-like glazes can leave no doubt in the reader's mind as to what is intended.

GLAZE DEFECTS

Crawling, running or *cut glazes* are those that have run off the surface of the wares during firing. Generally this is due either to a dirty surface to which the glaze was applied or to over-firing, that is to say, producing too fluid a glaze which has simply run off the surface. In many primitive glazed wares the occasional bare patch did not make the pottery un-saleable, but where the pots had been set one above another the glaze might run down between the base of one pot and the rim of the other so that on cooling the two would become joined. The more sophisticated potter might throw both away, but the primitive potter might sacrifice one and chip it away from the other, making little or no attempt to disguise the blemish.

Peeling, flaking, scaling, chipping or *shivering* of a glaze usually results from a failure to fit the glaze to the body, the contraction of the glaze being less than that of the body. The same result may, however, be due to too rapid cooling of the kiln. In either event such wares have no market value and are discarded.

Crazing results from too great a coefficient of contraction of the glaze. The crazing may be so bad that the wares cannot be sold; it may be no more than a fine crackle.

Pin-holes, pits, dimples, blisters, blobs and *spit-out* (fine, broken blisters) are most commonly due to the evolution of gases from the body during firing puncturing the molten glaze. Air or water in the body may have this effect, or the cause may be the break-down of carbonates or sulphates to give off carbon or sulphur dioxide gases. As in practice some gases must invariably be given off, these defects may be caused simply by firing too rapidly. Lead glazes are particularly prone to blistering if over-reduced.

Under-firing may result in *starved glazes* which have a dull appearance, or in *matt* or *eggshell glazes* which are dull and often full of small pin-holes.

Specks, if not due to poor grinding of the glaze materials, may be due to contamination of the glaze or even dust dropping on to the wares from the roof of the muffle.

Efflorescence, sulphuring, starring or *feathering* are normally due to the formation of lead or calcium sulphate on the surface of the glaze. The sulphur dioxide which causes this may come either from sulphates in the body or from the fuel, especially when coal is being used.

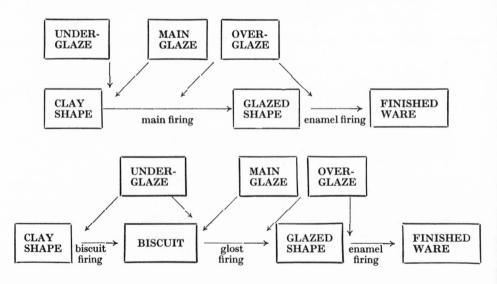

NORMAL MATURING TEMPERATURES OF BODIES AND GLAZES

Temperature		Bodies	Glazes
Cone No.	°C.		
0·019 0·016	650 800	Under-fired terracotta	Soft over-glaze colours (enamels)
0·015 0·011	900	Terracotta	Over-glaze lustres; hard over-glaze colours
0·010 0·05	1,050	Red earthenware	Glosses; lead glazes; soft alkaline glazes
0·04 0·01	1,150	Buff and cream earthenware; red stoneware	
1 4	1,200	Red clays *melt* – –	– – – Slip glazes
5 9	1,300	Grey stoneware	Salt glazes; ash glazes
10 16	1,450	Porcelains	Felspathic glazes

Chapter Three

GLASS AND ENAMELS

SYNOPSIS

General: Glass and Glazes. *Composition:* Formers · Modifiers · Colourants · Cullet. *Classification:* Simple · Compound · Complex · Classification based on modifiers · Clear · Opaque. *Shaping (Vessels):* Abrading · Flaking · Core-dipping · Core-winding · Glass-paste · Mould-blowing · Free-blowing. *Decoration:* Cutting · Engraving · Casing · Mosaic · Applied decoration · Inlay · Millefiore · False aventurine · Sandwich glass · Etching. *Other Glass Objects:* Cane and tubing · Beads · Window glass · Glass cameos. *Enamels:* Champlevé · Cloisonné · Plique-à-jour · Counter enamelling · Basse-taille.

GENERAL

GLASS DIFFERS FROM a glaze in the fact that it is used alone to form objects and is not supported by a body or any other backing. Chemically the two can be identical, but there is one very fundamental difference that militates against this being so in antiquity; the coefficient of contraction of a glass on cooling is quite unimportant, whereas in a glaze any such difference between glaze and body may cause the former to craze or peel. As a result the makers of early glasses tended to use a different set of criteria when formulating their material; for ease of working, a glass with a low melting point, and one that remained plastic as long as possible, was often to be preferred. Equally, transparency was commonly looked for in a glass, while in glazes sufficient opacity to mask the body was the more normal aim.

COMPOSITION

As with glazes, a glass may most conveniently be looked upon as a combination of network former, modifier and colourant. The common network *former* was, of course, quartz introduced either as sand or as crushed flint. In the Near East, quartz sands relatively pure and free from iron, which are fairly widely obtainable, were the commoner source; but in many parts of Europe the sands were too impure to be of use, and flint was normally used instead where clear glass was required. Sands of this kind can be used for making dark glass provided they are washed and then *burned*, or brought to red heat to remove any organic matter, before being used.

The principal network modifiers found in ancient glass are the oxides of sodium, potassium, calcium and lead. Sodium oxide was generally introduced either as sodium carbonate or as the nitrate, and in the Near East, where relatively pure deposits of soda ash and nitre occur, sodium oxide was the main modifier used. Potassium oxide was normally introduced as potassium carbonate or nitrate, the carbonate often being derived from wood or plant ash, in some regions the only readily available source of a modifier. Glasses composed of those modifiers alone are not stable to water and in practice some calcium or lead oxide had to be introduced to give a permanently insoluble material. Calcium oxide, today usually added as lime or limestone, could only be used in limited proportions since excess, as with glazes, would cause devitrification, but it is in fact doubtful whether it was ever deliberately added in antiquity and it seems likely that it became incorporated as an impurity in other ingredients. Lead oxide gives a particular brilliance and density to glass and was often used where these qualities were demanded. Where any choice of materials was available the glassmaker could balance the choice of modifier against the required properties; potassium compounds would provide a glass with a low melting-point and a wide temperature range of plasticity; sodium compounds a higher melting-point and a shorter range of plasticity, but the end product would be clearer and more lustrous. Alumina, which would raise the melting-point, was obviously to be avoided, but it nevertheless was introduced accidentally, usually from the walls of the crucibles or glass pots, possibly as an impurity, such as basalt, in the sand.

The common *colourants* for glasses were precisely the same as those used in making glazes and they present few technical problems. Indeed, the chief difficulty for the early glass-maker was to eliminate colour in order to make a water-white glass, and by far and away the main problem was to be free of iron oxide that tinted the glass yellow or green, although the pale bluish-green of sodium silicate or the yellowish tint of lead silicate might always remain. Today this is overcome by counter-tinting with a trace of purple manganese dioxide, and it seems almost certain that this was done deliberately in antiquity, at least by the Roman period. Scrupulous care in the selection of materials and thorough washing were, however, probably the more common steps taken to avoid this defect.

Unlike the potter who had only to alter the atmosphere of his kiln to produce oxidized or reduced colourings, the glass-worker had to achieve this effect within the material. Normally the colourants in a glass would be in a reduced condition, but many of the materials added as modifiers, such as potassium nitrate and red lead, produced free oxygen within the molten glass, and the oxidized colourings could be produced by their use. Doubtless early glass-workers understood this empirically.

In the making of glass one other ingredient was commonly added, broken scrap glass, normally of the same composition as the batch, called *cullet*. Its function is purely physical; it acts as a nucleus around which the new glass forms, and thus its presence helps to eliminate unevenness such as cords and striae in the new batch. Apart from this, the actual process of making glass was not complicated; it demanded, of course, an open furnace and crucibles of refractory materials—in practice, clays free from fluxes. The molten material once formed is known as *glass-metal*.

CLASSIFICATION

Unfortunately, today those engaged in glass-making sometimes classify glasses according to the actual ingredients used in their making. *Simple glasses*, apart from silica, contain only a single modifier, while *compound glasses* contain two modifiers as, for example, crystal glass which contains the oxides of potassium and lead, Bohemian glass containing potassium and calcium, or sheet or plate glass with varying proportions of sodium and calcium. *Complex glasses* contain many impurities, a large part of the modifiers often being derived from igneous rocks; common bottle glass, for example, frequently contains basalt and dolomite. The disadvantage of this system for the present purpose is that it demands a knowledge of the actual ingredients used in making the metal, while we are normally working backwards from a chemical analysis, and can seldom say with certainty the precise nature of the raw materials. In view of this, a classification according to the principal modifiers present would seem preferable. We may thus speak of a potash-lime glass, meaning that the principal modifier is potassium oxide with calcium oxide also present in a smaller proportion. Equally, one may use soda-lime or potash-lead, and so on, as a means of classification.

As with glazes, glass may also be classified according to its appearance —clear, semi-opaque, opaque, aventurine. This, while being adequate for purely descriptive purposes, fails to distinguish between specifically different types of glass. Thus, opacity may be due to the presence of tin oxide, for example, or may result from some recrystallization or, more simply, from the presence of minute air bubbles, while the spangles in an aventurine glass may be due to iron or copper oxide, as in blood-glass or haematinum, or to the presence of foreign bodies such as minute flakes of mica.

SHAPING

The following methods apply chiefly to the making of glass vessels; other forms such as beads and window-glass will be dealt with separately.

Once cold, glass can be treated as a stone; a solid lump of glass can be reduced to the required shape by *abrading* the unwanted parts (p. 105), and thus a flat slab of glass might be hollowed to produce a bowl, the outside being trimmed by the same method. Theoretically glass could also be shaped by flaking (p. 99), but there seems to be no record of this ever having been done in antiquity, although at one time the aborigines of Australia found the glass insulators used for telephone wires particularly suitable as a raw material from which to make arrowheads.

However, since glass must become plastic during its manufacture, it is only to be expected that nearly all shaping processes use glass in this condition. One of the simpler methods is that of *core-dipping* in which a core of clay, generally heavily filled with sand, is made around a rod, and this is coated with glass by dipping into the molten metal. Alternatively, the core might be made of compacted sand covered by a piece of cloth tied round the rod, or more simply still a small bag filled with sand. On cooling, the core is removed. In *core-winding* the glass was first drawn into rods (p. 61), known as *cane*, and these were reheated and wound round the core. The core and winding were then reheated and rolled backwards and forwards on a smooth surface, normally a flat stone, known as a *marver*, so producing a smooth face to the vessel.

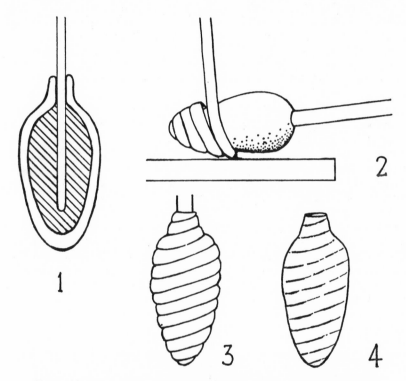

FIG. 5 CORE-DIPPING AND WINDING. CORE-DIPPED VESSEL (1). FORMATION OF CORE-WOUND VESSEL (2 AND 3), MARVERED AND ABRASION POLISHED (4).

The use of glass-paste (Fr. *pâte de verre*) does not depend upon the plasticity of molten glass. The metal is ground to a powder and then mixed with an adhesive to form a material that can be shaped as is clay —modelled, moulded or wheel thrown—and the object fired like pottery. The adhesive, being organic, would burn out while the glass particles would fuse, the final product being somewhat opaque.

These methods show a technical dependence on the craft of the potter; the use of glass-paste more so than the others, although in method there is a striking parallel between core-dipping and slipping, or core-winding and coil building. There is no such dependence in *glass-blowing*. A *gathering* (Fr. *paraison*) of glass-metal was taken from the crucible on the end of a blow-iron, an iron tube usually about four or five feet long and varying from half-an-inch to an inch in diameter, often with a pear-shaped end to hold the gathering. In mould-blowing a gathering is taken on the blow-iron, marvered, blown into a small elongated bulb, and this is introduced into a two-piece metal mould and blown to fill it. On cooling the mould is opened and the surplus glass-metal at the top and the flashes formed between the mould-pieces are trimmed away. (Today blowing is done mechanically, but the residual flashes are easily seen on bottles and cheap table-ware.) In *free-blowing* no mould is used. Instead a bulb of glass is blown on the end of the iron and shaped either by marvering, the marver itself sometimes having shaped hollows to help

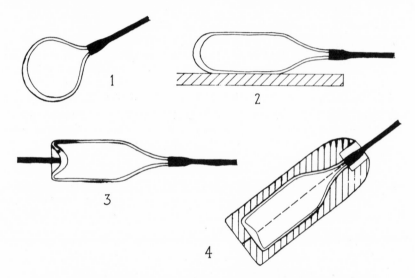

FIG. 6 FREE AND MOULD BLOWING. A BULB (1) IS MARVERED (2) AND THE BASE FORMED BY PRESSURE FROM THE PUNTY (3). SECTION THROUGH MOULD (4).

produce definite shapes; or it may be shaped with the aid of a flat board with a handle, a *battledore* (Fr. *pallette*). Bowls and drinking glasses may be produced by first sticking the bulb to a solid iron rod, a *punty* (Fr. *pontil*), opposite the blow-tube and then cutting free with *shears*; and the mouth may be further opened or reduced by using *tongs* (It. *pucella*). In blown glass generally there is a tendency for the material to become thicker the further it is from the blow-iron, and the same phenomenon can also be seen in toy rubber balloons. Bottles were most commonly made by blowing a bulb, marvering into shape and then pressing in the end opposite the blow-iron to give the characteristic dimple foot so carefully reproduced in machine-made wine bottles today. The bases of bottles were thus usually substantially thicker than their necks. All glass-blowing demands a good pair of lungs, but in the blowing of exceptionally large vessels a subterfuge was sometimes used. Having

blown a bulb, the worker took a mouthful of water and ejected it down
the blow-iron, quickly putting his thumb over the mouth-piece. The
steam generated inside the bulb then continued the blowing process for
him. Free-blowing naturally demands far greater skill than mould-
blowing but it does allow a very wide freedom of design. As in the case
of the potter's wheel, it is perhaps for this reason that the method was in
general used over a very long period of time.

Good glass-ware was often finally *polished* using a fine, hard abrasive,
and where this has been exceptionally well carried out much of the evidence that would suggest how the vessel was made—the rough surface
in contact with a core, or casting-flashes, for example—may have been
removed.

Decoration

Plain glass surfaces may be decorated by *cutting* with a lap-wheel or
engraving with a diamond point (p. 107). The actual treatment of the
design may vary considerably; one may find no more than a simple
linear pattern, or the whole surface may be elaborately facetted, or
again the design may be worked in low relief and the whole background
cut away. The latter technique was sometimes used to produce a cameo
effect in conjunction with *casing*, or *cupping*, in which a vessel of a glass
of one colour was blown into a vessel of another colour, often white, the
two then being annealed. The design was then worked in relief on the
outer glass which, for the background areas, was cut completely away to
expose the inner glass. Another method employing the use of different
coloured glass-metals and subsequent cutting was the making of *agate
glass* in which layers of differently coloured glass, usually of different
thicknesses, were fused and the whole block then ground down. The effect
is often remarkably like that of worked natural agate. *Mosaic glass* was
produced by arranging pieces of differently coloured glass either on a flat
clay surface or in a hollow clay mould and then heating until they fused.
The surface was then ground smooth.

Decorative detail was sometimes *applied* by fusing pieces of glass of
the same or different colours to the surface of the vessel. If the walls of
the vessel are reasonably thin, this can be a very difficult business, as
the process of applying and shaping the additions to the near-molten
vessel will tend to distort it. In practice this limits the style and complexity of the decoration to such an extent that blobs of various shapes,
or cane added as coils, wavy lines or zig-zags, are by far the most common
motifs.

Glass vessels can also be *inlaid* with a glass, or glasses, of another
colour. In *thread inlay*, glass threads were laid on the surface of the
vessel, and the whole was then reheated and marvered. The threads
might be partly or completely worked down to the surface of the glass
by marvering, and in the former case the whole surface might be worked
down on a lap-wheel so cutting away those parts of the threads standing
out from the face. The threads might be wound spirally round the vessel,
or by working a number of threads at the same time between the teeth
of a comb-like tool, they might be applied as chevrons, waves, festoons

or feather-patterns. *Combed* glass was produced by applying threads in the same manner to a gathering of glass-metal and then reheating, blowing and marvering. The threads were not necessarily each of a glass of a single colour. For this purpose *glass-filigree* was sometimes used, this being made by fusing rods of differently coloured glasses which were then reheated and drawn out, while sometimes twisting or interlacing at the same time. *Inlaid mosaic* glass could be produced by arranging small pieces of coloured glass on a marver, either randomly or in some definite pattern, followed by rolling the heated vessel over this surface, so picking up the glass fragments. The whole was then reheated and marvered or

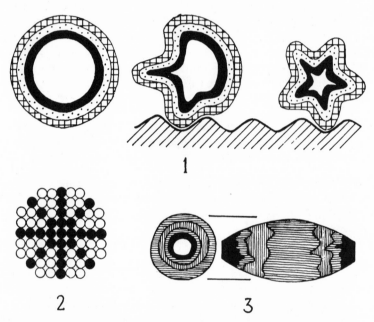

FIG. 7 MILLEFIORE AND 'AGATE' GLASS. STAGES IN THE MAKING OF A MILLEFIORE MOTIF (1). A MOTIF MADE BY FUSING GLASS RODS (2). SECTION THROUGH CASED GLASS TUBE AND 'AGATE' BEAD MADE FROM IT (3).

ground smooth. Alternatively the glass fragments might be picked up on the surface of a gathering which was then reheated and blown. As a final refinement the gathering with its mosaic pieces might be further cased with clear glass before blowing.

The distinction is not always clearly made between true mosaic glass and mosaic inlay although the two are quite different. In the one, obviously, the coloured glass pieces make up the whole thickness of the vessel, while in the other the pieces are backed by a glass of a uniform colour. Some modern glass-workers also incorrectly call any mosaic inlay *millefiore*. True millefiore is one of the more sophisticated inlay processes. As the name implies, the face of the vessel is inlaid with a mass of flower-like mosaic pieces. These were produced by casing either a tube or cane of glass with several layers of differently coloured glass, and then reheating and rolling on a corrugated surface and cutting into short lengths, the cross section of the tube or rod now being in the shape of a flower. For very small flowers the rods might be drawn out further after corrugating. The motifs were then inlaid as in mosaic inlay. Apart from flowers other designs were sometimes produced by laying together glass rods of different colours and fusing them, the whole then being drawn, cut and inlaid like millefiore. Both abstract and naturalistic motifs were made in this way, even small caricatures of human faces.

Glassware may also be decorated by making inclusions of non-vitreous materials in the glass-metal. Thus flaked mica may be used to produce an aventurine effect by sandwiching it between gatherings of glass-metal. Many materials, however, would become damaged if treated in this way. Gold is one of these, and in the making of gold sandwich-glass, the gold leaf was first applied in the cold and then covered with glass added drop by drop which was then polished. Alternatively, a glass with a low fusion temperature might have been powdered and the gold leaf covered with this material, the whole then being heated gently until the powdered glass fused, so coating the leaf.

Acid etching as a means of decorating glassware does not appear to have been used until the nineteenth century. This is hardly surprising since hydrofluoric acid—the only effective acid—is both difficult to prepare and dangerous from the health point of view. The method generally employed was to coat the glass with wax and scratch the design through this, the etching bath only attacking those areas in which the wax had been removed.

OTHER GLASS OBJECTS

Cane and Tubing. The simplest way of producing fine glass rod is to pour the molten metal very slowly from a crucible or ladle so that as it falls it cools and solidifies to give short lengths of rod. Longer and more even lengths of rod may be made by sticking a gathering of molten metal to an iron post or a plate in the wall and pulling out a length of cane with the aid of a punty by walking slowly away from the gathering. Glass tubing was produced in the same way save that the glass worker drew out the gathering with a blow-iron, and thus had to walk backwards and blow gently at the same time in order to maintain the cavity in the tube. Needless to say this required considerable skill.

Beads. Glass beads were made in a number of different ways, most of which have their parallels in the making of vessels. A small lump of cold glass might be shaped in the lap wheel or on a rubbing stone, and drilled using an abrasive. Alternatively, a lump of glass might be perforated with an iron rod while still plastic, and then cut to shape after cooling. Beads were also built up on an iron rod to provide the perforation. A length of cane might be made plastic and wound round the rod in a spiral; threads of glass might be twisted together and wrapped around the rod; or a small, flat rectangle of glass might be folded around it and the abutting edges fused or left unjoined. With the production of glass tubing, lengths could be cut off and then polished to provide simple cylindrical beads.

Beads were also made of glass paste. Like glassware made of the same material the beads were first modelled and then fired to cause fusion of the particles, the final product generally being more opaque than other glass.

The same methods of decoration were applied to beads as to glassware —thread inlay, mosaic inlay, millefiore, and so on. An agate effect was produced by casing glass tubing with layers of differently coloured glass and them chamfering down the ends of cut lengths to expose the various layers—'aggry' beads of the Orient.

Bangles. Most of the methods used in making glass beads can be applied to the manufacture of glass bangles. If not cut from a solid piece of glass, the two commonest means of producing bangles, however, are either by bending rod round and fusing the two ends, or by first blowing a hollow glass cylinder and then cutting it into short lengths. In the latter instance it is not uncommon to find that the glass gathering has been cased with several layers of differently coloured glass—an effect some-times faithfully copied in plastic materials today. All the methods of de-corating glassware can, of course, be applied to bangles.

Window glass. Early window glass, *crown glass*, was made by first blow-ing a hollow cylinder. A punty was attached opposite the blow-iron, and the blow-iron cut away with shears. The punty was then rotated rapidly so causing the glass to spread out into a circular disc. Only small sheets of glass could be produced in this way, the material being far thinner at the edges than in the middle. When the punty was detached it left a characteristic uneven thickening, the *bull's eye*, in the centre.

Larger and more even sheets of glass were produced by the *hand-cylinder* method in which a cylinder of glass was first blown and then placed on the marver. The two ends were then cut away with shears and the cylinder cut longitudinally and allowed to fall flat on the marver. Although of a more even thickness than crown glass, hand-cylinder glass remained very irregular by today's standards.

In making decorated glass windows the coloured panes might be of *pot-metal*, that is to say the colourant might be distributed through the whole thickness of the glass, but some colourants gave too opaque a glass if used in this way and to overcome this a plain glass was cased or flashed with a thin layer of coloured glass. This use of flashed glass had the double advantage that shading could be done by abrading different thicknesses of the casing. Dark lines and shading were also produced either by *glass-enamelling* or by staining. The enamel was made by fritting a potash-lead glass containing normally copper and iron oxides as colourants. The frit was often mixed with a gum to make it manage-able and painted on to the surface of the glass, which was then fired, so causing the enamel to melt and fuse to the glass pane, the gum burning out in the process. In *staining*, metallic silver was first heated in a crucible with sulphur to produce silver sulphide which was then ground to a fine powder and mixed with a fine clay, painted on the glass and fired. During the firing, the glass absorbed the colourant, silver oxide, and was thus, unlike enamelled work, actually stained. This work, how-ever, could only be done on the plain side of flashed glass since the silver sulphide would react with most other colourants, giving anything but the required results.

Glass Cameos. Glass has, of course, been used frequently to imitate gem stones. Cameo effects, simulating agate and other similar multi-coloured stones, were commonly produced by casing, say, a coloured glass with a white one, followed by cutting away the white glass in low relief.

ENAMELS

A true enamel is a vitreous substance fused to a metallic surface, although the term 'enamel' is frequently used to describe a similar material used to decorate ceramics and glass. Furthermore, not all vitreous substances applied to metals were true enamels, for many never actually fused to their metallic backing, and this is particularly true of most early 'enamels'. These were, instead, highly fusible glasses that were ground, applied to the metal and heated until they fused, and being basically either potash or soda glasses, their contraction on cooling was such that, unless the backing was designed to prevent it, they would fall away from the metal. A true enamel must, in fact, be so formulated as to satisfy two conditions; it must have a co-efficient of contraction roughly equivalent to that of the metallic backing; and its melting point must be lower than, but approximate to, that of its backing to ensure fusion. For these reasons most enamels are a lead-soda or lead-potash glass with, or without, colourants and opacifiers, the material being applied as a dried frit and fused in an enamelling oven. The surface of the cold enamel was normally polished level with an abrasive.

Enamels were seldom left with their surfaces standing above the level of the surrounding metal, but usually flush with it. This was achieved by providing a sunken area in which the enamel might be fused. These areas might be provided for in the original casting of the metal or cut out with scorpers, a technique known as *champlevé*. Alternatively, in *cloisonné* work, these areas were enclosed by a length of wire soldered on to the face of the metal. Enamels could also be applied without a backing, being held to the metal only at the edges. To do this type of work, *plique-à-jour*, the areas for the enamel were fretted and given a tem-porary backing of sheet mica or some similar material to which the enamel would not adhere. On very thin metal-work the contraction of the enamel on cooling might be sufficient to cause the metal to warp, and to counteract this the reverse face of the object might also be enamelled, a process known as *counter-enamelling* or *enamel backing*.

Apart from plain enamels, a number of techniques for decoration were employed very similar to those used on glassware as, for example, mosaic and millefiore. In *basse taille* work the metal backing was cut in low relief and a clear enamel applied over this, with the result that the enamel appeared darker over the deeper cutting and lighter over the shallow areas.

Chapter Four

COPPER AND COPPER ALLOYS

SYNOPSIS

General: Copper, bronze and brass.   *Ores:* 'Oxide ores' and 'sulphide ores'.   *Mining:* Fire-setting.   *Preparation of Ores.   Smelting:* Roasting · Bellows · Bowl furnace · Stückofen · Origins.   *Copper Alloys:* Bronze · Speculum · Tin ores · Brass · Zinc ores · Antimony, arsenic and lead bronzes.   *Casting:* Poling · Mould dressing · 'Open' moulds · Piece-moulds · False core · Lost-wax.   *Cold Working:* Annealing · Hammering · Sinking · Raising · Striking · Spinning · Turning · Drawing · Planishing.   *Joining:* Running-on · Burning-on · Soldering · Riveting · Seams.   *Decoration:* Repoussé · Tracing · Backgrounding · Engraving · Overlay · Inlay · Niello · Flushing.

GENERAL

PURE COPPER IS a relatively soft metal and as a result was never particularly effective as a material from which to make cutting tools. It can, however, be considerably hardened by mixing with other metals, such as tin and zinc, to produce the alloys bronze and brass. These alloys are not simple mixtures but complex crystalline structures in which quite small variations in the relative proportions of the ingredients can radically alter the properties of the material (p. 212). Before the discovery of bronze, and later brass, copper was, of course, used for the manufacture of tools, but since the working methods used in the preparation of both copper and its alloys are so similar, it will be most convenient to discuss them together.

In the production of a copper object there are five distinct stages of manufacture; the mining of the ores; the preparation and cleaning of the ores; the smelting to produce an ingot of metal; the refining and casting of the metal; and the final hot or cold working of the casting.

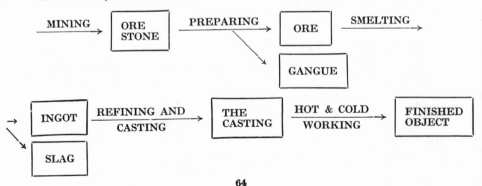

Ores

Relatively pure uncombined copper, *native copper*, occurs naturally in small quantities in the Old World and was presumably the earliest source of copper worked by man. Native copper is far purer than that normally produced by primitive metallurgical processes, but it is believed that its very limited occurrence may have made it a comparative rarity. It required neither smelting nor casting and could be worked into small articles simply by hammering, although of course, for larger objects, pieces of native copper could have been fused and cast, but to what extent this was done is a matter of debate.

The simplest copper ores to work are the so-called '*oxide-ores*' that appear in the weathered surface, or *gossan*, of copper-bearing deposits. Apart from the oxides of copper, *cuprite* (red oxide, Cu_2O) and *melaconite* (black oxide, CuO), this group includes the carbonates *malachite* (green basic carbonate, $Cu_2(OH)_2CO_3$) and *azurite* (blue basic carbonate, $Cu_3(OH)_2(CO_3)_2$), as well as the sulphate mineral *chalcanthite* (blue vitriol, $CuSO_45H_2O$) in arid regions only, the chloride mineral atacamite ($Cu_2(OH)_3Cl$) and the silicate *chrysocolla* ($CuSiO_32H_2O$). The brilliant colours of these minerals, the blues and greens of the carbonates and the liver red of cuprite, must have helped the primitive prospector considerably in his search for ores, although since they seldom appear in bulk save at the surface they would have been exhausted very early.

The so-called 'sulphide ores' are more difficult to work and come from the parent ore which is unweathered and from a zone of secondary enrichment between this and the gossan. This group includes the sulphide materials *chalcocite* (copper glance, Cu_2S) and *covellite* (CuS) from the zone of secondary enrichment, and the iron sulphide minerals *chalcopyrites* (copper pyrites, $Cu_2Fe_2S_4$) and *bornite* (peacock ore, Cu_5FeS_4).

Other copper-bearing ores of rather more restricted occurrence are important since they also contain the metals arsenic and antimony, and it may be through the use of such ores that these metals are found in some early coppers and alloys. These include the mineral *tetrahedrite* (fahlerz), a sulphide containing iron and antimony $((Cu, Fe)_{12}Sb_4S_{13})$; bournonite ($CuPbSbS_3$) containing lead and antimony; *tennantite* $((Cu, Fe)_{12}As_4S_{13})$ a sulphide containing iron and arsenic; and the sulphide of arsenic and copper, *enargite* ($Cu_3As . S_4$).

Mining

Apart from the very early stages when copper ores could be collected from the surface, *grubbing*, all copper ores had to be mined. For this purpose the simple tools used in quarrying (p. 109) were perfectly adequate. As mines grew deeper into the hillside a means of ventilation had to be developed, and this became even more essential where *fire-setting* (p. 108) was used as a means of breaking up the ore. For this purpose air-shafts, and very much later, air-pumps were introduced. In deep galleries supporting timbers also had to be used and in time many of these have become not only saturated with copper salts, but in some instances the salts have become reduced to metallic copper to give the effect of small flecks of copper embedded in the wood.

PREPARATION OF ORES

In the early exploitation of copper ores, since only the minerals themselves would have been collected, this stage was probably not a very complex one, requiring only the breaking down of the lumps of mineral into a size small enough to allow easy smelting. Deep-mined ores, however, contain a great deal of unwanted matter, chiefly silica, known as *gangue*, which had to be removed. The crude ores were broken down by pounding and the gangue removed, the large lumps by hand and the remainder by repeated washing, the gangue of lower specific gravity than the ore being carried away by the water. The relatively pure ore was then dried either in the sun or in an oven before smelting.

SMELTING

The finely divided 'oxide ores' are relatively simple to smelt, since in the presence of carbon the minerals will be reduced to the metal at a temperature of about 1,100°C.

$$2CuO + C \rightarrow 2Cu + CO_2.$$

As carbon, in the form of charcoal, is required to obtain this temperature, the mixed ore and charcoal need only be heated in the furnace together to provide the smelt; the liquefied metal will flow to the bottom of the furnace, while the siliceous matter will combine with any glass-modifiers present (soda, potash, etc.) to form a glassy material, *slag*, which being less dense than the copper will float on its surface.

The 'sulphide ores' cannot be so easily smelted, and it is essential to *roast* the ores first. In this process the ores are heated either in the open or in an oven with an ample supply of air. Some of the sulphide minerals become converted to the oxide:

$$2Cu_2S + 3O_2 \rightarrow 2Cu_2O + 2SO_2$$

and the oxides in turn react with the sulphides to form copper:

$$2Cu_2O + Cu_2S \rightarrow 6Cu + SO_2.$$

The resulting material, *matte*, is thus an impure mixture of copper and copper oxide which can be smelted like 'oxide ores'. Where the iron-bearing ores of copper, such as pyrites and bornite, are being worked, the process of roasting has the further function of removing the iron; the iron sulphide being first converted to the oxide:

$$2CuFeS_2 + 4O_2 \rightarrow Cu_2S + 2FeO + 3SO_2.$$

Following this, the iron oxide will, being a glass modifier, combine with any siliceous material present to form a slag which on cooling can be separated from the matte:

$$FeO + SiO_2 \rightarrow FeO . SiO_2.$$

If all the sulphides have not been reduced during roasting, the formation of sulphur dioxide gas during smelting will leave the copper full of blow-holes and give a very low-grade *blister copper*. The process of roasting has

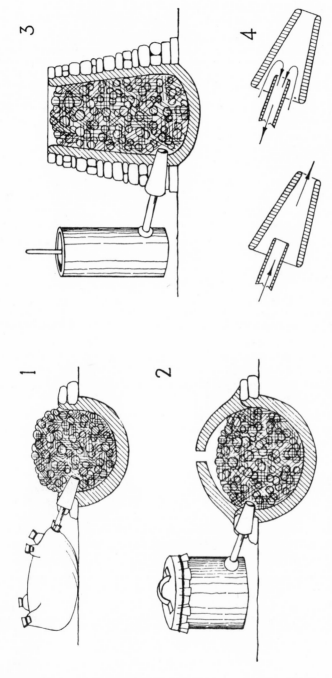

FIG. 8 SECTIONS THROUGH SIMPLE FURNACES. BOWL FURNACE WITH SKIN BELLOWS (1). DOMED FURNACE WITH DRUM BELLOWS (2). SHAFT FURNACE WITH CYLINDER BELLOWS (3). THE TUYÈRE ACTS AS A SIMPLE VALVE (4).

thus to be a very long one, the material requiring raking and turning if a reasonable quality metal is to result.

Primitive furnaces are not complicated structures, a simple clay-lined bowl in the ground being quite adequate for the purpose, but to obtain the required temperature a means of providing adequate draught is essential. In some areas this might have been possible by so designing the furnace that an aperture opened into the prevailing wind, but more commonly one supposes a blow-tube or bellows was used. *Drum-bellows* and *skin-bellows* are both used by primitive people today, the air being directed into the furnace by means of a clay nozzle, the *tuyère*, and although the organic materials have long since decayed, tuyères are not uncommon finds from archaeological excavations.

The chief disadvantages of the *bowl furnace* were its limited capacity, the high rate of heat loss, and the fact that it was impossible to tap off the liquid metal at the base as it was formed; the whole smelt had to be allowed to cool, and the metal removed as a cake from the furnace bottom. Many variants developed through the ages in different areas, but the most commonly evolved form was a chimney-shaped structure, the *shaft furnace* (*stückofen*), with a *tapping-hole* and inlets for the tuyères at the base. Such a furnace would allow a limited amount of recharging with charcoal and ore at the top, while the tapping-hole would permit removal of the molten metal during smelting.

The *domed-furnace* stands, functionally, halfway between the bowl and the shaft-furnaces. The ore and fuel were enclosed in a dome of refractory clay, part or all of which it was necessary to break away after each smelting, although in some cases recharging could have been carried out through the top vent when the furnace was cold, but not during smelting. A sloping floor and tapping-hole would allow the removal of molten metal during smelting.

Much has been written about the origins of copper-smelting, and most of what has been said is highly conjectural. It is generally accepted that the beginnings lie in some accidental smelting of copper from its ores, either in a camp-fire or in a kiln. The discovery is likely to have been a single event and our chances of ever knowing how this came about are remote indeed; but it is perhaps worthwhile commenting upon the conditions necessary for such an accident to occur. Ideally interest should be confined to those areas in which copper ores were already being used for other purposes, for example as pigments; while the high temperatures required almost certainly restrict the search to those areas in which fairly advanced pottery kilns were in use. Apart from this the possibilities are almost endless; copper might have been smelted as a result of attempting to fuse lumps of copper ore with the intention of making a workable decorative stone; as a by-product of glass-making; or by over-reduction of pottery in which copper ores were used as an ingredient, for instance if cuprite were used accidentally in place of haematite as a pigment.

COPPER ALLOYS

Early *bronzes* were essentially *binary alloys*, that is to say, alloys containing principally only two metals, in this case copper and tin. The alloy contained approximately 90 % copper and 10 % tin, although the proportions of the two metals varied very considerably in antiquity. By increasing the proportion of tin a white metal could be produced, and this alloy, *speculum*, normally contained about 70 % copper and 30 % tin.

The usual source of tin in antiquity was the mineral cassiterite, an oxide of tin (SnO). This is easily smelted in the same way as the 'oxide ores' of copper, and in principle could have been smelted either in the same furnace charge as the copper ores, or separately and added to the metallic copper. In fact, the first of these procedures would make the proportions very difficult to control and one suspects the metals were more commonly fused after smelting. An alternative source of tin might have been *stannite*, an ore containing both copper and tin. But it should be noticed that when smelted this mineral will not produce a 'classic' bronze, and one must make severe reservations as to whether this ore was in fact ever used.

Early *brasses*, which appeared at a very much later date than bronzes, were equally binary alloys containing 90-70 % copper and 10-30 % zinc, the metal becoming yellower as the proportion of zinc increased. The chief ore from which the zinc was derived was the carbonate, *calamine*, $ZnCO_3$. Metallic zinc boils and volatilizes at 927°C. As a result zinc was not smelted in antiquity, but the calamine was added to the molten copper in a crucible, the carbon and oxygen being then given off as gaseous carbon dioxide while the other impurities formed, with silica, a slag that could be skimmed off the surface of the molten metal.

Both *antimony* and *arsenic* are found in copper artifacts and some of the probable sources of these metals have already been discussed. In small proportions, in the region of 3 %, these metals have a considerable hardening effect on copper, while higher proportions will make the metal brittle. However, to what general extent these alloys were deliberately or accidentally produced is largely unknown. They were also used in conjunction with tin to give *ternary alloys*, that is to say, alloys containing three major constituents, sometimes referred to as antimonial and arsenical bronzes.

Lead was also added to bronzes to form ternary alloys, the proportion often rising to 10 % and more. Lead does not, in fact, enter into the crystalline structure of the cold alloy but remains free as minute globules, with the result that its presence somewhat softens the final metal. As opposed to this, lead increases the fluidity of the molten metal, and thus helps considerably in the production of high-quality casting. Today, for the same reason, lead is normally added to statuary bronze.

CASTING

The ingot metal formed after smelting is generally full of blow-holes owing to the formation of gases during the smelting process, and is frequently referred to as *blister copper*. The first remelting process is thus one in which the metal is initially refined. It is heated in a *crucible*—a deep cup-shaped container, often pyramidal in form to ease handling, and in which the surface area of the molten metal exposed to the air is kept to a practical minimum. Many residual inclusions left in the metal will float to the surface and are skimmed off as *dross*. If cast in this condition without further treatment, the metal will contain too much cuprous oxide, be very brittle, and break with a dull red fracture. To avoid this the metal is *poled*, or stirred with green wooden boughs, the copiously evolved reducing gases and to a lesser extent carbon from the wood reducing most of the oxide to the metal. Correctly poled copper, *tough pitch copper*, still contains a little cuprous oxide, is tough and malleable, and breaks with a salmon-coloured fracture. If, however, the poling is overdone, reducing hydrogen from the wood dissolves in the copper and causes it to be brittle, although exposure of the molten metal to the oxygen in the air for a period corrects this condition. Over-poled copper may thus be not only brittle but full of blow-holes.

After poling the metal is cast in a prepared *mould*. This may be of stone, refractory clay or metal, but before casting it must be perfectly dry, otherwise the moisture evolved from it as steam may again cause blow-holes. Often to ensure a good surface to the casting the mould face was given a *dressing* or *facing* of soot, wood-ash, flour or animal fat, especially when the material of which the mould was made was of a porous nature.

In antiquity four basic types of *mould* or *die* were used for casting: 'open' moulds and piece-moulds for casting in the solid; false-cored and lost-wax (Fr. *cire perdue*) moulds for producing hollow castings.

The *'open' mould* is the simplest of all, being little more than a depression made in the mould material to receive the molten metal. Such moulds were commonly made of stone, a rock being selected which would remain unaltered by the high temperature of the molten metal, for example soapstone or fine-grained argillaceous sandstone, although in areas lacking such rocks refractory clays were used. While termed 'open' moulds it would seem most likely that they were provided with a flat movable cover to be placed over the casting as it cooled to prevent excessive surface oxidation of the metal. The disadvantage of this type of mould lay in the fact that it was impossible to cast anything but the simplest of shapes, since undercuts would prevent the removal of the casting from the mould. It did continue in use, however, for a long time for the production of coin-blanks (p. 74) and ingots from which sheet metal was to be made.

More complicated solid forms could be cast in *piece-moulds* made of two or more fitting pieces. These were sometimes made of stone, the negative impression of the intended casting being cut into them, and accurate registration usually being ensured by means of opposing holes into which were fitted dowel-rods. Alternatively, the moulds might be made of refractory clay or of bronze. In the first case the mould-pieces were built up round an existing object or a model made of wood or clay, registration being achieved by making *keys* or *notches*, small pits and counter protuberances in the mould-pieces. Metal piece-moulds had, of course, to be cast themselves in piece-moulds, generally of refractory clay; the advantage of this type of mould lies in the far greater durability of the metal than of the clay: and where repetition work was required, as in the making of the common tools and weapons, this could have considerably eased the labour. Piece-moulds were generally made rather deeper than the intended casting, the additional height being to hold a small cup, the *sprue-cup, pour,* or *gate* (*jet, get, git*), into which the metal was poured until virtually full. The need for this was due to a phenomenon known as *piping,* in which the molten metal solidifies and contracts almost immediately as it comes in contact with the mould. The interior metal, away from the mould face, remains liquid, and since it cools and slowly contracts it requires an additional quantity of metal to make good this reduction in volume. If the sprue-cup is allowed to become empty, an actual hollow, called a pipe, forms inside the casting. On cooling, the excess metal which filled this cup, the *head* or *header,* was cut away. In some cases the mould pieces are provided with narrow channels, *air-jets, vents* or *lanterns,* to allow air displaced by the molten metal and the gases inevitably formed during casting to escape, but more

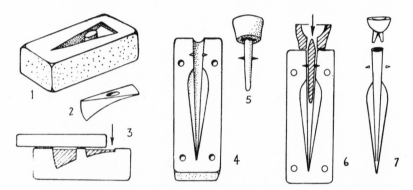

FIG. 9 'OPEN' AND FALSE-CORED MOULDS. 'OPEN' MOULD (1) FOR CASTING AN AXE (2). SECTION THROUGH MOULD AND COVER (3). FALSE-CORED PIECE-MOULD (4) WITH CORE, SPRUE CUP AND CHAPLETS (5). SECTION THROUGH MOULD AND CORE (6) AND CASTING (7) WITH HEADER AND CHAPLETS REMOVED.

commonly the mould materials were porous enough and the pieces ill-fitting enough to make this provision unnecessary. Narrow ridges of metal generally protruded between the mould pieces. These *flashes, joint-lines* or *casting-seams* were sometimes completely removed in the subsequent treatment of the casting, *fettling:* but where this was not done their presence is an almost infallible indication that the object was cast in a piece-mould.

Piece-moulds were also used in conjunction with a *false core* to produce *hollow castings,* as for example socketed tools and weapons. The core was generally made of refractory clay, which was initially made to fill the whole space of the casting. The clay was then removed and pared down, the amount removed corresponding to the thickness of metal required. Very frequently the false core and the sprue-cup were made all of a piece and channels, *runners* or *runnels,* were cut between the cup and the hollow to be filled by the metal; while in complex shapes it was sometimes necessary to make further channels, *risers,* to allow air and gases to escape, and up which the molten metal would ultimately rise and solidify. After casting the header and solidified metal in the runners and risers was cut away, and the core removed.

In the casting of very complex shapes, such as statues, by means of the false core the procedure was often somewhat different. The shape to be cast was first modelled in refractory clay, and on to this model was built up the piece-mould. If there were many undercuts the number of pieces might be so great as to demand a further outer mould piece, the *mother mould* or *case-mould*, to hold them all in register. When the piece-mould was complete it was removed and the model pared down to provide the core. After the metal had been cast the core might be removed, but was more commonly left in place. The rough casting would, of course, carry a number of flashes corresponding to the interfaces of the various pieces of the mould, but in high quality work these would all be removed in the final planishing (p. 76).

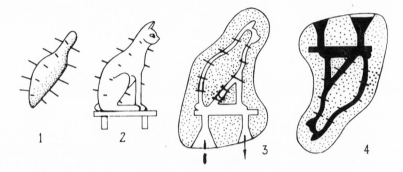

FIG. 10 LOST WAX CASTING. CLAY CORE WITH PROTRUDING CHAPLETS (1). OVER THIS IS MODELLED THE WAX FIGURE (2). THIS IS INVESTED WITH CLAY AND THEN HEATED TO REMOVE THE WAX (3) AND FIRED. BRONZE IS CAST INTO THE SPACE OCCUPIED ORIGINALLY BY THE WAX (4). HEADERS AND CHAPLETS ARE LATER REMOVED.

An alternative and somewhat simpler method of producing complex castings was to use the *lost-wax* (Fr. *cire perdue*) method. Over a core of refractory clay the object to be cast was modelled in wax, the thickness of the wax corresponding to the thickness of the metal required; and over this a single outer mould of clay was built up, incorporating the sprue cup and any runners, risers or vents needed. The whole was then heated and the wax allowed to run out, so providing the space into which the metal was ultimately to be cast. The core, however, needed to be held in register, or, once the wax was melted, it would inevitably shift; and to achieve this the core usually incorporated a number of protruding rods or wires of metal, the *chaplets*, the free ends of which became embedded in the outer mould. Being usually of the same metal as the casting, the chaplets ultimately became incorporated in it, the protruding ends being removed. The mould, of course, had to be broken away in order to get at the casting and hence could not be re-used, while the core was sometimes left in place. In most high quality work, however, a space was left through which the core could be raked out.

Very similar hollow castings could be produced by both the false-core and lost-wax methods, and while the presence of residual flashes on the one hand and chaplets on the other are indicative of the two processes, these have generally been removed. A very great disservice can be done to the study of the history of technology by assuming that either method of casting was used without any genuine evidence. The observation that an object appears to have been modelled in wax, for example, is a subjective one that has no real validity, and a far more critical examination (p. 220) should be made before any final conclusion is drawn.

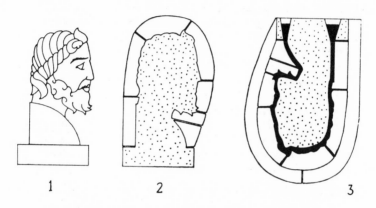

Fig. 11 Hollow casting. The figure is modelled in clay (1) and a piece-mould is built up around it (2). The model is removed, shaved down to provide the core around which the mould pieces and mother moulds are assembled (3).

COLD WORKING

Before discussing the cold working of copper and its alloys, it will be essential to say something about the physical properties of these metals. As cast, copper and its alloys are reasonably soft and can be hammered and drawn with relative ease. As hammering is continued the metals become increasingly harder and more brittle until, if the treatment is not stopped, the metals will crack. Stated briefly, the hammering distorts the crystalline structure of the metals, and a point can be reached where the distortion is so great that the crystals part. The metal-worker before reaching this point will *anneal* the metal by reheating gently to a dull red heat and allow it to cool. A fresh crystalline structure is formed as a result (although quite different from the as cast structure) which leaves the metal soft, malleable and ductile again. Where much hammering or other cold work is being done this process of annealing may have to be repeated quite often. The working of 10 % tin bronze differs in two major respects from that of iron and steel (p. 84): it is quite immaterial at what rate the metal is allowed to cool after annealing, for although sudden cooling, as when the hot metal is dipped in cold water, or *quenched*, produces a softer metal, it is not so much softer than slowly cooled metal to be of practical significance; also there is no advantage to be gained by hammering the metal while still hot (forging), and it is very doubtful if this was ever done in antiquity.

Hammering, apart from being a means of producing different shapes, as for example raising flanges and so on, had the great advantage that if the metal was left unannealed after the final treatment it remained hard and suitable for cutting tools; and this is probably why all copper and bronze tools and weapons appear to have been treated in this way. The greatest technical achievement of hammer-work was, however, the production of sheet bronze and bronze vessels. Beginning with a flattish ingot, the thickness of the metal was further reduced by hammering. Today the bronzesmith can make his selection from a number of different steel hammers for this work, but before the introduction of steel, hammers were generally nothing more elaborate than hand-held rounded stone pebbles of different sizes, usually well water-worn, and care should be taken not to discard them when excavating bronze-working sites.

Bronze sheet might be used simply as a cladding for wood, as for example over doors or wooden statues, but to produce vessels the bronze-worker might adopt one of two techniques, or a combination of them both. On the one hand the vessel might be produced by hammering from the inside—*sinking, blocking* or *hollowing*. The sheet metal was hammered either on the flat surface of an anvil, often made of wood, or more commonly hammered into a shallow concave depression cut into the surface of the anvil. The alternative method, that of *raising*, was the precise opposite: the vessel was produced by repeated hammering on the outside, the work being done over a small *dome-headed* stake or anvil. This is unquestionably the more difficult process, but by varying the sizes and shapes of the stakes it allows a greater variety and complexity of form.

Flat, jointless rings, bracelets and anklets were sometimes produced by first casting a small solid ring of roughly circular section, and placing this over a tapering rod, a *mandrel* (*mandril*) or *treblet* (*triblet*), against which the ring was hammered while being rotated the whole time.

The *striking* of coins and medals, sometimes erroneously called stamping (p. 85), is a rather different process. The impression required is first cut in negative in some very hard material and this die is placed over the coin blank and given a single, sharp blow, so compressing the metal of the blank into the recesses of the die. Before the introduction of steel, bronze coins could only have been struck using stone or bronze dies, although neither would have served a very long period of usefulness. Striking, incidentally, causes considerable stress in the crystalline structure of the metal, and in unfavourable surroundings this promotes the process of corrosion. For this reason many coins may be quite illegible, while other bronze objects from the same environment may be in reasonable condition. Today struck coins are normally annealed before being issued.

The method of shaping bronze vessels known as *spinning* is virtually a mechanical form of raising, which requires the use of a lathe (p. 117). A flat disc of the metal is forced down on to the *forme* or *chuck*, a solid block of hardwood, with round-ended burnishers. Since the metal is being compressed on to the forme, there is a very great tendency for the object to pleat; and although this could be avoided to some extent by the use of a second tool, the backstick, supporting the metal behind the burnisher, early spun work frequently shows some sign of pleating, especially near the rim. Normally only simple open shapes were made in this way, but by employing a chuck made of several sections that could be dismantled, closed forms could also be produced. Decoration was frequently no more than a few scored parallel lines made with a sharp tool while the metal was still on the lathe, although beadings could be produced by pressing hollow-faced wheels, *beading-tools*, against the moving metal.

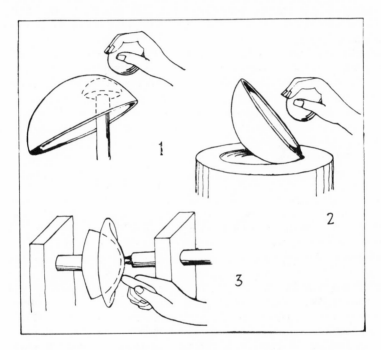

FIG. 12 MAKING SHEET METAL VESSELS BY RAISING (1), SINKING (2), AND SPINNING (3).

A second method of final shaping involving the use of the lathe is that of *turning*, in which the already cast shape is set up in the lathe and any irregularities removed by a sharp tool held against the metal. No forme need be used, and the turning may be done both inside and outside. Unless the work has been well cleaned up afterwards a number of small parallel lines, caused by the edges of the turning tool, can be seen; but a badly handled burnisher used in spinning can leave a very similar kind of blemish, and it may be very difficult to distinguish between the two types of work. Generally, turned work is thicker and of a more rigid metal, while the thickness of spun work usually shows an even graduation from base to rim. In both cases the base of the vessel will bear the mark of the lathe centre (p. 117), but it should be noticed that in spun work the inside of the base is in contact with the forme and will bear no centre-mark, while quite often, but not invariably, in turned work the inside of the base will carry a second centre-mark.

Wires were originally formed by hammering down a narrow bronze rod, but unless very carefully done the results were always very uneven. *Wire drawing*, in which the rods were passed through a plate with a series of progressively smaller holes, a *drawplate*, so repeatedly lengthening the rod and reducing the diameter, appeared early, it being perfectly possible to draw copper and its alloys through drawplates of the same materials. Generally the drawplate was only used for making wires of circular section, but the *swageplate* or *swageblock*, made of two plates that could be brought progressively closer together, and into the edges of which were cut notches of the section of the wire required, was sometimes used to make mouldings.

The finish of most metal work from antiquity is of a very high standard. Much of it was clearly carefully *planished* by going over the surface with a light hammer to remove any marks left as a result of previous cold working; while much of the fine finish could only have been achieved by a final *polishing*, first with a rubber of fine sandstone, followed by a polish with an even finer abrasive applied with a leather or wooden burnisher, or nodular haematite might be used as a burnisher without other abrasive.

JOINING

Molten bronze, if cast against a bronze object, will fuse with it to make a join as long as the face of the original metal is perfectly clean. This process of *running-on, burning-on* or *casting-on* was frequently used in antiquity when, for example, a handle was to be added to beaten or spun vessels. A small piece- or lost-wax mould was built up where required, and into this the new metal was cast. The method was equally used where two metal parts of the same object demanded different annealing and cold working. Thus we find bronze swords in which the blade and tang were first cast, hammered and trimmed, and on to which the handle was finally cast. Running-on was also extensively used for repairing broken castings, as when a new hilt was run on to an old sword blade. Welding, which involves heating two pieces of metal to somewhere near melting-point and hammering, so causing them to fuse, is very difficult to achieve with copper and its alloys owing to the rapidity with which their surfaces oxidize on heating, and was seldom if ever done in antiquity. Nevertheless, a form of cold hammer welding was occasionally used in which the faces of the pieces of metal being joined became burred into one another. Such joins lack any real strength and were used chiefly on decorative bronze-work such as statuary.

The use of a different alloy to join two pieces of metal, *soldering*, has the advantage that one can work well below the melting point of the metals being joined. In many alloys there is one particular proportion of the components, the *eutectic*, that has a lower melting point than any of the others. Thus an alloy of 55 % copper and 45 % zinc, *hard solder* or *brazing spelter*, has a somewhat lower melting point than 70 : 30 yellow brass, while an alloy of 67 % lead and 33 % tin, *soft solder* or *lead solder*, has a far lower melting point than either lead or tin. The soft solder might either be applied with a heated 'iron' (in practice generally made of copper) or be placed in position between the two pieces of metal to be joined, and then the whole heated until the solder melted. To prevent the surfaces of the metals oxidizing during the heating a *flux*, most commonly tallow or animal fat for soft solder and borax for hard solder, was used; while those areas on which one did not wish the solder to adhere could be stopped off with a luting of clay, whiting or jeweller's rouge. Sometimes, in the process known as *sweating*, the solder was first applied to both parts to be joined, following which the two were clamped together and heated, causing the two soldered areas to fuse.

Rivets were most commonly used in antiquity either to join non-metallic parts to metals or for joining sheet metal, although handles were also commonly added to cups and other metal vessels by riveting.

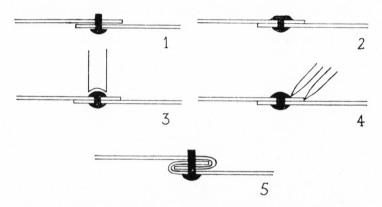

FIG. 13   SEAMS AND RIVETS. A LAP SEAM AND RIVET (1), HAMMERED DOWN (2). THE RIVET HEAD FORMED WITH A SNAP (3) AND THE HEAD AND SEAM FULLERED (4). A FOLDED SEAM (5).

Early rivets were simply short lengths of metal rod hammered down at both ends, but properly formed rivets with domed, conical or pan-shaped heads were clearly soon appreciated for their greater strength and decorative effect. The heads were either cast, or formed as the rivets were closed using *sets* (*setts*) or *snaps*, punch-shaped tools recessed at the end to form the required shape of the rivet-head. Bronze vessels of (riveted) sheet metal could be made perfectly watertight, even when the edges were joined by a simple *lap seam* in which one edge of the sheet overlapped the edge of the next, first by burring down the edges of the rivets with a blunt chisel and then by *fullering* the edge of the capped sheet metal, that is to say, thickening the edge, by hammering with a blunt-ended tool. A *groved seam* in which the edges of adjacent sheets of metal were folded into one another made a more satisfactory join from this point of view.

DECORATION

Bronze objects were decorated either by cold working the metal itself or by applying other metals or materials to the surface, apart, of course, from casting in the design in the first place. Thin bronze could be decorated by raising the design from the back, *repoussé work*, so that it stood out in relief; before beginning the raising, the design might be lightly sketched out with a sharp, hard point, the *scriber*, but this was not always the case. The areas to be raised were then worked up with hammer-struck round-ended punches, *bossing* or *cushion tools*. During this process the work could have been held against a leather pad or a sand-bag, although today most repoussé workers prefer to raise against a block of pitch, while where the design was confined to a series of small bosses a wooden block bearing hemispherical depressions, a *doming block*, into which the metal was sunk could have been used. Repoussé designs could also be raised on vessels with narrow necks into which it was ordinarily impossible to reach using a bossing tool and hammer. Such work was done with the aid of a *snarling iron*, a Z-shaped rod, one end of which is held in a clamp, and the other, free, end of which is rounded. This end is passed through the mouth of the vessel and held against the area to be raised. The middle section of the rod is then struck with a hammer, and as the whole free end of the rod rebounds from the blow so the rounded end in contact with the metal forces it out.

Repoussé work was usually worked from the face as well as from the back. The edges of the raised areas were often sharpened by going round them with a small chisel-shaped tool, *a tracer*, which each time it was struck made a short indented line. The spaces left between consecutive cuts with the tracer may be visible, but in really good work a traced line is perfectly even without interruption.

The tracer was, of course, equally used alone, without repoussé work, as a means of doing outline decoration. Areas in the design might be filled in from the face using a number of different *backgrounding* punches. Tracers could also be used for this purpose; or the punches might have a flat, granulated end, *matting tools*; small concave tips, *pearl-tools* (Fr. *perloirs*), or bear even more elaborate designs. Strictly speaking, a surface that has been backgrounded by stabbing all over with a small pointed punch is referred to as *pointillé*, although some archaeologists are in the habit of using the term to describe any surface with a fine dot pattern, be the dots bosses or pits. Equally, the term *chasing* is correctly only applicable to that part of repoussé work done from the face, but it is often used to describe almost any hammer or punch work.

In all of the decorating methods so far discussed it will be noticed that no metal is removed from the object, but in *engraving* the surface of the metal is cut away with *gravers* or *scorpers*. These are hand-held chisel-like tools, and are not hammer-struck. The blades are normally V-, diamond- or flat-pointed and must be very much harder than the metal being engraved. It is thus virtually impossible to engrave copper or its alloys with tools of similar composition and, in fact, gravers are normally made of hard steel. Engraving is thus not usually to be expected in the earlier metal periods of antiquity.

Other metals, such as tin or silver, may be applied to the surface of copper or its alloys either by keying it to the surface or by fusing it to the background. The crudest of these methods is that of *overlaying*, in which the surface of the metal to be decorated is stabbed all over, or *flinked*, so raising small, sharp projections. The metal to be used as the overlay is then placed on this surface and hammered down, with the result that some of the underlying projections will sink into the overlay metal and then be turned down, so holding it in place. In *inlay* work, the metal to be applied is either hammered or melted into prepared recesses in the surface and as a result normally lies flush with the surface of the object when finished, as opposed to overlay work. The recesses may be allowed for in the original casting or cut out later with scorpers, while in good quality work the edges of the recesses are undercut so ensuring that the inlay remains in place. Silver is often inlaid with a mixture of metallic

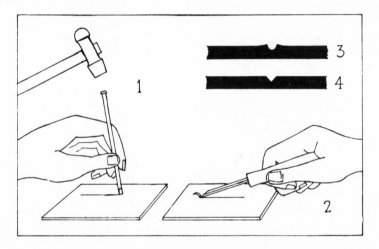

FIG. 14 THE USE OF THE TRACER (1) AND GRAVER (2) WITH PROFILES THROUGH A TRACED LINE (3) AND AN ENGRAVED LINE (4).

sulphides, *niello*, the white of the one contrasting well with the black of the other. The composition of niello varied considerably, but it was normally prepared by fusing sulphur with silver and copper, although lead and antimony might also be added. The prepared niello, being relatively soft, was cast into the recesses and then ground and polished flat. Both inlay and overlay work are frequently incorrectly referred to as *damascening* (p. 88).

Bronze objects in particular were quite commonly given a surface coating of another metal, *flushing* or *flashing*. This was virtually a soldering operation in which the covering metal was worked over the whole surface by using a soldering iron. The metal has, of course, to have a low enough melting point to make this practicable. Thus it is not possible to flush bronze with silver in this way. *Tinning* was at times common, a tinned brooch, for example, presumably giving to the uncritical of the period the impression of a solid silver one. Gold, on the other hand, was more normally applied by methods depending upon amalgam formation, and these will be discussed later (p. 92).

Chapter Five

IRON AND STEEL

SYNOPSIS

General: Iron and steel.   *Ores:* Oxides · Ironstones · Sulphides.   *Mining.*   *Preparation of Ores.*   *Smelting:* Slag · Fluxes · Bloom.   *Cementation:* Annealing · Quenching · Tempering.   *Forging:* Anvil · Anvil-tools.   *Joining:* Welding · Brazing · Riveting.   *Decoration:* Inlay · Flushing · Pattern-welding · Damascening.   *Cast Iron:* Blast-furnace · Moulds.   *Indirect Process:* Fining · Malleable iron.

GENERAL

THE WORDS 'IRON' and 'steel' are today generally so loosely applied that the distinction between them is often obscured. Iron is strictly speaking the pure metal while steel is an alloy of iron with a small percentage of carbon, the term also being used to describe alloys of iron with carbon and other metals. The pure metal is never met with in antiquity, and what we generally refer to as *wrought iron*, would to the modern metallurgist be more correctly termed *low carbon steel*, the alloy containing less than 0·5% carbon. Today one also speaks of *medium carbon* and *high carbon steels*, containing from 0·5% to 1·5% carbon, while *cast iron* actually contains the highest proportion of carbon of all, anything up to 5%. Most steels in which iron has been deliberately alloyed with other metals are of comparatively modern origin: *mild steel*, for example, although containing only 0·25% carbon, may contain greater proportions of metals such as manganese, while stainless steels may be alloys containing nickel and chromium with small percentages of molybdenum or other relatively rare metals. Mild steels of a kind may have been produced in antiquity as a result of working ores containing manganese, for example, and these are sometimes referred to as '*natural*' *steels*. Clearly the words 'iron' and 'steel' without qualification have no precise meaning, but to save repetition the term 'iron' will be used in this book to mean wrought iron which cannot be hardened by heat treatment, while the word 'steel' will be used to refer to alloys containing higher proportions of carbon which may be hardened and tempered (below).

Since by far the greater proportion of iron and steel was produced in antiquity by the *direct* or *bloomery process* this will be described first; the indirect or blast-furnace process, cast iron and crucible steels will be discussed at the end of the chapter.

In the production of iron four distinct processes are involved: (1) mining; (2) ore preparation; (3) smelting; and (4) forging:

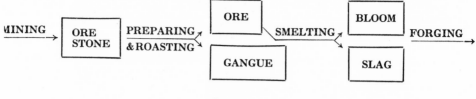

ORES

In most regions iron ores are far more readily obtainable than, say, copper ores and to obtain a workable iron it was not always necessary to locate a more or less pure mineral, since many rocks of high iron content could be smelted, even the 'hardpan' occurring in bogs and podsolized soils being a potential source of iron, bog iron ore being a very pure source.

Of the relatively pure minerals the red oxide, *haematite* (Fe_2O_3), and the hydrated form, *limonite* ($Fe_2O_3H_2O$), both contain a high proportion of iron, and being relatively free from sulphur and phosphorus are easily worked to give good iron. The magnetic oxide, *magnetite* or *lodestone* (Fe_3O_4), is also easily worked but is of rare occurrence in quantity, while the carbonate, *siderite*, *chalybite* or *spathic ore* ($FeCO_3$) although the iron content is lower, is equally readily worked.

In most '*ironstones*' the mineral present is one of the oxides of iron, but the other material present may be siliceous, argillaceous or even partly calcareous. Because of the other matter present the yield from these ores is naturally very low by comparison with the purer minerals, and many would be uneconomical to work today, but this does not mean that they were, therefore, ignored in antiquity.

The sulphide ores, *pyrites* or *marcasite* (FeS_2) and *pyrrhotite* (Fe_7S_8) were presumably less attractive to primitive man since any sulphur left in the metal would seriously affect its working properties and ultimate usefulness (p. 85). Phosphorus, also present in many sulphide ores, has the same effect although its presence was of value in the early production of cast iron. Iron and copper pyrites are very commonly found in association and it is never safe to assume that iron pyrites recovered during excavation from a foundry hearth indicates the smelting of iron for it is, if anything, even more likely that in early periods the ore was being smelted to recover the copper.

MINING

Because of its ubiquity iron seldom needed to be deep mined in antiquity and most early mining for the ore was of the opencast kind or *grubbing*. More important, in a way, than the ore itself was the need for fuel—charcoal—and hence timber; while very much later water-power was required. Early iron mines are thus most likely to be found not only where the ore deposit is reasonably superficial but also where forest cover was sufficient to provide adequate fuel, and perhaps where a steady wind was available to serve as a blast. But in some areas where the ore was especially pure and metal of exceptional quality could be produced, early *pitting* or deep mining did occur.

PREPARATION OF ORES

Most ores, especially those low in iron content, needed to be cleaned from as much of the *gangue*—clay, sand, limestone—as possible before smelting. To achieve this the ores were pounded to reduce them to as small a particle size as possible and then washed, often in running water, to remove the less dense gangue. Following this the ores were roasted to drive off the water which had been chemically combined with the oxides, and thus to render the ore porous. Neither process was, of course, from the chemical viewpoint strictly necessary, but by carrying them through the iron yield was vastly improved.

SMELTING

Although the temperature at which workable iron can be obtained (1,100°-1,150°C.) is much the same as that at which copper can be smelted, there are several important points of difference between the two processes. In the first place at this temperature iron, unlike copper, does not melt and although the particles of ore are reduced to particles of metal, the metal remains solid. Secondly, the chemical changes in the furnace are rather different. In the case of copper ores some of the carbon combines directly with the non-metallic elements present to liberate the copper; but iron ores are reduced at this temperature only by the presence of carbon monoxide gas:

$$2C + O_2 \rightarrow 2CO$$
$$Fe_2O_3 + 3CO \rightarrow 2Fe + 3CO_2.$$

In other words, the carbon in the charge provides both the heat and the gas essential to reduce the iron ore. From this it follows that unless the ore is adequately porous it will not be completely reduced, and a great deal of potential iron will be discarded since the carbon monoxide will be unable to reach all the ore. Equally, if the carbon is present in too large a particle size, the distribution of carbon in the charge may not be sufficiently uniform and the surface area may be too small to free an adequate quantity of carbon monoxide to ensure a complete smelt; better results are obtained if the charcoal is well broken up before charging. Finally, if too much oxygen is present, especially in the local absence of carbon, as for example when too great enthusiasm is shown in the use of the bellows, the already reduced iron may become reoxidized and the whole process be a failure:

$$4Fe + 3O_2 \rightarrow 2Fe_2O_3.$$

Below a temperature of 1,100°C. iron of a sort can be obtained although it is too full of impurities to be of any practical use, the impurities making it impossible to forge the spongy mass of iron into sufficiently ductile metal.

Silica is the principal impurity present in iron ores and this will combine with any fluxes (p. 42) present to form a glass-like *slag*. This will inevitably contain some iron and, if the ore were calcareous, lime. Indeed sometimes materials rich in *fluxes*, such as lime, dolomite or magnesia, were added deliberately to promote the formation of slag, and so rid the iron of its silica. Slags are a general feature of iron furnaces but very great care should be exercised in determining the use to which a furnace has been put from the nature of the slag. Depending on the ores being smelted, even after chemical analysis, it may be impossible to say whether a furnace was used for copper or iron smelting, especially where the ore employed contained pyrites.

Furnaces used for iron-smelting were similar to those used for copper ores (p. 68) in design, but not necessarily identical in function. Amongst primitive people today there are two rather distinct ways of setting about smelting iron ores. In the one, a small charcoal fire is kindled in the bottom of the furnace and a mixed charge of ore and fuel is placed on this, the temperature of the whole charge being raised by the use of bellows and the air supply being controlled in the later stages by watching the colour of the flame coming from the charge, a blue flame showing that carbon monoxide is present in excess. On the other hand, a charcoal fire may first be brought to white heat and on to this is thrown the charge of iron ore, but no further fuel, the bellows being kept working until a blue flame shows that conditions suitable for reduction have been attained. There is inadequate information to show whether these different methods are necessary for the working of different kinds of ore, or represent different traditions, but in antiquity either means could have been adopted and we are unlikely to recover sufficient evidence to show which.

After smelting, the furnace was allowed to cool and the spongy mass of metallic iron, the *bloom*, removed. From this could be detached the worst of the slag and other impurities, but to achieve workable iron it would now have to be *forged*, and since iron in this spongy state cannot be cold-worked economically, this meant reheating to red heat and hammering it while still hot on an anvil. The effect of this preliminary forging was not only to consolidate the metal but also to help squeeze out any slag remaining in it. Even so, inclusions of slag, oxides and other impurities are common in early wrought iron and these exist as fibrous islands in the metal, and are hence a potential source of weakness. As a result of the forging the iron takes on a fibrous structure, and is then ready for further shaping.

CEMENTATION

Wrought iron can be converted into steel by allowing it to absorb carbon. This process, variously known as *cementation, carburization* or *case-hardening*, depending on the end-product, is carried out above 900°C., the iron being kept covered with carbon. In antiquity this had to be done on the forge and since the rate at which carbon penetrates is slow the operation might take several hours, during which period, of course, the bellows had to be kept moving and the charcoal replenished. The production of steel was thus a hot, arduous and expensive process but the result was a far harder, though more brittle, metal. This is due to the fact that iron and carbon form a new chemical association in which the crystalline structure of the material becomes radically altered (p. 216).

Apart from its hardness, steel has the great virtue that its properties can be easily altered by appropriate *heat treatment*. Like copper and its alloys, steel can be softened by *annealing*, but unlike copper the cooling must be carried out slowly, the metal sometimes being buried in sand or ashes to achieve this slow cooling. If this is done the grain structure of the metal is again altered, but if the cooling is carried out rapidly the alloy takes on a completely different structure and the resulting metal will be hard and brittle. This rapid cooling was easily achieved by *quenching*, or thrusting the red-hot metal into a tank of cold water or oil, the *bosch*. Some of the hardness and brittleness of quenched steel can again be relieved by gentle heating, the higher the temperature attained during the limited period of the process the softer and more resilient the metal. The process of *tempering* can be controlled without the use of thermometers by watching the surface colour of the polished steel during re-heating, and then quenching as soon as the required colour appears. The typical temperatures, 'colours of temper', and uses to which a medium carbon steel would be put are:

220°-250°C.—Yellows · Razors, turning tools, scorpers.

250°-270°C.—Browns · Axes, wood chisels.

270°-290°C.—Purples · Swords, knives.

290°-330°C.—Blues · Saws, stone chisels, cold chisels.*

FORGING

Most metals can be shaped by cold hammering with periodic annealing, as is the case with copper and its alloys; but this is not practicable with iron and steel. Iron must be brought to a good red heat and *forged* while still hot. The forge itself need not be a very elaborate affair; any reasonably hot charcoal fire will suffice, but for the handling and hammering of iron very different tools are required from those used in working metals that can be hammered cold. In the first place it is essential to have *tongs* with which to handle the metal. Crucibles full of molten bronze could be, and in fact were, handled by gripping with pliable wooden rods, but this was done for only a very limited time, since to pour a casting took only a few seconds. On the other hand, iron had repeatedly to be returned to the forge, and to do this work without tongs would have been a very tedious business. The hand-held stone hammers of the bronzesmith would, equally, have been of little use and hafted iron-headed *hammers* would also have been essential. Finally the *anvil* itself would have needed to have been far more substantial than those used in bronze-working, and although the iron anvil was not used in the very earliest iron-using periods, a very large block of stone or an iron-clad wooden block could have served.

* This blueing should not be confused with that used today on such things as watch-springs, which is achieved usually by the use of a dye.

During the process of forging the inevitable repeated reheating of the metal results in oxidation of the surface, and the hammering causes the newly-formed black iron oxide (magnetite) to flake away from the surface in small *scales*, which if not cleared away can form quite a considerable accumulation over the years. Blacksmith's scale may be a very good indication of the site of an old forge as, too, may be fragments of *short* metal or iron that was too brittle to forge, due to impurities in the metal. *Hot shortness*, which leaves the metal brittle when red hot, was chiefly due to the presence of small quantities of sulphur; and *cold shortness*, which resulted in a metal too brittle for use when cold, was largely due to the presence of phosphorus, both these elements being present initially in the ores. In either case the fragments of metal would ultimately have been returned to the furnace for resmelting.

The preliminary forging of the bloom was normally carried out on the flat face of an anvil using a flat-faced hammer, and as a result the raw material from which the blacksmith would be making his final forgings would be in the form of rods of iron of square or rectangular section. Quite unlike the bronzesmith, who would have tended to produce designs that could be readily cast in a fairly simple mould, the blacksmith would have evolved patterns that could be made by thinning down and bending rectangular rods of metal, and the two technologies thus had a very definite influence on the shapes of tools and weapons.

While the *thinning-down* (*drawing-down* or *breaking-down*) and bending of iron can all be done on the flat or over the beak of an anvil, using only a hammer, a number of anvil tools were developed quite early for specific purposes. For cutting, chisel-shaped *sets* (*setts*) often held in a hooped handle of iron rod and hammer struck, were used on either hot (hot-set) or cold (cold-set, cold chisel) iron. The *pritchell*, a rather dumpy punch of square section, hafted and hammer struck, was used for the initial punching of holes; the final shaping being done, as for example in the making of hafting holes in hammers, axes and so on, with a short tapered rod of the required section, the *drift* or *stamp*. In thin or very soft iron this enlarging might be done cold by rotating a tapered square rod, the *reamer* (*rimer*) or *broach*, in the punched hole. Objects made of fairly thin iron were sometimes shaped by hammering into a form cut as a recess in some solid material. The Scottish crusie lamps, for example, were shaped by hammering iron sheet into a hollow cut into the face of a block of stone.

Many anvil tools were used in pairs, the bottom tool fitting into a hole in the anvil, the *hardy-hole*, the top tool being held in a handle, normally of bent iron rod and hammer struck. *Fullers*, like chisels with dull, rounded ends, were used in pairs to make corrugations or grooves in iron, often only as a preliminary to drawing-down; *swages*, squat tools with opposing hollow, semi-cylindrical surfaces, were used to reduce the diameter of rounded iron rod, several sets of swages being needed to produce rods of different size; while *flatters*, as the name implies, were similar tools with flat faces used to produce a smooth surface. The making of iron wire, however, demanded the use of either swage-plates or draw-plates (p. 76), but this very early became a specialist activity since the chief use of iron wire was in the manufacture of chain-armour.

Although the good blacksmith required an almost inexhaustible supply of brute force, the essence of success lay in being able to hit the iron being forged in exactly the right place while it was still hot, the tools themselves being by no means light. There were, in fact, very few 'tricks of the trade'; a smith was either experienced and produced good forgings, or inexperienced and turned out poor work. One of the very few tricks was that of avoiding *piping** when bringing iron rod to a point, for circular rod when hammered up on all sides about the end invariably produced a small cup-shaped hollow at the point. This could be avoided by

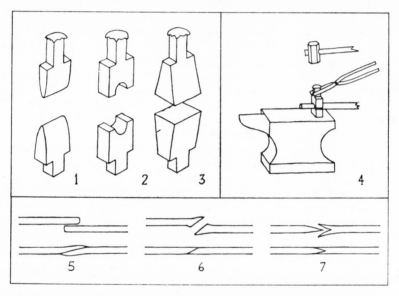

FIG. 15   ANVIL TOOLS AND WELDS. FULLERS (1). SWAGES (2). FLATTERS (3). SWAGES BEING USED TO DRAW DOWN AN IRON ROD (4). POOR LAP WELD (5). SCARFED AND UPSET WELD (6). FORK WELD (7).

squaring the tip of the rod before pointing, bringing the point up square in section and then rounding off. Many pointed tools, in fact, were never rounded off, as for example the pritchell, but left with a square point.

JOINING

For nearly all purposes the most effective way of joining iron was by *welding* or *shutting*, for when white-hot two pieces of iron can be joined by hammering. During hammering, however, the iron will also become drawn down and to overcome this smiths generally found it necessary to thicken the two parts being welded. This process of thickening, or *upsetting*, could be done either by hammering or by thumping the end of the hot iron on the anvil face.

* The term piping is also used to describe a phenomenon met with in casting (p. 71).

The simple *lap-join* in which one piece of metal was placed over the other and hammered to form the weld was not much used, especially where the final appearance mattered, since the method always resulted in a thickening at the join. Equally the *butt-join* not only gave a small area for welding but also was difficult to hammer, the plane of the joint being at right angles to the anvil face. More commonly the two pieces of metal were *scarfed*, or tapered down, upset, and then welded. This had the advantage of providing a larger welding area at a shallow angle to the anvil face. An even larger welding area could be allowed for in the *cleft* or *fork-join* in which one piece of metal was thinned down and this was welded into a cleft cut in the other piece. Sometimes additional strength was given to a weld by *layering* or *lining*, in which an additional piece of metal was welded to the outside or inside of the join; and it is not uncommon to find, for example, an iron hoop built up by welding one hoop inside another, the scarfed joins of the two bands from which the hoops were made lying at different points on the circumference.

Welding as a means of joining had, of course, the additional advantage that both iron and steel could be incorporated in the same object to provide a unified whole, the hard but brittle steel and the soft but resilient iron each being used where its properties were an advantage, these desirable properties being achieved by the appropriate heat treatment. Thus the shaft-hole and poll of an axe might be forged from a rectangular piece of iron and into this a steel bit, or cutting edge, might be welded; or the cutting edge of a sword might be of steel welded on to a complex core of iron and steel (p. 88). This process of welding steel to iron is sometimes referred to as *steeling*, but as the term is also occasionally used to mean cementation it is perhaps better avoided.

Iron and steel could also be joined by brazing. This is essentially a soldering operation using hard solder or brass spelter (p. 76). On the whole such joints lacked the strength of welds, but avoided the need for hammering and thus allowed the assembly of more intricate parts such as, for example, the wards of keys, which could be cut 'on the flat' and then brazed on to the stock.

Before the industrial revolution *rivets* were commonly used only for joining thin iron or steel parts. Iron rivets had to be worked hot, although an inferior form of riveting is to be found in which the end of the rivet has been burred over while cold and, naturally, such rivets lack any real strength. Where organic materials needed to be joined to iron, however, copper rivets, which could be satisfactorily worked cold, were normally used.

DECORATION

Iron and steel objects were often *inlaid* with gold, silver, bronze, copper and niello, the technique being the same as that used to decorate bronze (p. 79); while the whole or part of the surface might be *flushed* with either tin or with brass spelter. Gold or silver might be overlaid on to a previously prepared steel surface (p. 78), a method of decoration often erroneously referred to as 'damascening' (below). Virtually unique to iron and steel, however, were decorative effects depending upon the juxtaposition of alloys of differing composition welded together to produce a pattern. In this process, known as *pattern welding*, case-hardened bars of iron were *piled* or *faggotted* white hot and forged. Thus, after forging, each pile would be a laminated structure of iron and steel, the layers of steel being formed by the fusion of the case-hardened surfaces of the original bars. These piles might then be drawn down, case-hardened and piled yet again to produce an even finer laminated structure. Finally several such units might be twisted or folded, according to the pattern required, and welded together. On polishing, the differing hardness of the iron and steel would give a differentiation of surface, causing them to appear dimly as light and dark bands, so producing the

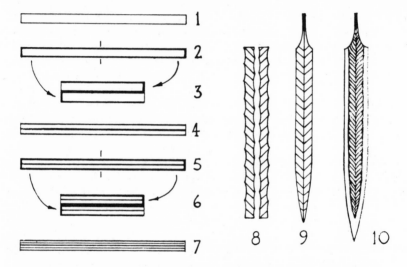

FIG. 16   AN EXAMPLE OF PATTERN WELDING. IRON ROD (1) IS CARBURISED (2), PILED (3) AND DRAWN DOWN (4). THE PROCESS IS REPEATED (5, 6 AND 7) TO PROVIDE A LAMINATED ROD OF IRON AND STEEL. TWO SUCH RODS ARE TWISTED (8) AND WELDED (9) TO FORM CORE OF SWORD. AN EDGE IS WELDED TO THE CORE (10) AND THE BLADE POLISHED AND ETCHED TO BRING OUT THE PATTERN.

pattern; while by etching with a corrosive solution the surface of the polished iron, being the more readily attacked, would be slightly eaten away, thus heightening the pattern effect. Alternatively the polished surface may have been allowed to rust for a limited period, followed by the removal of the products of corrosion in a dilute acid.

Pattern-welding should not be confused with *damascening*, in which a watered pattern is produced in the metal before the forging takes place. Although there were probably many different methods of achieving this, in one of them the production of the bars from which damascened blades were made, *wootz*, required three separate stages. In the first, the ores were reduced to wrought iron as in the normal bloomery process. Following this, the iron was broken up and placed in crucibles with wood or charcoal and these were then luted with clay and allowed to dry. The crucibles were then heated for a long period at a high temperature and allowed to cool slowly. The metal that resulted from this process was a high carbon steel too brittle for immediate use, due to the absorption of carbon. In the final stage some of the absorbed carbon was removed by heating the steel in a current of air with intermittent forging. The bar of wootz was then ready for the final forging. In this case the pattern in a sword blade made from such bars was due not to alternative layers of iron and steel, but to the fact that the metal was now composed of grains of cementite distributed in pearlite (p. 217), which on forging became arranged in laminae to give the watered pattern.

CAST IRON

Since pure iron does not melt until a temperature in excess of 1,500°C. has been reached, the production of cast iron made a number of high demands of the craftsman who produced it. The furnace itself had to be constructed of materials sufficiently refractive to withstand temperatures of this order, while if charcoal were being used as fuel a system of forced draught had to be devised that was far more powerful than the simple hand-operated bellows of antiquity. The first of these prerequisites was overcome by using highly siliceous clays free of iron or other glass modifiers to line the furnace, and the second by the use of water-power to drive the bellows. The greatest obstacle to be overcome, however, was that of heat loss. In all the early forms of furnace a great proportion of potentially useful heat was lost in the escaping gases. To an extent this was rectified in the shaft-furnace by increasing the height, and thus preheating fresh charges of fuel and ore as they descended into the reducing area. To produce cast iron the ratio of furnace height to width had to be increased still more. Even so, the *blast furnace* remained wickedly extravagant of fuel, while the cast iron that was obtained from this process, although hard, was far too brittle for making tools. This difference between cast iron and steel is essentially due to the presence in the structure of cast iron of flakes of soft graphite which divide up the metal so greatly that a blow will shatter it. The graphite does serve, however, as an internal lubricant and this makes it an excellent bearing material, as well as allowing it to be turned (p. 75) readily.

Since high temperatures are more easily reached with coal than charcoal (p. 168) its use as a fuel would in principle have simplified matters, but for the fact that most coals contain a considerable proportion of sulphur which has, as has already been said (p. 85), the effect of producing even greater brittleness if the sulphur combines with the iron. Anthracite however, is relatively free from sulphur and it is worth noticing that one of the few instances of really early cast iron comes from China where high quality coals were to be found as outcrops and where the iron ores are rich in phosphorus, the presence of which can greatly reduce the melting point of iron. Curiously, the object is a piece-mould for the casting of bronze axes, the cast iron itself being too brittle to use for cutting tools.

Cast iron was used in Europe initially for the manufacture of cannons for which its high cost of production and brittle nature were of little consequence, although later it found its way into domestic use as fire-backs, cauldrons and so on. The higher temperatures necessary made the moulding media used for bronze unsuitable and instead sand packed into a frame, or *flask*, was used. Some 'sharp' sands, made up of very angular particles, remain in place when packed down in this way, although binding agents, such as loam or horse dung, were normally added, the mixture being *tempered* with water, packed into the flask and allowed to dry, the shape of the casting, of course, being formed by a wooden pattern. In piece moulding, register of the mould parts was obtained by dowels and sockets on the flasks, the lower part being referred to as the *eye-side* or *drag* and the upper part as the *peg-side* or *cope*. In hollow castings the cores, too, had to be of casting sand, and these were produced in special wooden moulds of their own, usually called *core-boxes*. Otherwise, the arrangement of vents, risers and so on was much the same as in bronze casting (p. 71).

THE INDIRECT PROCESS

The discovery that some of the carbon could be removed from cast iron to give a softer, malleable steel led to a different method of iron and steel production allowing a separation of processes. After the production of crude cast iron in the blast furnace, the *pig-iron*, it was remelted in a hearth, the *finery*, while being subjected to a forced draught of air with the result that some of the carbon in the molten pig iron was removed by conversion into carbon dioxide. In the fining of pig iron the metal was heated to a pasty mass and kept in motion by raking so that other impurities present, such as silica, would rise to the surface and could be removed. After rough forging the refined pig iron, often called *malleable iron*, was then ready for the final forging.

Chapter Six

GOLD, SILVER, LEAD AND MERCURY

SYNOPSIS

Ores: Native gold · Silver · Galena · Cinnabar. *Mining and Extraction:* Panning · Smelting. *Refining:* Amalgamation · Cupellation · Pattison's process · Liquation · Conversion to silver chloride or sulphide · Gold refining · Silver refining. *Alloys:* Gold · Carat · Touchstone · Sterling silver · Pewter. *Working:* Gold leaf · Filigree · Granulation · Solders · Pickling. *Gilding and Silvering:* Leaf-gilding · Amalgamgilding · Silvering.

ORES

UNLIKE THE OTHER metals worked in antiquity, gold occurs more commonly as the native metal than as an ore, and in early periods the native metal appears to have been the only source of gold known. The metal is found either as veins in quartz rocks or in sediments, known as *placer* deposits, derived from the weathering of these rocks. In these, the gold may be present either in the form of *nuggets*, or more finely divided as *gold dust*, in which case its recovery depends upon the possibility of separating it from the sand particles.

By contrast native silver, in the Old World at least, does not appear to have been an important source of the metal. Native silver, furthermore, generally contains a fairly high proportion of alloyed copper. Silver does, however, occur with gold in the natural alloy *electrum*, from which it can be separated. There is little evidence that the common ores of silver, *horn silver* (silver chloride, $AgCl$), *silver glance* (silver sulphide, Ag_2S), *ruby silver* (silver antimony sulphide, $3Ag_2S.Sb_2S_3$) or *silver copper glance* ($Ag_2S.Cu_2S$) were smelted in antiquity and apart from native silver and electrum the principal source appears to have been the lead ore *galena* (lead sulphide, PbS) in which small quantities of silver sulphide are almost invariably present.

Galena was, equally, the principal source of lead in antiquity. Other lead ores such as *cerussite* (lead carbonate, $PbCO_3$) and *anglesite* (lead sulphate, $PbSO_4$) may have been worked, but were relatively unimportant.

Mercury occurs native in small quantities, normally with copper, zinc and lead as impurities; but the chief source was the sulphide ore, *cinnabar* (HgS) which was sometimes found mixed with the chloride, *calomel* (Hg_2Cl_2).

91

MINING AND EXTRACTION

The simplest, although the most tedious, method of recovering the metallic content of gold-bearing sands was by *panning*, in which some of the sand was placed in a shallow dish with water and made to swirl around by a rotary movement of the hands in such a way that the lighter quartz and other rock particles were brought to the edge of the pan and allowed to slop over the edge, while the heavier gold particles remained in the bottom of the dish. Slightly more advanced were water-driven rocking devices, usually wooden troughs moved by an eccentric wheel, which performed the same function. Alternatively the gold-bearing sand might be washed down a long wooden trough in which the heavier gold particles would settle, and which often also contained some material to which the smaller particles of gold might adhere; hides, cloth, fleece and branches of the prickly rosemary bush have all been used for this purpose. Fundamentally the same methods were also used for recovering mined gold, especially where the veins were thin, the gold-bearing quartz being crushed to a small particle size and then washed to recover the gold, the crushing being done either by hand-operated equipment or by water-driven stamping machinery.

Galena was generally crushed and roasted before smelting to convert the sulphide to lead oxide:

$$2PbS + 3O_2 \rightarrow 2PbO + 2SO_2.$$

The oxide was then smelted under reducing conditions, the lead, having a low melting point, being tapped off from the furnace. On the other hand, cinnabar could be smelted directly, the mercury having a very low boiling point ($357°C.$) and vaporizing during the process. The liquid metal could be collected by allowing it to condense on a cool surface, as for example a jar filled with cold water, from which it could be scraped.

REFINING

Before discussing the refining of gold and silver it will be necessary to describe four simple chemical processes that may have been involved in the refining methods:

(1) Mercury very readily forms alloys, called *amalgams*, with a number of metals including gold, silver and copper. For example, the copper amalgam that is soft when first mixed and later sets hard was at one time used for stopping teeth in dentistry. When an amalgam is heated most of the mercury is given off, because of its low boiling point, leaving behind only the metal with which it was amalgamated. The mercury, of course, can be recovered by allowing the vapourized metal to condense on a cold surface.

(2) Some metals, for example copper and lead, oxidize readily when heated in an ample supply of air, and the oxides may either be carried away by the draught or be absorbed by the crucible in which they are heated, or by some other porous material such as clay, brick dust or bone ash, while the noble metals, gold and silver, remain unoxidized. Porous

crucibles designed for this purpose are called *cupels* and the whole process is referred to as *cupellation*. Even so, cupellation was not always a crucible process, and furnaces were designed for the purpose, usually with a thick bed of bone ash to absorb the oxides being formed.

(3) When an alloy of lead with silver is melted and then allowed to cool pure lead tends to crystallize before the bulk of the alloy, and at this stage the still fluid alloy may be decanted. If this process is repeated many times, the decanted material will become progressively richer in metals other than lead. This method of enriching a lead alloy is now known as *Pattinson's process*, named after the nineteenth-century metallurgist. To what extent the process was practised before this is frankly unknown; but the method should not be confused with that of *liquation* in which a metal may be separated from others, or extraneous matter, by virtue of its lower melting point. Gold, for example, could have been separated from quartz rock simply by heating until the molten gold ran free, leaving the quartz unaltered.

(4) While silver is not easily converted into an oxide by heating in a current of air, it is readily turned into a chloride or into a sulphide by heating with the appropriate salts of other -metals. Thus, if silver is heated with common salt (sodium chloride) silver chloride is formed; while if it is very gently heated with a sulphide, as for example stibnium (antimony sulphide), silver sulphide is produced. Although in modern chemical terminology both these processes may be referred to as oxidations, it will be less confusing if they are here called conversions to sulphide or chloride.

Native gold is seldom found even in a moderately pure state, but is normally an alloy of gold with copper or silver, or both, as well as traces of other metals. The refining of gold thus often demanded two separate stages; in the first, the copper and other base metals were removed to provide an electrum; and in the second the gold-silver alloy was treated to remove the silver. The first stage might be achieved simply by melting the alloy in an ample air supply, the copper oxide and other base metal oxides formed during heating being removed as dross or simply blown away in the current of air. Again, some of the base metals might first be removed by amalgamating the crude gold with mercury, the base metals not being taken up by the mercury as readily as gold and silver. The more or less pure gold-silver amalgam was then heated to drive off the mercury.

The silver could be removed from the electrum by converting the silver to either the sulphide or the chloride. Both these compounds could be removed by flotation in a stream of water, neither being appreciably soluble in water. More efficient than washing by flotation was further cupellation in which these silver compounds were absorbed by the cupel.

The two stages of gold refining may be summarized as on page 94.

Both these stages could, however, be carried out in one process. Thus, if gold were heated with common salt and charcoal in a closed cupel, the silver would first be converted into the chloride, and if, after this, air were blown into the cupel, the silver chloride and oxides of other metals would be absorbed by it, leaving only the pure gold.

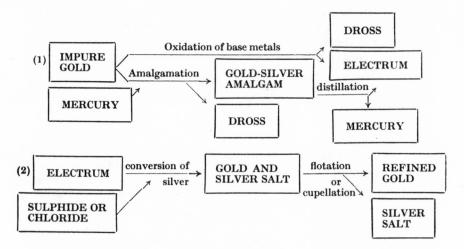

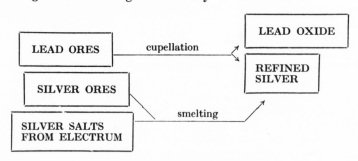

The refining of silver must clearly depend upon the source of the metal. Silver may be obtained from lead ores either by the use of Pattison's process, followed by cupellation, or directly by cupellation; the silver salts absorbed by the cupel during the refining of gold from electrum could readily be reduced to the metal by smelting, and silver-lead ores might equally be smelted to provide crude silver. This, in turn, would require refining by cupellation.

The stages in the refining of silver may be summarized:

GOLD, SILVER AND LEAD ALLOYS

Pure gold is rather too soft for most practical purposes and for making jewellery it was generally alloyed either with copper or silver, or with both; the silver tending to make the metal white, and the copper reddening it. Today, the proportion of gold in an alloy is indicated in carats, a *carat* being a twenty-fourth part of the metal. The disadvantage of using this system when referring to ancient gold alloys is that it takes no cognizance of the other alloyed metals. Hence, eighteen carat gold, apart from eighteen parts of gold, might contain varying proportions of silver and copper—six parts of silver, six parts of copper, or a balance of the two to make six parts. For this reason it is preferable when referring to gold alloys from antiquity to state the metals present as a percentage of the whole.

The purity of gold could be estimated by measuring its specific gravity, gold having a higher specific weight than either silver or copper, but this was often difficult to do, and *assaying* was more commonly done with the help of *touchstones*. These were made of extremely hard, fine-grained stone against which the gold was lightly rubbed, the colour of the streak giving an indication of the nature of the alloy by comparison with streaks made on the same stone from needles of gold having a known composition.

As with gold, pure silver is too soft for most purposes and the metal was commonly alloyed with copper. *Standard English (sterling)* silver contains a maximum of 7·5 % alloying metals other than silver, but here again it is always preferable to state the percentage of alloyed metals when speaking of ancient silver.

For many functions lead was used unalloyed, its softness often being an advantage as, for example, when used as a roof covering, for lining water conduits or as lead piping. The use of lead as an ingredient of ternary bronzes (p. 69) and of soft solder (p. 76) has already been mentioned, but the metal was also alloyed with tin to provide *pewter*. The alloy normally contained about 80 % tin and 20 % lead, although the composition varied considerably, and some silver might be included in the alloy. The merit of the material lay, of course, in its relative cheapness, its resistance to corrosion and its strength compared with other materials used for making vessels, dishes and so on. Modern pewter, it should be noted, has a quite different composition, being made of an alloy of tin and antimony with a very small percentage of copper. Lead is excluded because its salts are cumulative poisons.

WORKING OF GOLD AND SILVER

Gold is exceptionally malleable, and can be beaten into very thin *leaf* without the need to anneal. While the metal is being reduced in thickness a stage is reached when it is no longer possible to beat the metal directly and in antiquity the final beating to produce leaf metal was carried out with the gold interleaved between sheets of thin leather or vellum, which might be piled into a pack in the final beating.

The malleability of gold makes it an easy metal to work, and equally allows exceptionally delicate shaping. Apart from shaping by hammering and piercing, however, much ancient gold jewellery was produced by soldering gold wire (*filigree*) or by soldering small spherical drops of the metal on to a backing (*granulation*). The wire used in filigree work might either be plain or vary in section or thickness throughout its length, wires of different section usually being made by drawing through draw-plates with perforations of various shapes; while wires of varying thickness, as for example beaded wires, were prepared in specially designed swages. Granules of gold were presumably made by melting the metal and pouring it slowly into cold water, the droplets afterwards being sorted for size, probably by sieving, or by cutting short lengths of wire and heating until a drop formed.

The solder used in this kind of work was normally a gold-copper alloy, the eutectic proportions being 18 % copper to 82 % gold, giving a melting point of 878°C., which is 185°C. below that of pure gold. Gold solder might be prepared before use and applied by the normal methods (p. 76), or the alloying might be carried out on the surface of the gold. One such process, which was re-discovered and patented in this century, employs an animal or vegetable adhesive mixed with a copper compound. The mixture was used to stick each granule exactly in position and was then heated with a blow-pipe. The adhesive first decomposed to give free carbon and as the temperature was raised this in turn promoted the re-duction of the copper compound to metallic copper. Finally, the copper in contact with the gold surfaces became alloyed with the gold to provide a gold-copper solder.

Silver is not as malleable as gold and after prolonged hammering requires annealing. It was thus not practicable to produce silver leaf, although the other methods applied to gold working were employed in the making of silver jewellery. The normal solder was a silver-copper alloy, the eutectic being 71·5 % silver and 28·5 % copper, giving a melting point of 779°C., which is 181°C. below that of pure silver. Both the methods of soldering described for gold were apparently used.

The appearance of both gold and silver alloys could, in the final stages, be 'improved' by *pickling* (Fr. *mise-en-couleur*). Copper oxides are soluble in a number of acids and if the completed object were heated in air to form a thin film of oxides and then treated with an acid the copper at the surface could be removed, to give the impression that the metal had a higher gold or silver content than it indeed had. The surface en-richment of gold alloys could also be carried out by removing the silver as well as copper. Hence, if the object were heated in a mixture of common salt and brick dust, the copper and silver would have been con-verted to the chlorides by the salt and these compounds would have been absorbed, as in cupellation, by the brick dust.

GILDING AND SILVERING

The surface of many objects may be covered with gold leaf no matter what they are made of—wood, ivory, metal—using a suitable adhesive, such as size (p. 163), to hold the leaf in place. This process is perhaps better described as *leaf-gilding* than as gilding when applied to metal objects, since the gold is not in contact with the underlying metal, as is the case with other forms of gilding.

True gilding was most commonly applied to copper or its alloys. In *amalgam-gilding* one of two procedures might be followed. The gold might first be mixed with mercury to form an amalgam, and this was applied to the surface of the object, following which the whole was heated to expel the mercury. Alternatively, a copper or bronze object might be treated with mercury to form a copper amalgam on the surface to which gold leaf was applied, the whole again being heated to get rid of the mercury.

An alternative system of gilding has been suggested in which a copper object was supposedly first flushed with gold solder, and afterwards pickled to remove the surface copper from the solder. To what extent this was practised is a matter of conjecture.

Silvering was carried out by similar means. Clean copper or bronze might be rubbed with mercury to produce an amalgam and to this was applied silver amalgam, the whole being heated to remove the mercury. Alternatively the surface might be flushed with silver solder and then pickled to remove the copper.

The use of dipping solutions for gilding and silvering in which one of the noble metals as a salt in solution replaces the baser metal on the surface of the object, because of the lack of chemical reagents capable of dissolving the noble metals, appears to have been unknown in antiquity, as too, of course, was the practice of electro-plating. Sheffield plating, in which copper is sandwiched between sheets of silver and rolled hot to form a weld, is equally a relatively recent technique, demanding fairly elaborate equipment.

Apart from pickling, one other deception was practised on silver objects in antiquity. If the surface of silver was smeared with arsenious sulphide (orpiment) and heated, the surface appeared to be gilded due to the formation of a thin layer of silver sulphide.

TABLE OF MELTING AND BOILING POINTS OF SOME METALS AND ALLOYS
OF ANTIQUITY

°C.

183	Lead solder melts (lead 38%; tin 62%).
232	Pure tin melts.
327	Pure lead melts.
357	Mercury boils.
420	Pure zinc melts.
779	Silver solder melts (copper 28·5%; silver 71·5%).
878	Gold solder melts (copper 18%; gold 82%).
907	Zinc boils.
960	Pure silver melts.
1,000	12% tin bronze melts.
1,063	Pure gold melts.
1,083	Pure copper melts.
1,150	Lead boils.
1,525	Pure iron melts.

Chapter Seven

STONE

SYNOPSIS

General: Flaking · Abrading · Pulverizing · Cutting · Hardness · Resilience · Selection. *Flaking:* Flakes · Methods of flaking · Percussion · Pressure · Cores · Blades · Secondary flaking · Natural and mechanical fracture · Surface alteration. *Abrading:* Rubbing · Sawing · Drilling · Cutting · Polishing. *Cutting:* Carving · Turning · Engraving · Intaglio. *Pulverizing.* *Splitting:* Fire-setting · Frost-splitting. *Sculpture and Masonry:* Quarrying · Facing · Building Stone.

GENERAL

ALTHOUGH SOME ASPECTS of early stoneworking have survived virtually unaltered into the present day, generally the introduction of suitable steel tools so changed working methods that it will be most practical to consider the two periods—pre- and post-steel—separately. Even so, there are only four basic ways of shaping stone: by *flaking* (chipping, knapping), by *abrading* (of which polishing is one aspect), by *pulverizing* (pecking, hammering, crumbling), and by *cutting*. A fifth method, *splitting* or *cleaving*, whether it is done mechanically, by *thermal fracture*, or by *frost splitting*, is not easily controlled and is generally only an adjunct of mining and quarrying.

The success of any particular method of shaping stone depends on two properties of the material itself, its *resilience* and its *hardness*. Some stones, such as flint and obsidian, while being very hard, are not resilient, and fracture readily even when struck with a relatively soft object such as a wood or bone hammer. Stones of this kind are most easily shaped by flaking. In contrast quartzite, for example, while being hard, does not flake easily; but it can be shaped by hammering away the surface. Obviously it is best to use a hammer as hard as, or harder than, the stone being worked, but a rather softer hammer can be used, although admittedly it will wear at too great a rate to be thoroughly practicable. In the process of abrading the abrasive must be as hard as, or preferably harder than, the stone being worked, no matter whether the abrasive is a solid block or in the form of a sand. Thus nephrite (jade stone), which is about as hard as quartz, can be abraded using quartz sand, but it is a very slow process and a harder material such as garnet sand or corundum was most commonly used. Where the abrasive is being used in the form of sand or dust, the tool carrying the abrasive need not be as hard as the stone being worked since it is only a vehicle for the abrasive; a bone-pointed drill can be used with quartz sand to bore a hole through granite. This process of abrading is frequently referred to as cutting, being the method used to shape gemstones ('diamond cuts diamond') and in decorating glass. In the strict sense of the word stone can only be cut by a tool considerably harder than the material itself. Soapstone (steatite) can easily be cut with a sharp-edged tool of flint or one of the harder metals, quartz not at all.

Any discussion of stoneworking methods, therefore, must take into account these two properties of the material being shaped. Degree of hardness is generally established by reference to the Mohs' Scale (p. 179); but resilience is less easily measured, and liability to fracture can normally only be assessed in vague terms. Undoubtedly these qualities were well known to primitive man, who established them empirically. Any attempts to flake or trim by pulverizing would only have caused nephrite to shatter; it was too hard to be cut even by steel tools; it could be abraded only with the utmost difficulty using quartz sand, more easily with corundum, and so ultimately the working of jade led to the development of specialized abrading tools and a search for suitable abrasives.

Appreciation of these qualities also led to a selection of suitable materials for specific purposes. Obviously an axe of nephrite, while being aesthetically satisfactory and durable, would have been little used for everyday purposes since the time taken to shape it would make it highly valuable. On the other hand, some fine-grained igneous rocks could be roughly shaped by flaking and reduced to their final form by abrading on quartz sandstone to give an axehead that was resilient enough and kept a good enough edge for general work. Equally, soapstones, which could be cut easily and yet would withstand relatively high temperatures, were ideal for making lamps, cooking vessels and moulds into which to cast bronze. In fact, the search for, and distribution of, stones with properties ideal for specific duties was clearly well developed even in the most primitive communities, and the tracing of these raw materials to their sources has been one of the most enlightening aspects of recent archaeological work.

FLAKING

Because they not only flaked easily, but also fractured to give a sharp edge, flint, obsidian and chert were the favoured stone materials of early man. In areas where these stones were absent other fine-grained rocks were made to serve, but for all practical purposes what may be said about the working properties of flint is equally true of these other materials.

Although flint is a micro-crystalline form of quartz, in many physical respects it behaves as a super-cooled fluid (p. 42). If one gives a slab of flint a sharp blow at right angles to its surface, the shock will be transmitted at an equal but increasing distance in all directions from the axis of the blow, with a result that it will fracture to give a cone, the apex of which was the point of impact. Depending upon the density of the flint, the angle between the axis of the blow and the sides of the cone varies from 120° to 160°. If the blow is directed at the edge of the block of flint, only a part of a cone will be produced, while as the angle between the direction of striking and the face being struck is decreased, smaller and increasingly narrower and flatter segments will be formed. Any piece of stone detached in this way is called a *flake*, while the parent block is referred to as the *core* (Fr. *nucléus*), and the surface that is struck the *striking* or *flaking* platform. Because this type of fracture roughly resembles a limpet shell it is termed *conchoidal fracture*. The fracture face is never flat but shows a series of concentric rings, rather like ripples, that radiate from the point of impact, and it is a draughtsman's convention to show these clearly when illustrating flint objects. Apart from these, the flake normally has a clearly distinguishable swelling, the *bulb of percussion*, immediately below the point of impact, presumably due to compression of the material at the moment of striking. The bulb may bear a small scar, the *bulbar scar* (Fr. *éraillure*) and a number of straight

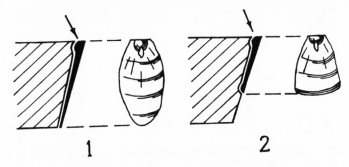

FIG. 17   FEATURES OF A TYPICAL FLAKE (1) AND A DUB FLAKE WITH
HINGE FRACTURE (2).

fissures may be seen on the face of the flake radiating from the point of impact, but these features are not invariably to be noted. The face of the flake formed by the fracture is generally called the *bulbar, main* or *positive flake surface*, while the face of the core is termed the *negative flake surface, flake-bed* or *flake scar*, and bears a depression corresponding to the bulb of percussion on the flake, the *bulb pit* or *negative bulb of percussion*. When the flaking blow is too weak the line of fracture, instead of running straight through the core, turns sharply outwards some distance below the bulb so that the flake ends in what appears to be an exaggerated conchoidal ring. This is known as *hinge fracture* to the archaeologist, and more succinctly as a *dub flake* to the Brandon Knappers.

Methods of flaking

There are basically two methods of detaching a flake; one by striking the core, *percussion flaking*, and the other by applying heavy pressure at a point, *pressure flaking*.

In percussion flaking there is a number of possible variations. The core being flaked may be struck against another stone lying on the ground, the *anvil stone*, or the core may be held against the anvil stone and struck above with another stone. This is variously known as *anvil flaking, block-on-block flaking*, or *direct rest flaking*. The core may be held in one hand and struck with a hammer held in the other. The hammer may be of stone, wood or bone, the process being known as *hammer-flaking* or *direct freehand flaking*. The core may be placed on the ground and a wooden or bone punch struck with a hammerstone to detach flakes, generally known as *punch flaking* or *indirect flaking*.

In pressure flaking the core may be held in one hand and flakes detached by pressing hard with a stone, wood or bone tool held in the other hand, *freehand pressure flaking;* or the core may be placed on the ground

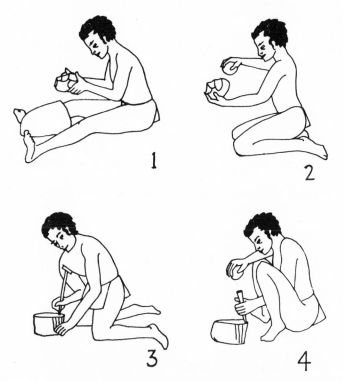

FIG. 18   FLAKING METHODS. ANVIL FLAKING (1). DIRECT PERCUSSION
(2). PRESSURE FLAKING (3). INDIRECT PERCUSSION (4).

and pressure applied by means of a point, usually of bone, and often hafted so that the craftsman can put the weight of his chest or shoulder against the end, a process known as *rest* or *impulsive pressure flaking*.

As has been said above, sometimes flakes break off short with a hinge fracture. To prevent this happening, where a long flake is intended, the fingers of the supporting hand may be held firmly against the outer surface of the core, or the core may be gripped firmly between the knees to achieve the same effect. This is really an adjunct of general flaking methods, and *controlled flaking* of this sort can be used with all methods save anvil flaking.

In examining flint artifacts it is usually difficult to determine beyond broad generalities what methods of flaking have been used. Flakes struck on an anvil normally show a wide angle between the striking platform and the main flake surface, while the bulb of percussion is large and semi-conical, and the same is true of hammer flaking where a stone hammer has been used; but where a soft hammer of bone or wood has been employed the bulb of percussion is usually more diffuse and the flakes longer and thinner. This is equally true of punch and pressure flaking. Even so, diffuse bulbs and slender flakes can result from hard hammer flaking when, for example, the point of impact coincides with an existing ridge on the striking platform.

Cores

Archaeologists often distinguish between *core tools*, in which, starting with a nodule or large pebble, flakes of unwanted material are struck and discarded as waste; and *flake tools* in which the flakes struck from the core are either used directly or reworked to form implements. This is obviously not a distinction to be interpreted too literally; a large flake may perfectly well serve as the raw material from which to form a core tool.

In the making of flake tools the core may be struck in a random way, depending very much on the shape of the core at the moment, and this is commonly the case in anvil flaking. On the other hand the core may be very carefully flaked in preparation so that ultimately one final blow will detach a flake tool of the required shape, and these *prepared cores* are generally the result of hammer, punch or pressure flaking. Particular attention is often given to the striking platform, the process varying from removing a single flake to produce a platform, *dishing;* to roughening the whole surface by removing a number of small flakes to give a *faceted platform*, presumably to prevent the flaking tool from slipping, and to ensure that the platform is at the correct angle to the flaking surface.

Blades

Many flint implements depend in the first instance on the production of blades, which are long, narrow flakes, the edges of which are approximately parallel. The *blade cores* from which these are produced normally have a flat, common striking platform at the top and become fluted as the blades are detached, developing a cylindrical, conical or prismatic shape. As more blades are struck off, the ridges between previous flaking surfaces naturally appear on the backs of fresh blades, and generally in antiquity only *single-ridged* or *double-ridged* blades were produced. The Brandon flint workers referred to these as *single-backed* and *double-backed* flakes, but the word 'backed' has a different meaning for archaeologists (p. 104). Near the striking platform these ridges often become strongly developed due to the close proximity of neighbouring negative bulbs, and these projections or *spurs* are commonly flaked away before fresh blades are struck, so that on these new blades spur-trimming scars may be seen.

As the angle between the striking platform and the sides of the blade core approaches a right-angle, it becomes more difficult to strike off new blades. If the core is reasonably large at this stage, a new platform may be produced by flaking away the original one at an angle. Generally this can be done by removing a single large flake, and these *core rejuvenation flakes* are often a common feature of the waste on sites where blades have been made.

FIG. 19 DIAGRAM TO SHOW THE PROCESS OF CORE REJUVENATION. THE PRODUCTION OF A FRESH PLATFORM ALLOWS FURTHER FLAKES TO BE STRUCK FROM THE CORE.

Secondary flaking

The initial roughing out of a stone tool is usually referred to as *primary flaking*, while any later working designed to thin down or otherwise improve the look or function of the implement is called *secondary flaking* or *retouch*. On crude flint tools this often amounts to no more than a rough trimming of the edges with a light stone hammer or a wooden or bone baton. The result is a mass of small flake scars on the edge of the tool, each ending in a hinge fracture, a style of trimming generally referred to as *step-flaking* or *resolved flaking*.

For the most part secondary flaking is done by pressure methods using either bone or wooden points or pieces of stone with thick right-angled edges which acquire a characteristic crushed or scaled appearance as a result of this use and are often called *fabricators*. A great variety of terms have been coined to describe secondary flaking of this type; *feather-edge, fish-scale, shallow, ripple* and *free-flaking* all seem to have been used as general descriptive terms; *invasive retouch*, to describe tools in which the entire primary flaking has been removed by secondary work; *serial* or *fluted flaking*, in which flakes have been removed in sequence across the face of the tool, each flake-scar cutting into the edge of the last (ripple-flaking is often given this meaning too); *collateral-flaking*, in which flakes have been removed from either edge of a tool and the scars meet in a clearly defined rib; *transverse-flaking*, in which the flake scars either run right across the face of the tool, or those from either edge merge without producing a rib (also known by some as fluting); *oblique flaking*, in which the flake scars run at an angle across the face of the tool; and *channel-flaking*, in which one or more flake scars run down the length of the tool.

Notching either along the edge of a blade to give a saw-edge, or in a more exaggerated form at the base to provide a means of hafting, is also usually done by pressure flaking. One edge of a flint blade may be blunted by removing a series of flakes at nearly a right-angle to the face of the blade. These *battered-backed* blades are not necessarily evidence of pressure flaking, since the same effect can be achieved by light hammering.

Natural and mechanical fracture

In dealing with early artifacts especially it is vital to be able to distinguish between fractures that are man-made, or *mechanical*, and those that occur naturally. In the first place it is important to appreciate that fractures may occur as a result of natural forces, for example during land-movements or when stones are moved rapidly by water; while lesser movements may produce a certain amount of flaking along fresh flake edges that may look deceptively like deliberate step-flaking. Since all tools are the result of a logical process conditioned by traditional practice, it seems a reasonable procedure to ask first the two salient questions: Is this a logical shape? Does it conform to a known tradition? In fact it is better to examine critically the flake scars and to determine first from which point each flake was struck.

Flint is particularly prone to fracture if exposed to sudden temperature changes, especially cooling. A nodule of flint exposed to the sun all day may become quite warm and if there is a sudden evening fall of temperature roughly circular patches of the surface (pot-lids) may flake away due to the sudden contraction of the surface while the centre remains unchanged. An oval pebble that has suffered in this way may look remarkably like a hand-axe, but the flake scars will show no negative bulbs of percussion and no conchoidal rings. Flint that has small fissures on the surface may absorb water which may freeze. The expansion on freezing may be sufficient to crack the flint, often producing columnar rods, a phenomenon known as *starch fracture*. Many of these fragments may look like known tools, such as blades, but again examination will show no bulbs of percussion or conchoidal rings.

Thermal fracture has been used to shape tools, but only in fairly sophisticated societies. The flint was warmed gently and cold water allowed to drop, usually by means of a hollow stalk, on to areas from which a flake was to be removed. As a result a small pot-lid was formed, the process sometimes being repeated all over the surface of the tool.

One form of mechanical fracture does not produce conchoidal rings or bulbs of percussion—*quartering*—but since it can only be used to break apart large nodules of flint it is not liable to result in any confusion. The nodule is placed on a stone or the flint-worker's knee and one end is grasped firmly, the other end being struck obliquely away from the centre, with the effect of virtually pulling the nodule apart.

Surface alteration of flint

The surface appearance of flint usually depends entirely on the conditions under which it has lain buried. Freshly struck flint often shows a slight bloom on the surface, but this disappears with age and old flake surfaces are normally glass-like. Under alkaline conditions, such as are met with in lime or chalk soils, the minute quartz crystals tend to dissolve and this causes a diffraction of the light, with the result that the surface appears white or mottled. In iron-rich soils this surface layer, usually known as *patina*, becomes stained yellow, brown or red. The degree of surface breakdown and staining naturally depends partly on the time the flint has remained buried, and in theory, were the conditions under which any flint remained under the earth known with some accuracy, it would be possible to suggest how long the flint had remained buried. As it is, it is simply not possible to arrive at adequate data to allow this kind of calculation; flint from the same stratigraphical horizon often shows considerable variation in degree of surface change. More success along these lines seems to have been achieved with obsidian, itself a more uniform material, from habitation sites of reasonably even soil composition.

Flint that has become buried in shifting sands, as in dunes or some desert conditions, often acquires a very high gloss which is nothing more than a natural polish. This should not be confused with *corn* or *sickle gloss* which results from cutting the stalks of corn or grass or from shaving wood. In these cases the polish is generally confined mainly to the cutting edge of the tool.

ABRADING

As has already been said, stone may be abraded using either a solid block of abrasive material or by using a powdered abrasive and a tool as vehicle for the abrasive. For producing simple shapes, such as stone axes, solid blocks of abrasive (*grinding-stones, whetstones, polishing stones* or *rubbers*) are perfectly satisfactory, most commonly a sharp-grained quartz sandstone being used. During the rubbing down some water is generally used to act as a lubricant and so ease the work, and to emulsify and carry off the waste. The tool being shaped is usually hand-held and worked against a stationary rubber since greater pressure can be exerted this way than when the rubber is hand-held. Laminae of shallow-bedded sandstone have been mounted in a frame and used for sawing stone, while solid drill points of sandstone have also been used with a bow-drill (p. 107) for boring holes, but both these methods are unusual.

With powdered abrasive, *sawing* can be done using a string or thong of leather held taut in a bow. Because of the heat generated by friction water must be used as a coolant (as well as a lubricant) but even so the string or thong is fairly short-lived, and a metal wire serves better. For this purpose, in fact, a flat metal blade has disadvantages as compared with a wire, for not only does it make fretting difficult, but actually increases the friction area, and hence the work to be done, without in any way increasing the efficiency of the cutting edge.

Drilling may be done with either a solid or a hollow drill point. The solid drill may be no more than a piece of wood or a splinter of bone, or it may be tipped with flint or some other hard stone, but unless the stone being drilled is exceptionally soft the drill will wear with use, and in so doing produce a tapering drill hole, or, where drilling has been done from both sides of the object, a characteristic 'hour-glass' perforation. Hollow

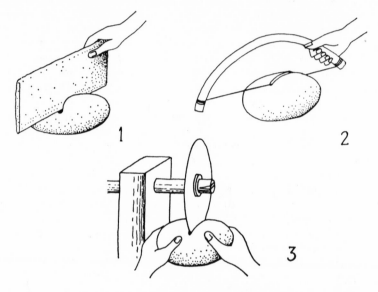

FIG. 20   ABRASION SAWS. BLOCK OF SANDSTONE (1). WIRE-STRUNG BOW-
SAW (2). LAP-WHEEL (3).

drills may be of wood (jade has been successfully bored using a bamboo drill) or the middle section of a long bone or, of course, a metal tube. For wide bores, hollow drilling is far more practical than solid drilling since less material needs to be worn away. Apart from making the task simpler, there is less wear on the drill and the bore holes are more or less cylindrical, often with only the slightest taper. As a waste product of hollow drilling there are the solid cylinders of material that filled the hollow of the drill during boring. If the material is precious these may be reworked as beads or amulets, and unworked they may be used as gaming pieces, or stoppers, but they are not of necessity deliberate artifacts.

Drill holes may have to be enlarged, as would be the case when forming the interior of a narrow-necked stone vase. This can be done by abrading with a hooked-bit of metal, usually rotated in a lathe (p. 117), and where the interior is excessively undercut progressively larger hooked-bits may have to be used.

Abrasion-cutting, such as is done by lapidaries and glass-workers, is generally achieved with the edge of a thin metal disc, a lap-wheel, again normally lathe-rotated, although thin discs of hard stone have been used for this purpose; while *polishing* may be done on the flat surfaces of similar, though usually somewhat thicker wheels. For a really high final polish *buffing wheels* of wood or leather are used with a very fine-grained abrasive although, of course, in societies in which the lathe was unknown polishing would have to be done by hand using the rounded end of a stick or piece of bone, or a piece of leather, to work the fine abrasive.

In most primitive societies quartz sand was the abrasive commonly used simply because of its ubiquity, and this in practice limited the

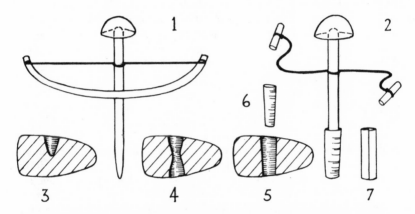

FIG. 21 BOW (1) AND STRAP (2) DRILLS FOR ABRASION DRILLING. AXE PARTLY DRILLED (3) AND COMPLETED (4) USING SOLID DRILL POINT. AXE PERFORATED WITH HOLLOW BIT OF BONE (5) AND CORE FROM DRILL-ING (6). HOLLOW BIT OF METAL (7).

stones being worked to those with a hardness of 7·0—the hardness of quartz—or less. More sophisticated people learned to look for, or even manufacture by crushing stones, harder abrasives such as Chinese 'red sand' (crushed garnets, hardness 7·5) and emery (crushed corundum, hardness 9·0), or even the hardest of all, diamond dust, so allowing the working of the harder gemstones.

CUTTING

Cutting implies the shaping of stone with a tool so much harder than the material that there is little or no wear on the tool itself. The simplest method is, of course, *carving* or paring, and while for some purposes knife-shaped blades could be used, chisel-ended blades were infinitely to be preferred. Many of the softer stones—steatite, calcite, alabaster—could be cut with flint or early metal tools, while using the same materials for pointing a drill, boring presented no difficulty. The introduction of the lathe allowed the *turning* of rounded shapes, and it is interesting to notice that for the working of soft stones flint lathe-tools continued to be used into comparatively late periods. Equally, the true *engraving* of soft stones was possible with tools of flint or metal, while the introduction of diamond splinters for pointing tools allowed an even harder range of stones to be drilled or engraved, but it should be remembered that the small size and large cost of diamonds has never allowed their use for the coarser work of carving or turning.

When examining fine stone decoration, such as *intaglio* work, it may be difficult to decide whether the work has been done with abrasive and a small lap-wheel or whether it has been truly engraved. The lap-wheel has one serious defect as far as the artist-craftsman is concerned in that it is extremely difficult to cut anything approaching an abruptly curving line, and the whole design has thus to be executed in terms of straight, or gently curving, lines. Apart from this, the lap-wheel tends to cut a relatively wide line compared with a diamond point, while the line itself generally has a U-section, the point being able to give a sharp V-section; and the lap-wheel must of necessity give a characteristic semi-elliptical end to any line cut by it, while an engraved line may end abruptly.

PULVERIZING

Pulverizing probably demands the least skill, and often the most patience, of any of the methods of shaping stone. The method is that most commonly used by primitive people for dressing building stones, making stone monuments and decorating flat stone surfaces, although it is a method that has been used to perforate stone mace and axe heads by repeatedly hammering in the same area. Unless it is very heavily weathered the characteristic 'pecked' surface that results from hammering is not difficult to recognize. Technically the process is of little interest, although estimates of the time involved to produce results, and the corollaries of such calculations, may be of interest.

SPLITTING

Rocks with a clearly defined bedding plane are easily quarried by splitting along the plane with wooden wedges, and once quarried the blocks may be further reduced by the same method. Some freestones, too, that have no obvious bedding plane, may be treated in this way, but even the most skilled quarrymen and masons have little control over the process, and few would care to predict what precise shape or dimension of stone block would result from it; at best it is a rough and ready method of producing stone blocks of approximately the right shape and size.

An even cruder method of breaking up large rocks is that of *fire-setting* in which a fire is built up against the rock, so warming it and causing it to expand. The rock is then doused with cold water, so making it split. The process was largely used by miners, who obviously were unconcerned about the shape in which ores left the mine, and farmers who wished to remove large boulders too big to manhandle from their land.

Frost-splitting was also used as a means of breaking up finely laminated rock to make slates. When a cold spell was anticipated the blocks were well soaked with water to ensure penetration between the laminae. On freezing, the expansion of ice would force the laminae apart, so forming slates of roughly the required thickness.

SCULPTURE AND MASONRY

Until the recent introduction of explosives, power-driven tools and steels hardened with other metals, the equipment of quarrymen, sculptors and masons had changed little over the past two millennia: the hand tools listed by Vasari and Cellini are almost identical to those used by a sculptor and mason today; none would have caused Pheidias much surprise. Fashion, however, has changed and it is chiefly, although not entirely, in determining how the craftsman has attempted to produce what is asked of him that our interest in this field must lie. From this point of view masonry is as a whole more informative than sculpture, since careful polishing too often has removed every last tool mark from a statue, although inaccessible corners may retain enough to be o." value. Even so, the sculptor and mason have always worked with the same tools and in the same way; what is true of one is generally true of the other.

Quarrying was a blend of skill and brute force. Deeply fissured rock could sometimes be quarried in manageable lumps by inserting a lever, often a steel bar with a chisel end, or *paddle*, and so inching the block out. More commonly the rock had to be cleft first, in which case a row of wedge-pits or triangular slots was cut along the line in which the splitting was to be done with an axe-shaped tool (*race, gad* or *jad*). Into these pits were fitted wedges (also sometimes called gads), and these were driven down with a heavy hammer little by little in series until the rock split. Small steel plates, *wedge-slats*, were sometimes placed each side of the wedge. Because it is easier to drill a hole with machine tools than to cut a tapering pit, in recent years the slats have been replaced by semicircular rods (*feathers*) and the wedge by a tapering steel rod (*plug*).

Once quarried, large blocks were often split again using the same method, or a deep groove, or *chase*, might be cut across the block which was then raised slightly from the ground and struck a heavy blow, so causing it to break along the chase line. Alternatively the blocks might be sawn. A toothed saw could be used only on the softer stones, otherwise a *grub saw*, a frame saw (p. 116) with a toothless but corrugated blade, was used, and this had to be fed with sand and water.

In antiquity stone for the better buildings was seldom used straight from the quarry (undressed), *rock faced*, unless as a footing for walls. Apart from an axe-like hammer, the *walling hammer*, most of this work was done with a variety of punches and chisels, hammer or mallet struck. Punches varied from heavy, blunt-nosed *pitchers* to light, sharp *points;* while chisels ranged from wide-bladed *boasters* (bolsters) to narrow-ended *querks* (quirks) as well as *toothed chisels* or *claw tools.*

In dressing, the usual process was to hack away first the worst of the protruding lumps with a walling hammer, or a pitcher, simply to make it reasonably level. Sometimes the dressing was taken no further than this *poled* or *scabbled* facing, or the whole face might be cut lightly all over with the walling hammer, usually at right angles to the bedding plane, to give a *hammer-dressed* face. Alternatively, the face might be gone over with a light punch to produce fine parallel scored lines across the face, or be *battered* with a chisel or claw tool to give much the same effect, work traditionally only done by right-handed men if the lines were to run obliquely across the face, since the left-handed men would naturally produce lines at right-angles to the others. *Drags*, steel combs for smoothing the surface, rasps and rifflers, although used by sculptors, were not commonly employed by masons, but for a smooth finish, rubbing down with a fine sandstone rubber was more normal.

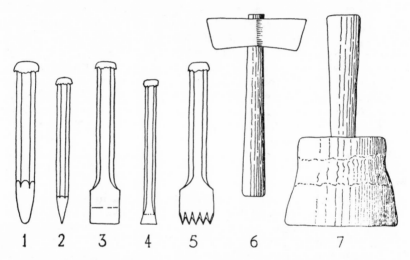

Fig. 22   Mason's Tools. Pitcher (1). Point (2). Boaster (3). Querk (4). Claw (5). Walling hammer (6). Mallet (7).

In the process of squaring up a stone prior to facing, the block was placed on the *banker*, a level block of stone which served as a bench, and beginning at the lowest corner a draft an inch or so wide was cut with a chisel along the edge to the next lowest corner, and so on round the whole face to produce a rock-faced stone with a level margin all round. Normally the rock-faced centre would then be cut away, but stones in this state have been used for quoins and facing buildings—the effect even having been copied in plaster and concrete in recent years!

Building stone may be so accurately cut that there is no space in the joints for mortar, in which case each stone needed to be tied to its neighbour by a metal *cramp* usually fitting into a dovetailed recess at the edge of the stone. Iron cramps have often rusted and caused the stone to split. The difficulty of joining stones, in fact, often places limitations on the mason that are not met with by the woodworker, and the translation of architectural forms from wood to stone often had curious results. Thus, in the case of a flat-lintelled door-frame with moulding, the carpenter can make a mitred joint where the moulding turns at the corner; for the mason this is impossible, and the turn of the moulding must be cut in the lintel.

Masons use a number of generic terms to describe building stones that are apt to be confusing because they are applied haphazardly, but for the following terms the meanings are more or less generally accepted. Any stone composed of sand or grit that occurs in thick beds and can be cut freely in any direction is called a *freestone,* and once hewn for facing it is

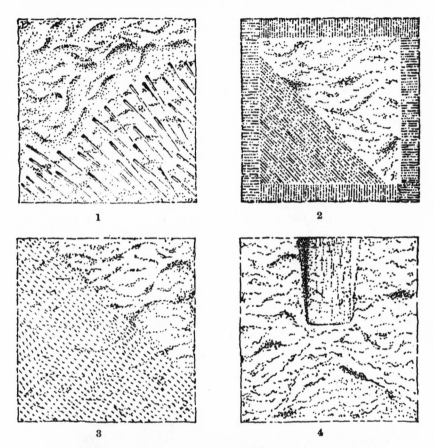

Fig. 23 Rock-faced stone partly scabbled (1) with walling hammer. Stone with levelled edges and partly battered with a point (2). Stone partly faced with claw (3). Rock-faced stone with mark left by gad when splitting (4).

termed *ashlar. Gritstone* and *ragstone* are terms usually applied to sandstones with coarse, angular grains that cut with a ragged fracture. *Flagstones* are thin-bedded sandstones ideal for flooring, but *hardstones* are hard limestones which will take a polish, and not just any stone that is hard. Building stone laid with the strata horizontally, in the orientation in which it was deposited, is said to be *base-bedded;* but when laid with the strata upright is said to be *face-bedded.* The latter is an easy but often fatal way of producing a smooth face since frost fracture may cause it to flake away.

Chapter Eight

WOOD

SYNOPSIS

General: Standard and coppice wood. *Felling:* Thinning out · Facing. *Seasoning* Heartwood · Sapwood · Grain. *Shaping:* Cleaving · Burning · Hewing · Shaving · Sawing · Drilling · Turning · Bending. *Joining:* Lashing · Sewing · Pegging · Nailing · Joints. *Decoration. Selection of Timber:* Oak · Elm · Ash · Alder · Bir.ch · Beech · Sycamore · Chestnut · Willow · Hazel · Yew · Box.

GENERAL

To many archaeologists, especially those whose chief interests lie in the remote past, a knowledge of wood and wood-working methods may at first seem of doubtful value since so little of the material has survived. Apart from actual artifacts, however, many excavated sites could, if examined critically, produce some evidence about the type of timber used and its preparation. This is particularly true of dwelling sites, in the building of which some wood was almost invariably used. The arraugement of the packing stones around a since decayed post might suggest whether it were a whole timber, one that had been squared, or one that had been cleft, for example; or the presence of a low, level stone footing for a wall could mean the use of a squared wall-plate.

On the whole one must suppose that primitive man appreciated the different behaviour of different timbers, and that provided enough timber of the type was available, he would select the appropriate material for the purpose in hand. Indeed the principal interest in identifying the various woods used in antiquity would seem to be in demonstrating the availability or lack of suitable materials. In some areas a lack of timber may have been due to a natural scarcity of woodland; in others, especially those in which cities appeared early, it may have resulted from deforestation due to the heavy demands for timber, fuel and agricultural land. Indeed, man's approach to woodland may take one of several forms. All the standing timber may be felled and the land either be allowed to revert to forest or be converted to farmland; all the timber may be felled and, as is done commonly today, the land replanted with young trees; or instead of using the whole tree, *standard wood*, the woodland may be thinned from time to time, branches of some trees being lopped and other trees cut back near the ground to produce *coppice wood*. The last simple method of preserving woodland naturally yielded smaller timber on the whole, but in areas where wood was in constant demand it did ensure a steady supply.

FELLING

As a general rule the woodman's tool was the axe. There are reports from various remote parts of the world of other means used by primitive people to fell trees, such as burning around the base or *stamm* of the tree, or using thongs and abrasive to saw through the trunk, but only from areas in which suitable stone for axe-making is not to be found. The stone axe, despite its somewhat frail appearance, is a most effective tool if properly used. The saw, on the other hand, was little used for felling because of the tendency for movement of the tree to close the cut and so 'bind' the blade.

Once felled the tree was *thinned out* (*shrouded*, *headed* or *snedded*); that is to say all the branches were cut away at the *spurs* or *stop* at the top of the trunk. If large enough, these branches might be used as timber; if not they would provide fuel, sold today by the 'cord' and hence known as *cord-wood*. The trunk, now known as the *butt* or *stick*, might then be *barked*, and the bark itself used for some other purpose such as tanning (p. 150) or simply burnt. Where the bark was required whole or in large sheets it was usually removed by splitting down the whole length of the butt and levering away with wedge-shaped barking tools. At this stage the butt might be used immediately as it stood or be roughly squared up with an axe or adze (*facing* or *broking*) and used without delay, but if it were to be used for any other purpose than crude building it would need first to be seasoned.

SEASONING

To understand fully the need for seasoning wood, and indeed much of its behaviour, one requires some knowledge of the structure of the material itself. Like all plant tissues wood is composed of a number of cells, the walls of which are made originally of cellulose and the centres of which initially contain the living matter of the tree. Unlike many plants, however, trees grow by laying down layers of new cells in the cambium layer immediately below the bark, and since this growth normally only takes place in the spring and summer the growth is intermittent and gives rise to the familiar tree-rings. In time the older cells lay down a new material chemically somewhat similar but more stable than cellulose, lignin, within the cell walls while at the same time the living cell substance dies. As a result, if one sections a tree of any great age one will find the wood in the middle, the *heartwood*, relatively dry and free of sap while the wood around the perimeter is moist and sappy, the so-called *sapwood*.

In different species of tree the shapes and sizes of the various cells, and their relationship to one another, differ. There are also chemical differences, some trees, for example, containing high proportions of resins or oils. It is these differences that account for the quite distinct behaviour of the various woods and their usually equally distinct colour, grain and odour.

All trees, however, even when felled in the autumn, when the sap has virtually stopped flowing, are relatively moist throughout and the seasoning process is largely one in which the wood is allowed to dry out.

If this process of drying is carried out too rapidly the outer sapwood may become relatively dry while the heartwood remains moist, and since the wood will shrink on drying the sapwood will almost invariably crack as a result. Equally, if the timber is kept too moist it may take a very long time to season, too long in fact for all practical purposes, and it was thus common practice to quarter large butts by splitting or cutting them longitudinally and then to stack them in such a way that the air could circulate through the wood pile. Today, where planking is required, it is more common to rough saw the butts into planks and stack these between cross-timbers to allow ventilation.

In a manner of speaking, however, wood is never seasoned: or at least it is never completely stable. With large changes of relative humidity it will absorb or lose water, so swelling or shrinking, and this ultimately may lead to warping. A plank cut radially, that is to say cut straight through the centre of the butt, may swell and shrink, but will seldom warp since the grain lines or bands of tree-rings are virtually all at right angles to the face of the plank; but one cut tangentially is very liable to distortion as the grain lines run through the wood obliquely to the face Craftsmen in antiquity were well aware of this, and selected for carving or panel-painting planks that had been cut radially.

Shaping

Some woods, but by no means all, can easily be split longitudinally. This process of *cleaving* can be done with no more elaborate equipment than a number of wooden or iron wedges and a woodman's mallet or *beatle* (*beatel, bitel, bittel*), although the cleaver or *froe** (*frow, throe*), an iron tool with a straight knife-like blade and a handle at right-angles to the back of the blade, driven down with a beatle, is of considerable antiquity. As a general rule cleaving is only used for quartering or halving butts, although lighter timber may be split in this way to make fencing spars and roofing battens. Some woods, however, in the hands of really experienced craftsmen, can be cleft into moderately thin planking. Since the lines of cleavage must follow weaknesses in the grain, cleft wood is not difficult to distinguish, the face of the timber always following any slight irregularities there may be throughout the length of the grain.

Where cleft timber has been used in early buildings, either as sunk posts or as wall infilling, and has since decayed, on excavation the packing may well show an outline that is either semi-circular or a quarter-circle in plan.

On the whole the more sophisticated woodworkers do not *burn* wood as a means of shaping it, although a heated iron rod was occasionally used to remove roughnesses left after drilling with an auger or bit. Even so, there is good reason to believe that fire was used quite extensively in the more remote past for hollowing such things as dug-out canoes. Eye-witness accounts of the making of these boats by primitive people today are almost without exception in agreement on two points, no matter

* The number of terms for this tool is unusual: frammer, frummer, froward, fromard and thrower (clearly the same name), as well as reamer, divider, dillaxe, side-knife, and splitting knife.

whether the work was done in Malaya or the Amazon: the major part of the hollowing was done by kindling a fire on the log and burning out the interior, and this was followed by cutting away every last piece of charred wood with an axe or adze. If the same practice were followed in antiquity we should, of course, be quite without the vital evidence that such canoes were initially hollowed by burning. This method of hollowing was probably not only restricted to canoes. There are reports, for example, of the hollowing of narrow-necked water bottles using iron burners by even fairly sophisticated peoples today, and indeed without a lathe it would seem to be the quickest and most efficient means of hollowing wood, although of course this does not imply that it was therefore the only or even the commonest way in which such work was done in antiquity.

For all rough trimming, especially for woodwork that was not intended to be inspected at close quarters, timber was generally *hewn* with either an axe or adze. Thus, a butt that had already been broked before seasoning might be further trimmed with an adze afterwards, and used as part of a frame building without further treatment. Timber that has been trimmed in this way is, again, not difficult to distinguish since the whole face is covered with small facets or scars that result from the chipping away of unevennesses. It is often said that this work can only be done satisfactorily with an adze, and the scars are often referred to as 'adze marks'. This is certainly true of planking, but in trimming a squared timber it is often simpler to support it just off the ground and work down the two vertical lengths with a light axe and then to roll the timber over and work down the other two lengths. From superficial appearances it would be difficult, if not impossible, to distinguish wood treated in this way from that hewn with an adze.

The faces of a piece of wood may be made even smoother by shaving, for which a variety of tools may be used. The simplest of these is the *draw-knife* (*draw-shave*) a stout, long knife-blade with a handle at both ends. The blade may be straight or curved (*round-shaver*) according to the work being done, but it is an open bladed tool with no device to determine the depth of shaving being removed. This is something that the craftsman must control himself, and on the whole the tendency is to remove broad, sweeping shavings with this tool. In a somewhat similar tool, the spoke-shave, the blade is short and set at an angle in a slot between the two handles, with the result that, according to the setting of the blade, the depth of shaving is limited. As the name implies, the tool is only really useful for shaving down spokes, chair-legs, and similar small, rounded shapes. The *plane*, fundamentally a chisel-ended blade set at an angle in a slotted stock, is of course today the commonest shaving tool used by carpenters. Planes have a bewildering variety of shapes and names, but there are perhaps half-a-dozen basic types: the coarse-set *jack-plane* for rough smoothing; the *smoothing-plane* for producing a relatively level surface; and the *trueing-plane* (*trying-plane*) for the final levelling. Other planes are designed for more specific purposes: the *fillister-plane* for cutting rebates to take the edges of window-glass or panels; the *jarvis*, a hollow-bladed plane for shaping spokes, chair-legs and other rounded forms; and *moulding-planes* with profiled blades for cutting mouldings. All these tools are normally used for working down the length of the grain of the wood. The *rung-engine* (*smoothing-engine*, *stail-engine* or *nug*) however is used to produce rounded shapes, and cuts across the grain, the stock having a cylindrical opening into which protrudes the cutting edge of the blade. The roughly prepared wood is placed in the cylindrical opening and the plane rotated, the effect being very similar to that of turning (see below), although of course it is the cutting tool that rotates in this instance. All these planes are hand-held tools, but coopers use a fixed bladed tool, the *jointer*, for bevelling the edges of staves, the staves themselves being passed over the cutting edge of the tool, as by this means a more precise angle of bevel can be achieved than by using a conventional plane.

The efficiency of the *saw* depends not only upon the quality of the metal and the size and sharpness of the teeth, but also upon their 'set' or the angle at which they are bent out of the plane of the blade, for the cut made by the teeth (the *kerf*) must be wider than the blade, otherwise the blade would 'bind' in the wood. Since there is a greater tendency for wood to bind in this way when cutting down the grain it is necessary to make a wide kerf and hence the teeth of a saw used for this purpose, the *rip-saw*, have a coarse set, while for cutting across the grain the set can be more shallow, the *cross-cut* setting. The design of most early saws also was affected by the fact that simple steels when worked thin enough to make an efficient saw were prone to buckle. To overcome this the blade was either held in tension in a bow or frame (*bow-saw* and *frame saw*) or was provided with a handle at both ends, and so required two sawyers. For cutting across the grain with a two-handle *thwart-saw* this presented no difficulties, but for sawing down the length of a butt it necessitated a *saw-pit* over which the timber was supported, the top-sawyer standing above pulling the saw upwards, the pit-man below pulling the blade downwards and incidentally becoming smothered with the falling sawdust. Until the introduction of mechanical band and circular saws this was virtually the only means of producing wide planking, panels and veneers.

For *drilling* holes the simplest tool of all was the plain pointed *awl*, but since this pierced without removing any wood, it could only be used for making small holes. Spiral, screw and twisted drilling tools appeared on the whole remarkably late, and the *auger*, a tool with a cross-handle at one end and a spoon-shaped or gouge cutter at the other, continued in use for a long period, especially for drilling wooden water-pipes and pumps. For more rapid drilling a number of different devices have been used in different areas during the ages. The *strap-drill* and *bow-drill* both work on the same principle: a strap or thong passed around the shaft is moved backwards and forwards, so producing a reciprocal rotation of the drill. In the case of the strap-drill the ends of the thong are free and thus need either both hands of a separate craftsman to work the drill, or a mouth- or chest-piece with which the carpenter can control the upper end of the drill, leaving his hands free to work the strap. With the bow-drill the ends of the thong are attached to a bow of wood or horn which can be worked with one hand, leaving the other free to control the shaft.

The *pump-drill* or *archimedean drill* had a shaft of square section that had been twisted, and a rider with a square hole in it to fit the shaft was pushed up and down, again causing reciprocal rotation. The screw or twisted drilling point would not have been effective in any of these drills because of their reciprocal movement, but with the introduction of the carpenter's *brace* or *stock* their use became possible. The brace is, in fact, only a cranked shaft into which could be fitted interchangeable *bits* (*bitts*, *bittes*) of various types and sizes. One hand turned the crank while the other controlled the free end. Removable bits of the appropriate kind could, of course, also be used with the other types of drill discussed, and today it is common to distinguish three main classes: *centre-bits* which

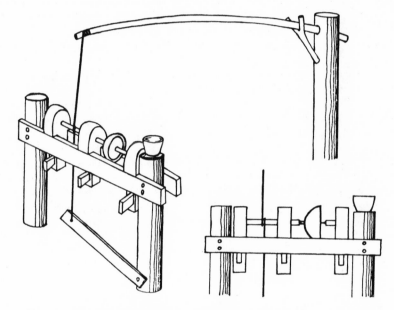

FIG. 24   DIAGRAM TO SHOW THE FUNCTION OF A SIMPLE POLE LATHE.

are little more than sharp points, sometimes with spurs, used normally to start a drill-hole; *hollow-bits*, spoon-, gouge- or shell-shaped; and *twisted-bits* including twisted, spiral and screw shapes.

For rounded work the *lathe* was very commonly used in antiquity. In this the wood to be *turned* was held between two horizontal mandrels, one being free and ending in a point, the *cup centre*, the other taking the drive and ending in two or more projections, the *spur centre;* although sometimes the drive mandrel was squared at the end, and this was let into a corresponding square hole in the wood being turned. The mandrels were free to rotate in two bearings, the *stocks* or *poppets* (*puppets*), the head-stock of the driving mandrel being fixed, the tailstock being adjustable to take different lengths of wood; both stocks being supported in a bench-like *bed*. Before the invention of the crankshaft or the introduction of water-power, the lathe was driven either by two pedals or a single pedal and pole. With *double-pedal drive* a thong was carried from one pedal around the drive mandrel and down to the other pedal, and by pressing on each in turn a reciprocal rotary movement was given to the wood to be turned. The same kind of movement was also given by the *pole-drive* in which the thong was carried from the free end of a flexible pole fixed above the lathe, around the drive mandrel, and so down to the pedal. On pressing down on the pedal the work rotated one way, and on releasing the pressure the pole sprang back, carrying the work around in the opposite direction. Working with these lathes was very much a stop-and-start business since turning could only be done when the wood was rotating towards the craftsman. The turning tools were mostly chisels or gouges, but for cutting out the inside of bowls a knife with a curved blade, the *inside-knife* or *hooking-knife* was commonly used. Turned wooden vessels, or *treen*, frequently carry a mass of small parallel scars across the surface, somewhat akin to the rilling on pottery (p. 29), although these may have been removed by later sanding, and centre marks are very commonly present as well.

Some timbers may be shaped by *bending*, but to do this the wood must normally be either unseasoned or steamed. Light, unseasoned wood needed only to be bent and kept in position until seasoned to remain permanently curved; but heavier timber, even though unseasoned, needed to be heated before attempting to bend it. Reports of primitive people today making 'dug-out' canoes invariably show that the hollowed log is heated thoroughly before attempting to open out the sides. Seasoned wood must be heated in a *steam chest* before bending, and after drying out it will then keep its shape, although thick timbers are normally *kerfed* as well before bending. A series of parallel saw-cuts are made on the inside of the curve, and these close on bending, but of course the strength of the timber is drastically reduced by this treatment.

JOINING

To the modern eye the use of *lashings* of either rope or thong as a means of joining wood appears a strictly temporary measure. Nevertheless it must be remembered that in most early building this was probably the only means of securing timbers, and any conjectural reconstructions by archaeologists should be made with the low tensile strength of such lashings in mind. Planks were also *sewn* together, especially in early boat building, holes being drilled at intervals along the edges of the planks and thongs or cords passed through them, the holes finally being caulked. The technique is still in use for boat construction in some parts of the world today.

Wooden *pegs*, *pins*, *dowels* or *treenails* were commonly used in heavy timber construction, without glue, the pegs being made longer and tapering to a wider 'head' than initially necessary. The heads were frequently left projecting, and as the timber aged, the pegs were from time to time driven deeper in, but in finer work they were cut off flush, although apt to work loose and require replacing. Early iron *wrought nails*, because they had to be hand forged, were commonly square in section. Their manufacture was a slow process, and it was not until the introduction of *cut-nails*, stamped from a flat piece of steel, that nail-making became sufficiently economic to allow the ubiquitous use of nails

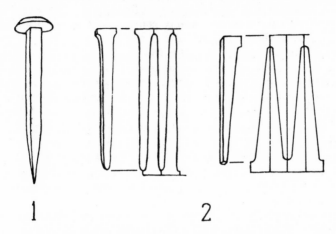

FIG. 25   HAND FORGED (1) AND CUT NAILS (2).

in wood-working. Later, drawn iron wire was cut into lengths and a head forged on these to give *wire nails*. Steel screws, like the twisted bits, were a comparatively late introduction.

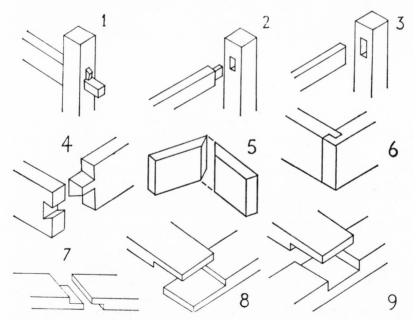

FIG. 26   WOODWORKER'S JOINTS. KEYED MORTICE (1). MORTICE AND TENON (2). HOUSED MORTICE (3). DOVETAIL (4). MITRE (5). DADO (6). REBATE (7). END-LAP (8). MIDDLE-LAP (9).

Joints in woodworking are strictly speaking joins made by cutting one timber to fit accurately in a recess made in another, although most cabinet makers today would also consider that jointed work must be glued. The simplest type of jointing is that found in *stick furniture*. In this the legs, arms, and so on are simply rounded and tapered and passed through holes in the main part of the furniture, the protruding ends sometimes being split and wedged before being cut off flush. Almost as simple as this is the *keyed mortise* and *tenon*, in which the squared end of a timber (the tenon) passes through a corresponding square hole (the mortise) and protrudes beyond. Into this protruding tenon is cut another small mortise into which is driven the small wedge or key so that the mortise cannot be withdrawn. Neither of these joints require glueing, although they may well need tapping up with a mallet from time to time, but the other joints illustrated need either glue or pegs.

DECORATION

The principal method of decorating wood was, of course, by *carving*. and the chisel is found in very remote antiquity. It is in fact practically impossible to carve without an end-bladed tool, and many flint 'gravers' of pre-neolithic age were probably as much designed for working wood that has since perished, as for carving the bone artifacts that have survived. In relief carving of later periods, punches were also used to give a broken background, the punches sometimes having patterned points similar to those used in metal working (p. 78). The pronounced grain of many timbers is itself of no little aesthetic merit, and it is the manner in which the craftsman adjusted his design to suit the grain of a piece of wood that distinguishes the artist from the mediocre woodworker.

Some highly grained woods, quite unsuitable because of their lack of strength for general use, were applied to a *carcase* of more durable timber as a *veneer*. Contrary to popular usage today, veneers were thus not necessarily a means of disguising an inferior framework. The immense labour of cutting, glueing down and polishing a veneer in antiquity never allowed the process to become the cheap deceit it may be today. Apart from simple veneers, and mirror veneers made by laying side by side adjacent cuts from the same butt, two different woods might be counter-cut. Usually a light and dark veneer were placed together and cut with a fret-saw, so that after cutting the one veneer might be inset in the other. The widespread belief that after counter-cutting two veneers result—a light wood inset with dark, and a dark wood inset with light, for example—is a complete myth. If the fret-saw were worked vertically, the kerf would be wide enough to prevent an accurate fit of one veneer in another, and to overcome this all the cutting was carried out at an angle. This process of inlaying one veneer with another is sometimes referred to as *marqueting*, while the inlaying of non-veneered wood with other pieces of wood is sometimes called *parquetry*. Both terms, however, have lost any precise meaning they may once have had. Parquet, in fact, originally only referred to flooring made of different woods; while marquetry described any inlaying of wood, including the use of ivory, mother-of-pearl, tortoiseshell, and so on. Under the circumstances it would seem less confusing to speak of inlay and veneer inlay when describing these different types of work. The term *boule*, less correctly *buhl*, refers to a type of inlay work of brass and porcelain made popular by André Charles Boule (1642-1732).

Wood may be *stained* either to bring the grain into greater relief or to conceal completely the nature of the wood. In many highly grained woods some areas will absorb stains more easily than others, and when lightly stained the colour distinction between these areas is heightened. Heavy staining in dark brown, red and black was sometimes used to imitate oak, fruit-woods and ebony. Wooden objects were also commonly painted. The paint was, however, often not put straight on to the untreated wood surface, but a covering of *gesso*—a mixture of size and plaster—was first applied to the wood. Many wooden statues, for example, that have since lost their surfaces, have survived from the medieval period, and a careful examination of cracks and crevices will often reveal traces of the lost gesso and paint surfaces.

SELECTION OF TIMBER

It is obviously impossible to review here all the types of timber available to man in different parts of the world throughout the past, but to those who wish to understand fully the significance of any wooden objects that may have survived, it is advisable to list the timbers that were available and to study their special qualities. The following is a very short list of ten of the main *hardwoods* (timber from deciduous trees) and two *softwoods* (timber from coniferous trees) common in Western Europe, with their particular properties and the normal uses to which they were put.

1. *Oak*. The heartwood is strong, hard, durable and quite heavy with a characteristic gnarled grain. The sapwood is more perishable and was generally avoided. Unseasoned oak tends to warp and at all times it is liable to split longitudinally. Oak was used wherever strength was required, save where splitting would prove disastrous: frame buildings, joists, flooring, ships, heavy furniture, carvings.

2. *Elm*. Hard, tough and durable with a typical twisted grain, it is a heavy wood which, although liable to warp under variations of temperature, does not split easily. Elm was used where splitting would be calamitous and its weight relatively unimportant: wheel-hubs, ships' keels, pulley-blocks, mallets, water-pipes and pumps, chair seats.

3. *Ash*. Hard, tough and quite heavy with a close and remarkably straight grain, ash is singularly flexible. It was used where elasticity was essential: handles, hafts, shafts, oars, barrel-hoops, coachwork frames.

4. *Alder*. Soft, weak and perishable when dry, alder is nevertheless very durable under water. It was thus frequently used, unseasoned, for revetting river banks, and when dry for turnery where strength was unimportant as, for example, for platters.

5. *Birch*. Tough, moderately hard and fine-grained, birch has a very pleasant 'satin' finish when sanded. It was extensively used for turning.

The bark, incidentally, is quite easily removed whole, and was used for making vessels, canoes and for roofing.

6. *Beech*. Rather soft and brittle, beech is inclined to warp and crack if not well seasoned. It is also very prone to woodworm. It was commonly used for turnery where strength was not vital.

7. *Sycamore* (Great Maple). Similar to beech in most of its qualities, sycamore was used for much the same purposes.

8. *Chestnut*. Rather soft and open grained, chestnut cleaves easily and, unseasoned, withstands the weather well. It was used chiefly for posts, poles and fencing, but also as a substitute for walnut and fruit woods in cabinet making.

9. *Willow*. Soft and straight grained, willow shaves easily into thin strips. The strips were used for basket-making (p. 146) as too were the one- and two-year growths, or osiers.

10. *Hazel*. The bigger timber is virtually useless but the young growths are flexible and quite durable. Hazel roots were extensively used for basketry, fascines, hoops, thatching-spars.

11. *Yew*. Technically a softwood, being coniferous, the heartwood of yew is hard, close-grained, and flexible, and little prone to warping when seasoned. It was used for turnery and handles, and was *par excellence* the wood for making bows in both the Old and New Worlds.

12. *Box*. Also technically a softwood, boxwood is hard, dense and very heavy. It has a fine, close grain without figures and once seasoned never warps. Used for rulers, musical instruments, small handles, it was prized as the material for the finest carving and turnery: chessmen, plaster moulds, woodcut blocks.

Chapter Nine

FIBRES AND THREADS

SYNOPSIS

General: Fibres · Sources.　*Hair and Wool:* Staple · Bracts · Shearing · Parting · Combing · Carding · Blending.　*Silk:* Cultivated · Tusseh.　*Seed Fibres:* Cotton · Lint · Kapok · Bombax · Coir.　*Bast Fibres:* Flax · Hemp · Ramie · Nettle · Jute · Wood.　*Leaf Fibres:* Sisal · Raffia · Esparto.　*Spinning:* Thigh spinning · Spindle · Distaff.　*Ropes and Cordage:* Lay.　*Unwoven Fabrics:* Tapa · Papyrus · Paper · Felt.

GENERAL

NATURALLY OCCURRING *fibres*, the basic units from which all yarns are spun, are exceptionally diverse in both structure and origin, so diverse in fact that it will be possible to give only a summary of the principal types used by early man. In order to provide a satisfactory yarn, a fibre must possess a number of properties: it must be flexible, or be capable of being made so by some treatment; it must be durable; and it must exist in sufficient length to make spinning practicable. Where fineness rather than strength is required of the thread, the fibre, too must be fine. Many naturally occurring fibres, although used by early man, lacked one or more of these properties, and in practice one finds that the more satisfactory threads were made from fibres derived from cultivated plants and domesticated animals, often deliberately bred to improve fibre quality.

Fibres derived from animals are normally hairs, of which the wool of sheep is the most important single example; but people living in areas in which suitable plant materials were not obtainable frequently used the tendons or sinews of animals to provide coarse, strong threads. Of considerable importance in antiquity were silks made from a continuous filament extruded by the silk-worm and similar insects.

Fibres derived from plants tend to be more varied in origin. These may be filaments attached to seeds, as in the case of cotton and kapok, or hairs growing on the fruit, as with coconut. Fibres may be derived from the leaf of the plant, such as sisal or esparto, or from the stem. Stem fibres are most commonly bundles of bast cells, as in the case of flax and hemp, but the bark of some trees and plants, such as the elm, was occasionally a source of fibres. Finally, the whole stem or leaf might be used, without further treatment, to provide a thread, as in the case of grasses.

Hair and Wool

The coat of most wild animals is made up of two distinct types of hair, a top coat of long, coarse hairs, and an undercoat of shorter, finer hairs. With domestication and breeding the top coat may partly or even completely disappear, to leave a coat composed of only undercoat, or *wool*. The length of hair or wool is usually referred to as its *staple*, the longer hairs sometimes being called *topwool*, and the shorter *noil*, a staple number frequently being given to different grades, the number being an average length for the sample. Other systems of staple numbering, however, take into account the fineness of the hairs, the finest hairs being reckoned at 100, and the coarser hairs being given lower numberings. This can be confusing, and for choice length and thickness should be given as average measurements.

The surface of all hairs is covered with very small horny scales, *bracts* or *imbrications*. During spinning these bracts tend to become interlocked, so holding adjacent hairs together, and preventing the thread untwisting. The finer and shorter the hair, the greater the number of bracts, and hence the better the spinning qualities. Excessive heat or strong alkalis will damage them, and hence ruin the hairs for making yarn. The shape and number of bracts on the surface of the hair vary greatly with the species of animal from which it came, while the number of bracts will vary, even from the same animal, depending upon the staple of the hair. The number, shape and configuration of the bracts are the chief features by which the hairs of different species of animal may be identified (p. 224).

Wool may be *shorn* from the sheep, as is common today, but in antiquity it may equally have been *plucked*. Plucked wool will, of course, still have the hair root on its proximal end, while shorn wool will have a cut end. Plucked hairs, and those from animals that have never previously been shorn, *teg* or *hog wool*, will have a tapering distal end; but the hair from previously shorn sheep, *wether* or *ewe wool*, will have far blunter tips—the healed growth from previous shearings. *Kemp*, the dead but unshed hair in a fleece; *skin wool*, cut from a slaughtered animal; and *gathered wool*, collected from bushes, are harsh and brittle and as a result will not spin well. Their use may account for some of the poorer quality yarns from antiquity.

Before wool can be spun it was normally considered essential to carry out a number of cleaning and sorting operations. The naturally matted wool was usually first *teased*, or pulled out by hand, while the more obvious foreign bodies were removed. At the same time the hairs might be *sorted*, or *parted*, into grades of hard and soft, long and short, locks of wool. Following this, much of the grease and adhering dirt was removed by *scouring* either in cold, running water or in warm, soapy water. The dried wool was then frequently *willeyed* (*willowed*) or *bowed*, beaten with sticks or a bow, to remove any residual dust and to disentangle the single fibres. The final preparatory process, that of either *combing* or *carding*, was designed to make all the hairs lie in a single direction, while at the same time further parting could be done. The hairs might be drawn out lengthwise with a comb, or with *cards*, opposed flat boards from the faces of which projected short spikes, the two boards being drawn across one another with the wool between them.

Although in the Old World one tends to think exclusively in terms of sheep when one speaks of wool it is vital to remember that many other animals produce a soft undercoat that was available to early man. Such animals include not only goats, such as the Angora (mohair) and Tibetan goat (Kashmir wool), but also the camel, and certain rodents, such as beavers and rabbits. Furthermore, *blending* was not uncommon: the finer hairs of both cattle and horses, for example, were occasionally mixed with sheep's wool before spinning.

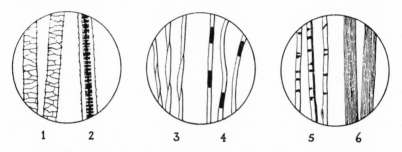

FIG. 27 TYPICAL FIBRES. THE SURFACE OF SHEEP'S WOOL (1) AND WOOL IN LONGITUDINAL SECTION (2). COTTON (3) AND KAPOK (4). LINEN (5) AND HEMP (6).

SILK

Cultivated silk is a continuous filament extruded by the grub of the mulberry-feeding moth (*Bombyx mori*) around its cocoon. The filament is usually collected by unwinding the cocoon, a process known as *throwing*, and reeling the fibre, which is then used without spinning. Inevitably some filaments snap, and break away in short lengths. These shorter lengths are normally combed or carded, and spun to provide *spun silk*, the very short rejects from the process being spun separately to provide an inferior quality thread, *silk noil*.

Wild silk, or *tusseh*, even when derived from *Bombyx mori* cocoons, is somewhat coarser than the cultivated variety. Furthermore, there are other insects of the *Bombyx* and similar genera, from the cocoons of which a silk of sorts can be obtained. The filaments are generally coarser and more brittle, and hence difficult to throw, and more commonly found as spun silk.

SEED FIBRES

Cotton fibres are hollow growths attached to the individual seeds, and are gathered when the fruit, or boll, has ripened and burst open. Normally the fibres have a staple of about five centimetres, but their shape depends on how mature the fruit is when the cotton is picked. The fibres are hollow, and taper to a closed tip, and in the immature state, the fibre walls being thin, the lumen remains closed so that the individual fibre appears to be a flat ribbon. As the seed matures, so the walls of the fibres thicken by laying down cellulose on the inside, with the result that the lumen is reduced, and the fibre remains rigid and circular in section. Cotton fibres also, if picked at the right stage, tend to twist in a cork-screw manner, which is an advantage when spinning. Immature or over-ripe fibres, however, lack this property, apart from which the immature fibres are too flaccid, and the over-ripe fibres too rigid, to allow easy spinning. Thus cotton picked at the right degree of ripeness is naturally twisted, and oval in section.

After the bolls had been gathered, the fibres, or *lint*, had to be picked from the seeds by hand. Until the introduction of machinery to carry out this operation, it was considered a good day's work for a single person to seed a pound of cotton. Seeding was followed by combing or carding, in which the short, useless fibres, the *linters*, were also removed.

Cotton was derived from a variety of different plants of the genus *Gossypium*, of which the most common were Egyptian cotton (*G. barba-dense*), Levant cotton (*G. herbaceum*), and Tree cotton (*G. arboreum*). Cultivated cotton can be distinguished from the wild varieties not only by its fineness, but also because in the cultivated varieties the tendency for the fibres to twist is more exaggerated. Other seed fibres somewhat similar to cotton are kapok and bombax. *Kapok* is derived from the seed of *Eriodendron anfractuosum*, a tropical tree. The fibres are exceptionally smooth and difficult to spin. *Bombax ceiba*, the silk-cotton tree of tropical America and the West Indies, was a common source of seed-fibres in antiquity in the New World.

Coir, the fibres growing on the outside of the husk of the coconut, is the commonest of the fruit-derived fibres. The material is very coarse and used, for choice, only for the making of matting, cordage and similar products.

BAST FIBRES

Bast fibres, more commonly referred to as phloem by botanists today, are the cells that in the living plant carry the food in solution from the soil. Each fibre is made up of a number of long, cylindrical cells, the end of each cell abutting on to those of similar cells above and below. In the prepared fibre, the junction between cells is normally of a rather greater diameter than that of the cells themselves; and thus, under sufficient magnification, the fibres appear rather like the canes of a bamboo. The presence of these swellings, or nodes, makes the identification of bast fibres, as distinct from other types, a relatively simple matter; but many bast fibres from widely different species of plant are very similar and can easily be confused. To differentiate between the various bast fibres thus requires considerable specialist botanical knowledge (p. 225), and if the material has become too decayed, it may not be possible to do more than classify the fibres within very broad limits.

Flax is the bast of the linseed (*Linum*) plant. Normally the plants are gathered when the seed is ripe, and dried, it being usual to pull the plants from the ground rather than cut them. After drying the bundles are combed, or *rippled,* to remove the seed pods. There follows a partial rotting process, *retting,* in which the stems are exposed to dew or soaked in water, until much of the non-vascular plant material has decayed. The stems are then beaten, normally with a wooden blade or sword, to detach the fibres from the woody core, remove the bark and separate the fibres, a process known as *scutching (skutching)*. Finally, the fibres are again combed or *hackled (heckled, hatcheled)* to remove any remaining wood or bark, the cleaned fibres, or *flax lint,* then being ready for spinning.

In antiquity these processes were not always carried out with the greatest efficiency and it is not uncommon to find a certain amount of bark or woody material left adhering to the fibres, while due to inadequate retting and scutching the fibres were not always completely separated, with the result that it was not possible to produce even threads.

Hemp is a bast fibre derived from a wide variety of plants native to Asia, of which *Hibiscus cannabinus,* Deccan Hemp, is one of the more common. The preparation of the fibres is very similar to that of flax, although the fibres themselves are coarser.

Ramie (ramee, rhea, china grass), is derived from a number of different plants of the nettle family, and is again of Asiatic origin. Although white, the fibres are far thicker than flax, while the method of preparation is similar.

The *stinging nettle (Urtica dioica)* was quite commonly used in Europe until recent periods as a source of fibres, which were again prepared like flax.

Jute fibres are amongst the coarsest bast fibres obtained from annual plants, the jute plant often growing to a height of fifteen feet. The plant is of Asiatic origin, and the prepared thread is normally referred to as *hessian.*

Many trees will yield adequate fibres, although generally these fibres are far coarser than those derived from annual plants. Normally the fibres are obtained by stripping the bark, the fibrous vascular material underlying the bark being stripped away with it, and later being separated from it. In Europe bast fibres from lime, elm, cedar, birch and willow have all been used to prepare threads, usually for rope manufacture. The process normally adopted was similar to that of preparing flax, namely retting followed by scutching and hackling. In rarer cases the wood itself might be the source of fibres. Thus pine wood was occasionally soaked in hot water, followed by beating to separate the fibres. Many of the fibres derived from trees, particularly the finer ones, such as those from the lime, are not easily distinguished from the coarser fibres from annual plants, such as hemp.

LEAF FIBRES

The leaves of many trees, more particularly those of tropical and subtropical areas, will also yield fibres. In some cases, as with sisal and the date-palm, the leaves may be soaked and beaten to separate the fibres, but very commonly the leaves were more simply shredded and the strands so obtained used unspun, the fibres never being separated. The leaves of raffia-palm and banana were commonly treated in this way, as too were those of the maguey (*Agave*) in Meso-America.

The leaves of many grasses and rushes might equally be treated in either way. Both papyrus and esparto grass might be soaked and beaten to provide fibres that could be spun, while the papyrus reeds might also be cut into strips and used unspun, and the esparto grass, uncut, might be used spun or unspun.

SPINNING

In its simplest form spinning requires no equipment at all. The threads to be spun may be placed on any flat surface, generally the thigh, and the palm of the hand passed across them, so causing them to twist together. Simple spinning of this nature, usually referred to as *thigh spinning*, has its limitations. It is difficult to produce even threads in this way and the fibres tend to untwist again to give a rather loosely spun yarn. It should, however, be noticed that the absence of any spinning devices cannot be taken as evidence that a people were ignorant of the use of yarns.

Better thread can be produced with a *spindle*. This normally takes the form of a short rod with a flywheel or *whorl* mounted near the distal end. In operation the fibres being spun are attached to the proximal end of the spindle either by a half-hitch or by being held in a notch, and the spindle is then spun until the length of fibres has been given a sufficient twist. This length of yarn is then wound on to the spindle and the process is repeated. The spindle may, of course, be made to rotate in either a clockwise or anti-clockwise manner. If, viewed from above, the movement of the spindle is clockwise, the resulting thread will have spirals conforming to the slope of the central part of the letter Z, and is referred to as *Z-spun*, or, by analogy with the thread on the carpenter's screw, *right-handed*; while if the spindle is made to rotate in the opposite direction, the resulting thread will be referred to as *S-spun* or *left-handed*. It is often stated that flax is more easily spun with an S-twist, while the preference for hemp or cotton is a Z-twist. This is undoubtedly the case, but caution is required when commenting upon unusual spinning. In thigh spinning, for example, a right-handed person will almost always produce Z-spun yarn, a left-handed person S-spun; with a spindle, the same is true unless the spinster is corrected. Unusual spinning may thus be as much a matter of personal idiosyncrasy as of a tradition stemming from the use of a different fibre; the presence of S-spun cotton thread does not of necessity imply that the spinster was more accustomed to working with flax.

When using the spindle it is normal to prepare the fibres before beginning work. The roll of carded or combed fibres, the *rolag* or *sliver*, may be wound round a second rod, the *distaff*. This may be short and held in the other hand from that working the spindle, or it may be longer, the lower end being tucked into a waist-band, so leaving both hands free for spinning. Sometimes the rolag may be drawn out to a thickness approaching that of the required thread, and even given a slight twist before winding on to the distaff. Prepared fibres in this state are usually called *rovings*.

The nature of the yarn produced will, of course, depend upon many factors other than the skill of the spinster. Extraneous matter and tangles due to poor washing or combing will naturally produce a thread that is uneven and full of lumps—*slubs, snarls* or *knops*. While the manufacturer today may deliberately produce uneven yarn of this type to give a 'decorative' or even 'handmade' look to his products, it seems unlikely that this was ever done in antiquity. The degree of twist given to a thread will depend largely on the quality of the fibres. Excessively twisted, or *hard-spun*, yarns may kink or curl up on themselves when in use, while *soft-spun* threads with little twist may untwist further and snap as a result. Generally, harsh fibres that resist twisting in the first place require to be harder spun than those which twist naturally or do so easily.

Several threads may be laid together and spun again to give a *ply* or *doubled yarn*. Commonly the direction of twist of a ply will be the opposite to that of the threads used. Thus, if the threads are S-spun the ply will normally be Z-spun.

ROPES AND CORDAGE

Ropes and cords—the distinction is one of size, cordage being of less than one inch in diameter—are simply coarse plies and were, naturally, not produced with a spindle, although the individual yarns from which

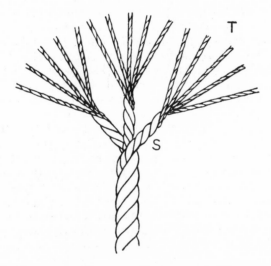

FIG. 28   THREE-STRANDED ROPE. THE THREADS (T) AND ROPE ARE OF Z-TWIST; THE STRANDS (S) ARE OF S-TWIST.

the rope was made might be spun. In the hand-making of rope, the rope-maker normally walked backwards down a rope-walk twisting the strands together as he moved. The ends of the strands were usually attached to a simple cross-bar handle which the rope-maker turned, but after the introduction of the cranked brace (p. 117), a similar device, the twist, was often used for this purpose.

9

The twist of a rope is generally referred to as its *lay*, and analogous with hard and soft spun threads are hard and soft laid ropes. Generally, where flexibility was required soft laid ropes were produced, while hard laid ropes had better wearing qualities. As with threads, however, the lay also depended to a degree on the nature of the fibres being used, but an adhesive, such as size (p. 163) could be used to maintain the twist of those strands that naturally resisted it.

In *standard-lay* rope, the yarns are first spun right-handed, and these are then twisted to form a left-handed strand. The strands are then laid right-handed to provide the rope. A three-stranded rope is referred to as *plain-lay*, four-stranded as *shroud-lay*, while three three-stranded ropes laid together form a *cable-lay*.

Short lengths of rope and cordage could also be produced by *plaiting* (*sennit*), but perhaps because of the need to pass the whole of each un-plaited strand over the others, the method seems to have been little used for making long lengths.

UNWOVEN FABRICS

Many fabrics, although made of fibrous materials, required neither spinning nor weaving. The simplest of these to produce was the *tapa* cloth of the Pacific Islands. The bark from a variety of mulberry (*Broussonetia papyrifera*) was removed as a large sheet and soaked until the hard outer bark could be stripped off by hand. The fibrous material was then beaten to the required thickness and allowed to dry. Since the fibres were held together by the natural gums, this cloth had the dis-advantage that prolonged wetting would make it disintegrate.

Papyrus was very similar in character. Thin strips of the papyrus leaf were laid edge to edge, one layer of strips at a right-angle to another, and these were beaten hard. Here again a natural gum in the leaves caused the strips to adhere.

Early *paper* was made of a variety of fibrous plant materials, depend-ing upon the quality required. In the Far East bamboo pith, mulberry bark and the pith of the shrub *Fatsia papyrifera* (rice paper) were the common sources. In these cases the natural gums or starch in the plants acted as binding agents; but where, for example, macerated cloth was used, additional starch, gum or resin had to be added to the fibres. In the making of paper the fibres were first soaked, beaten and shredded and allowed to steep. A gauze-covered frame was then dipped in the vat, with-drawn and shaken to ensure that the fibres were evenly spread over the gauze. After being allowed to drain, the sheet was carefully removed and *couched* until dry. Couching in China was commonly nothing more elaborate than sticking the paper against a flat wall to dry in the full sun, but in Europe the paper was usually laid between cloth pads and heat-dried by ironing. In order to be able to identify the paper they had made, the paper-makers often drew a number of threads from the gauze to make a pattern that was transferred to the sheet as a *water-mark*. Papers that contain only fibres and a binder are generally porous, as is blotting-paper, and to give a better writing surface an inert white filler, or *loading*, such as chalk, kaolin or talc, was added. The nature of the fibres, binders and fillers naturally varies with different areas and periods of production, and often allows identification of the source of an early paper, even when no water-mark survives.

The manufacture of unwoven *felt* depended on the fact that wool, fur and some fine hairs will naturally mat when heated, beaten and pressed. This is due very largely to the interlocking of the bracts on the surfaces of adjacent fibres, but oils and sizes may have been added to help felting. Despite the widespread manufacture of felt in antiquity and amongst underdeveloped people today, there are remarkably few data on the subject. Generally, however, two methods appear to have been followed.

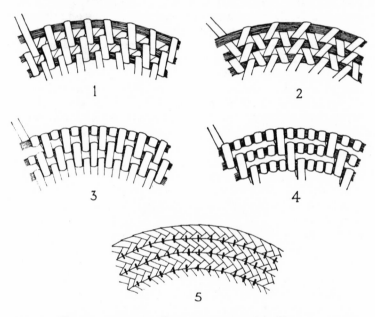

FIG. 29   COILED BASKETRY.   PLAIN WRAPPING (1).   FIGURE-OF-EIGHT (NAVAJO) WRAPPING (2).   LONG AND SHORT (LAZY SQUAW) WRAPPING (3). PERUVIAN COIL WRAPPING (4).   SEWN COILS (5).

In the one, the wool was spread out on a mat, sprinkled with oil and rolled firmly. Repeated rolling and unrolling made the wool cohere. Finally the felt was washed, stretched and allowed to dry. In the second method, which conforms more nearly to the common industrial practice today, the wool was washed, laid out as a layer and hammered with flat, spade-shaped clubs. The wool was then damped down and heated either by rolling hot stones over it or by passing it over a fire. This was followed by further hammering or *fulling*; the whole process of steaming and fulling being repeated many times.

Matting and some kinds of baskets may be made by *coiling* a continuous length of fibrous material. The coil may be a pre-formed rope or plait, or a long natural growth such as *rattan* (cane palm) which grows wild in many tropical countries. The coil may be joined either by wrapping or by sewing. In *sewn* coil-work a thread is passed through adjacent edges of the coil, and hence the method can only be applied to materials soft enough to allow the needle to be passed through the coil, as, for example, ropes and plaits. In *wrapped* coil-work the join is made by passing a wrapping completely around adjacent parts of the coil. Many different wrappings (confusingly often referred to as *stitches*) may be used. In *plain wrapping* the wrapping thread is passed over adjacent coils, the wrapping of each new coil passing between those of the previous coil (Fig. 29); while in *figure-of-eight wrapping* (Navajo stitch) the wrapping is carried over adjacent coils in a figure of eight (Fig. 29). In *long-and-short wrapping* (lazy squaw stitch) the wrapping is carried first over one coil and then over two in regular sequence (Fig. 29); and this principle can be carried further by varying the sequence of long and short stitches to produce many different patterns (Fig. 29).

Other unwoven fabrics include *netting* made by knotting continuous threads, and *knitting* and *crochet*, made by looping continuous threads. *Lace* was made by laying out a pattern of threads either on canvas or on a hard 'pillow', held in position with stitches or pins. The pattern threads were then joined by looping, knotting or sewing, and the lace freed from its backing by cutting the retaining stitches or removing the pins.

Chapter Ten

TEXTILES AND BASKETS

SYNOPSIS

Looms: Warp · Weft · Beam-looms · Body-looms · Weighted-looms · Shed · Heddles · Shuttles · Tablet-looms.　*Weave Recording Systems:* Semi-diagrammatic · Graph-type.　*Pattern in Weaving:* Tabby · Basket · Twills · Broken twills · Satins · Gauze · Twined · Wrapped · Pile · Double-weave · Stripes　and　bands · Tapestry · Brocade. *Finishing:* Fulling · Shearing · Bleaching · Degumming.　*Woven Basketry:* Rods · Sticks · Skeins · Clefts · Chips · Stakes · Slath · Randing · Slewing · Pairing · Waling · Borders.

LOOMS

WEAVING DEMANDS THE use of two distinct groups of parallel threads. One set, the *warp, chain* or *ends*, is kept under tension during weaving, while the second set, normally referred to as the *weft* or *woof* (but also known as the *abb, shot, shute, shoot, picks, filling* and *tram*), is passed over and under the threads of the warp, at right angles to it. The *loom* is fundamentally a device to keep the warp-threads under tension during weaving. Looms vary very considerably in their design and function, and it is customary, when describing simple looms, to refer to vertical and horizontal looms, depending on whether the threads of the warp are maintained upright or parallel to the ground. In many respects, however, what dictates the type and size of fabric produced is not the orientation of the warp, but the means by which it is kept under tension. In the beam-tensioned loom, the warp threads are held at each end by a bar or *beam*, and the beams are secured to maintain a taut warp. The construction may be very simple, each beam being lashed to a pair of pegs driven into the ground; or the beams may be supported in a frame, with the warp lying in either the horizontal or vertical position. In a more sophisticated form the beams may be provided with stub axles and some kind of ratchet or securing device so that a length of warp greater than that of the frame may be wound on to one beam (the *warp beam*) and as weaving proceeds the finished fabric may be wound on to the other, the *cloth* or *breast-beam*.

In making fabrics of small dimensions, the warp may be kept under tension by pressure from the body of the weaver. In the *body-tensioned loom* or waist-loom the warp-threads are commonly attached to a short beam at each end. The warp-beams may be lashed to any available upright—a tree or a post—while the breast-beam is secured by a belt or back-strap to the wearer, who, by adjusting the position of the body can alter the tension of the warp. While a loom of this type cannot be used to produce large pieces of cloth, it is exceptionally mobile and can be set up almost anywhere.

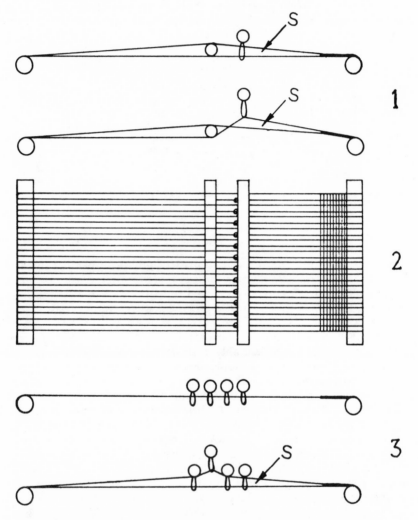

Fig. 30 Diagram to show the function of a simple loom using shed rod and single heddle (1 and 2) to provide sheds (S). A four-heddle loom (3).

The warp may be kept under tension by the use of a number of weights. In general the warp-threads are attached at one end to a warp-beam and at the other end to clay or stone weights, several threads being attached to each weight. The *warp-weighted loom* is, of course, a vertical loom, and suffers from the disadvantage that the length of cloth produced must be less than the height of the frame, but it also has one particular advantage that probably accounts for its extensive use in antiquity. As weaving proceeds, successive weft-threads cause increasing tension on the warp if it is secured rigidly, as in a beam-tensioned loom, since the weft forces the warp to bend slightly, and if this tension is allowed to become excessive, the warp-threads may snap. With evenly spun thread, this danger is not great, since all the threads will tighten at the same rate, and the beams may be slackened when a danger point is reached. With poorly spun yarn, however, one warp thread may become taut while others remain relatively slack, but if the tension is evenly maintained by

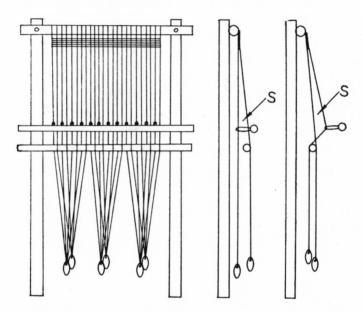

FIG. 31 DIAGRAM TO SHOW THE FUNCTION OF A WEIGHT-TENSIONED LOOM. SHEDS (S) ARE FORMED WITH A SHED-ROD AND SINGLE HEDDLE.

weights rather than by a fixed beam the difference is less critical, and the danger of snapping threads is greatly reduced.

In the simplest form of weaving—and also the most laborious—the weft-thread is wound on to a shaft, the *spool, bobbin, quill* or *pirn*, and this is darned in and out of the warp. However, by inserting a rod, the *shed rod*, behind every second warp-thread, these threads may be pulled away from the remaining warp-threads to produce a gap, the *shed*, through which the spool may be passed. This arrangement will only allow the weft to be passed in a single direction, and if no other device is used, the return weft must be darned. If, however, a second rod is used, and to this is attached a thread passing between each thread separated by the shed-rod, and looping each unseparated thread, by pulling this rod away from the warp a new shed may be formed, and the weft passed as a single movement. This rod is called a *heddle* (*headle, heald*), or *leaf*, while the looped thread is termed the *leash*. In some looms the combination of shed-rod and heddle was retained; in others the shed-rod was replaced by a second heddle; while in pattern weaving three, four, or even more heddles were employed (p. 139). In the very simple looms the heddles were hand-operated, but in the more advanced types they were moved by treadles to which they were attached by a system of pulleys, each treadle working a single heddle. The attachment of treadles to heddles is generally referred to as the *tie-up*.

After the weft-threads had been passed through the shed they needed to be beaten down hard against the already woven cloth. A flat-bladed wooden *sword* might be used for this purpose, the blade being passed through the shed; or a toothed comb-shaped tool of wood or metal, the

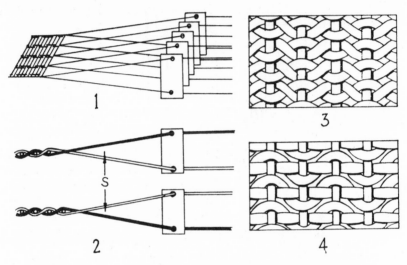

Fig. 32   Tablet loom (1) and diagram to show how sheds (S) are produced by rotating tablets (2). A typical gauze (3) and gauze with doup warp (4).

fork-beater (sometimes called a weaving-comb by archaeologists) might be used against the face of the cloth. More even beating in, however, was achieved by the use of the *reed*, batten or sley. This was a rectangular wooden frame, originally threaded with reeds, a warp-thread passing between each reed. The frame was pulled hard against the cloth after the passage of each weft-thread. The reeds were in later periods often replaced by metal wires, while by making these wires bear a small loop or eye through which the warp threads were passed, the reed might ultimately be made to function as both heddle and beater-in. During the setting-up of a warp, a toothed or notched rod, the *raddle*, was sometimes used to prevent the warp-threads becoming crossed, but it was not used in the actual process of weaving. However, two rods, one passing behind the even warp-threads, the other behind the odd threads, and then lashed together near the warp beam, were sometimes used to prevent the warp-threads becoming displaced. These are called the *lease* or *lazerods*.

Anthropologists generally distinguish between two different types of spool; those in which the thread is wound on the long axis—and thus normally a rod notched at each end—and those in which the thread is wound at right angles to the long axis. The importance of this distinction lies in the fact that only the second type can be encased in a *shuttle*, a boat-shaped wooden container that can be thrown through the shed, and hence allow really rapid weaving.

One form of weaving employed neither shed-rod nor heddle. This was *card-weaving* or *tablet-weaving* in which the warp-threads were passed through holes in small discs which were rotated a half-turn clockwise and counter-clockwise, so forming the sheds. The tablets were generally oval or rectangular with a hole, or a pair of holes, at each end. Tablet-looms, because of the need to rotate the tablets, are not really suitable for the making of wide cloths, and in practice one finds their use restricted to the making of narrow gauzes (p. 141).

WEAVE RECORDING SYSTEMS

Before discussing weaves it will be necessary to mention the various systems that have been devised by weavers to record patterns.

When examining a cloth, or a fragment of textile, the first feature to be recorded should be the *count*, which may be defined as the number of threads per unit of length. This is very commonly given as a simple two figure notation, as, for example, 18/24. This can be taken to mean 18 warp-threads and 24 weft-threads to the inch, but it is advisable to state the unit of measurement since 18/24 might be taken to mean 18 and 24 threads to the centimetre. Although it is customary to record the count as warp followed by weft, it certainly makes for greater clarity if the words are not omitted. In the great majority of textiles, the count is higher for the weft than the warp, since the weft-threads have been beaten in to provide a compact fabric. Hence, when recording fragments of textiles in which no selvage remains, it is normally assumed that the lower count will represent the warp, the higher the weft; but it must never be overlooked that this is only an assumption. If, however, there is a far greater degree of bending of those threads with the higher count, then it may be assumed that these are the weft threads with more certainty.

When it comes to illustrating textiles, there can be little doubt that the semi-diagrammatic drawing (Fig. 33, nos. 1 and 2), although the most tedious to produce, is the least open to misinterpretation. Most weavers, however, to save time, use graph-paper on which to record patterns, each square of the paper being taken to represent the crossing of a warp and a weft-thread, some squares being hatched, or filled in solidly, the others left blank. The hatched squares may either represent the crossing of a warp over a weft, or *vice versa*, and it is hence essential to state which is intended in this type of diagram (Fig. 33, nos. 3 and 4). This system of recording weaves has the additional advantage that it can readily be transliterated into type or print by using letters in place of the hatched squares (Fig. 33, no. 5). Other systems of illustrating weave depend upon omitting those parts of threads that pass behind others (Fig. 33, no. 6);

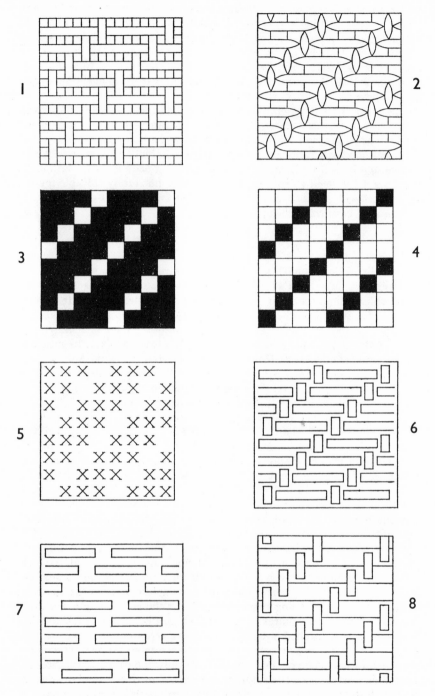

FIG. 33 METHODS OF RECORDING WEAVES. SEMI-DIAGRAMMATIC (1
AND 2). GRAPH PAPER (3 AND 4). TYPOGRAPHIC (5). SIMPLIFICATIONS
OF SEMI-DIAGRAMMATIC METHODS (6, 7 AND 8).

while this line of simplification may be continued even further by completely omitting either the warp or weft threads (Fig. 33, no. 7), or only indicating their existence by a thin line. On the whole this system has very little to commend it, and it could mistakenly be taken to illustrate tapestry weave (p. 145).

Normally, as most weavers are familiar only with beam-tensioned looms, the first line of weave is that at the bottom of the diagram, the last at the top, since this would be the order of weaving on such a loom. This is not, however, universally accepted, and it is preferable to number the lines of weave. It is also usual to indicate the number of heddles and the position of the leashes or ties on each, above the weave diagram.

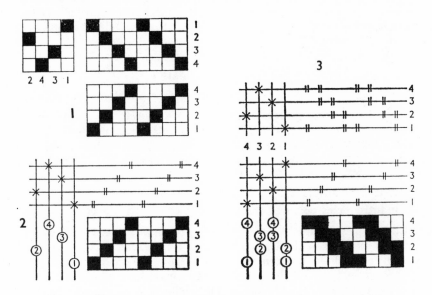

FIG. 34 PATTERN WEAVES WITH HEDDLE DIAGRAM AND TREADLE TIE-UP.

The heddles may be shown as a number of lines of squares on graph paper, the position of the leashes being hatched (Fig. 34, no. 1). Alternatively, the heddles may be drawn as ruled lines with the leashes indicated as short vertical dashes or crosses (Fig. 34, no. 2). A further set of squares or vertical lines to the left of the heddle diagram may be used to indicate the tie-up between heddles and treadles. Again, most weavers use the treadles in the order: outer right, outer left, inner right, inner left, but this is also not universally accepted and the treadle orders should thus invariably be stated.

Since the indication of a treadle tie-up suggests *ipso facto* the use of treadles, it should only be included in those cases where a treadle-operated loom is known to have been employed. To include a treadle tie-up on the analysis of a weave created on a hand-operated loom can only invite confusion. Even the inclusion of the heddle diagram may be purely speculative. In the first two cases illustrated (Fig. 34, nos. 1 and 2) the position of the leashes on each heddle can reasonably be assumed to correspond to the position of the raised warps in the lines of weave. In the third example (Fig. 34, no. 3), however, there are two possible ways of arranging the leashes. In the one, each heddle and its leashes correspond to a line of weave, but this has the disadvantage that it necessitates tying a leash to a number of pairs of adjacent warp threads, and this can be very troublesome in operation. As an alternative, each heddle might be tied to every fourth warp thread in sequence so that any required line of the weave may be produced by operating two heddles simultaneously. On a treadle-operated loom this is almost unquestionably the course that would be followed, but on a hand-operated loom the weaver might find it simpler to manipulate a single heddle than two for each weft. Faced with a fragment of cloth one cannot say which system the weaver followed; one must either give all the possibilities or omit any mention of them.

PATTERN IN WEAVING

Pattern may be introduced into weaves by four principal means:

1. By so arranging the crossings of warp and weft that a pattern is formed, while using identical thread in both warp and weft. This is generally referred to as *pattern weaving*.
2. By using different threads in warp or weft, or a mixture of threads in either or both.
3. By using multiple warps or wefts.
4. By introducing coloured threads in any of these systems.

The simplest of all weaves is the *tabby* or *plain weave*, also known as *taffeta weave*, and in the United States as *cloth weave*. In this the wefts pass over and under adjacent warps in one row, the order being reversed in the next and so on. Where, instead of a single weft interlacing with a single warp thread, the threads cross in groups of two or more, the weave is generally referred to as *basket* or *canvas weave*, *ordinary hopsack* or *matt weave*, but some weavers reserve the term 'basket weave' to refer only to those cases where warp and weft cross in pairs, while a plain weave based on three threads is sometimes called *Panama weave*.

Greater variety can be achieved by the use of *twill weaves*. In these, the weft passes over two or more warps and under one or more warps in one row, while the sequence is moved one warp space to the left or right in all subsequent rows. In its simplest form, the 2 : 1 twill, or *prunella*, one weft thread crossed two warp threads and under the next, this sequence being repeated a space to the left or right in the following row. The simplest twill thus requires three heddles, with a repeated line of weave after every third weft. In plain twills the exposed threads of the warp form an oblique line, the *wale*, running across the fabric, normally from the bottom left-hand corner to the top right, while in a *reverse twill* the line of the wale runs from bottom right to top left. Plain twills may be based on any regular sequence of crossing warps and wefts—2 : 3, 3 : 1, 3 : 2 and so on—but in loose weaves long *floating threads*, that is to say weft threads that cross a large number of warps, had to be avoided since they would tend to get caught in service and pull out. For many early cloths the 3 : 2 twill appears to have been the longest practicable unit.

Plain twills may be varied by using regular sequences of twill and reversed twill to provide a *plain zig-zag twill* (Fig. 35, no. 7), while if the twill is also reversed at regular intervals throughout the single weft, a *plain diamond twill* can be produced (Fig. 35, no. 9). If the twill sequence is reversed only at regular intervals throughout the single line of weft, a *plain wave twill* results (Fig. 35, no. 8).

Broken twills are made by moving the successive wefts two or more warp spaces to the right or left, with the result that the wale either does not appear (Fig. 35, nos. 4 and 5) or runs more obliquely across the cloth than in the case of plain twills (Fig. 35, no. 6). These breaks may be made with each weft, but they may also be made at regular intervals during weaving. If a plain twill is broken in this way the wale becomes interrupted and appears as short lengths running across the face of the cloth to give a *half-herringbone twill* (Fig. 35, no. 13), while if such a break is made in a plain weave twill, a *herringbone wave* results (Fig. 35, no. 11). Twills may also be broken in the vertical; a plain zig-zag twill broken at intervals will give a *herringbone twill* (Fig. 35, no. 10), while a plain diamond twill broken both horizontally and vertically will produce a *herringbone diamond twill* (Fig. 35, no. 12).

The majority of twills are *weft-faced*, that is to say they are intended to be used with the floating weft threads on the outer surface. Some twills, however, are *warp-faced*, often broken vertically, as, for example, the *whipcord twill* (Fig. 35, no. 14) and the *corkscrew twill* (Fig. 35, no. 15).

Twills may also be combined with other weaves. There are many such weaves, often most intricate and with long floating threads. These are commonly traditional patterns with a great variety of local names. *Bird's eye* or *Honeycomb weave* (Fig. 35, no. 16) and *Barleycorns* (Fig. 35, no. 17) are typical examples.

Satins are cloths woven with long floating warp threads on the face, tied at intervals by a single weft thread, and thus appear to be made up almost entirely of warp threads on the face of the cloth. The weave is in fact a broken twill, the floating warps crossing at least four wefts. Satin weaves are spoken of either as four-end, five-end, eight-end satins or as 4 : 1, 5 : 1, 8 : 1 satins. Since satins are commonly woven with the face downwards, many weavers when illustrating satins depict the reverse side, and unless clearly stated this practice can be most confusing. Satins with short floating threads are often called *satinettes*, while those in which the floating threads are in the weft, instead of the warp, are termed *sateens*, or *reverse satins*. True *Damask* weaves include areas of satin and sateen in the same cloth, often forming elaborate patterns.

Some weaves cannot be produced using conventional heddles. *Gauze* or *leno*, most easily made on a tablet loom, is produced by crossing adjacent warps before passing the weft, and re-crossing the warps again before passing the next weft. As a result, in the finished fabric, adjacent warps cross and re-cross, being held in position by the wefts. Variation may be introduced into this kind of weave by using different combinations of right-over-left and left-over-right crossings in adjacent warps, while in some cases the warps are so arranged that in any pair there is

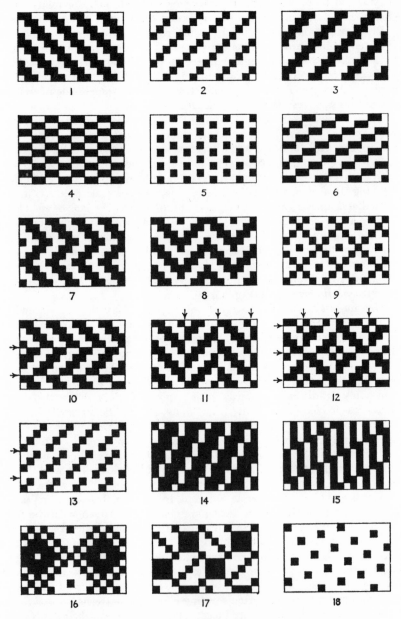

FIG. 35   PATTERN WEAVES. 2×2 REVERSED TWILL (1); 3×1 TWILL (2);
3×2 TWILL (3); 2×2 BROKEN TWILL (4); 3×1 BROKEN TWILL (5);
3×2 BROKEN TWILL (6); 2×2 PLAIN-ZIG-ZAG (7); 2×2 PLAIN WAVE
(8); PLAIN DIAMOND (9); 2×2 HERRINGBONE (10); 2×2 BROKEN WAVE
(11); BROKEN DIAMOND (12); HALF-HERRINGBONE TWILL (13); WHIP-
CORD TWILL (14); CORKSCREW TWILL (15); BIRD'S-EYE OR HONEYCOMB
(16); BARLEYCORNS (17); EIGHT-END SATIN (18).

one taut, or *standing warp*, and one slack or *doup warp*, with the result that after weaving the doup warp appears to be coiled around the standing warp.

In *twined weave* each warp thread is interlaced with two crossing weft threads, a process that has a precise counterpart in pairing in basketry (p. 146). The process can only be done by hand manipulation (Fig. 36, no. 2). The same is true of *wrapped* or *Soumak weave* in which the weft threads are carried completely around the warps. Both twined and

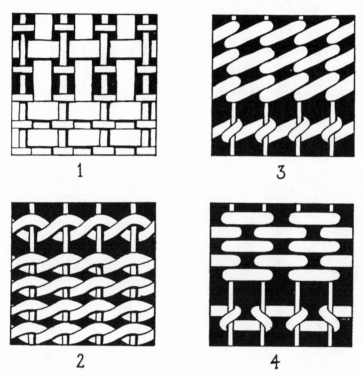

FIG. 36 REP (1) IN OPEN AND CLOSE WEAVES. TWINED WEAVE (2) IN OPEN AND CLOSE WEAVES. WRAPPED (SOUMAK) WEAVES (3 AND 4) SHOWING FACE AND SINGLE LINE OF REVERSE.

wrapped weave may be used in conjunction with tabby weave, the tabby wefts acting more or less as a skeleton to support the other wefts.

The use of a tabby weave skeleton of *binder threads* is, however, far more common where threads of different quality or composition are being used in the same cloth. A thick weft thread may thus be used alternately with a thin weft, and woven into a thin warp so that in effect the thick weft predominates on the face of the cloth, usually referred to as *brocade weave*; or both warp and weft may be made up of alternate thick and thin threads to form a *rep* (*repp* or *ribbed tabby*) weave (Fig. 36, no. 1), although the term 'rep' is also used to denote a plain weave with a higher count of warps than wefts. Pattern may equally result from uneven spacing of the warp threads, or weft threads, or both; while uneven tension on the warp threads will produce a crinkled face to the cloth, as for example in *seersucker*. A striped appearance, generally known as *shadow stripes*, can be produced by using groups of Z- and S-spun yarns in either the weft or warp, while if the same sequence of differently spun threads is used in both warp and weft, *shadow checks* result.

Fabrics with a *pile* were most commonly produced by passing wefts over a rod, so that when it was removed loops protruded from the surface of the cloth, these being held in place by the warps and a binder

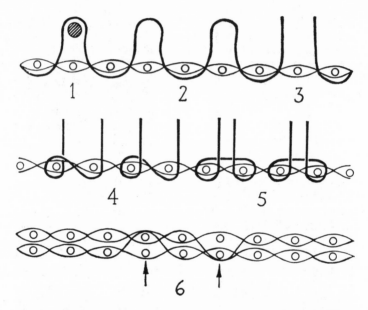

FIG. 37 SECTION THROUGH PILED FABRIC SHOWING PILE-ROD (1) TO PRODUCE LOOPED (TERRY) PILES (2). THESE MAY BE CUT (3) TO GIVE CUT (VELVET) PILES. HAND TIED PERSIAN (4) AND SMYRNA (5) KNOTS. SECTION THROUGH FABRIC IN DOUBLE WEAVE (6).

row of weft. If the loops are left uncut, the fabric is referred to as a *terry weave*, commonly seen on towelling or Brussels carpets today. On the other hand, if the loops are cut after weaving to form projecting ends of thread the fabric is referred to as a *velvet weave*. Fabrics with a pile were, of course, not only used for clothing; most carpets were made of pile fabrics. Not all carpets, however, could be produced by lacing around a pile-rod, for in both Smyrna and Persian carpets the pile was knotted around the warps and this work had to be done by fingering (Fig. 37, no. 4).

Exceptionally thick cloths could be made by double weaving. In this two sets of warp threads were used, one set lying in front of the other. During weaving an occasional warp thread was transferred from one set to the other by means of a special heddle, and held by the passage of the new weft thread. The final fabric thus appeared as two distinct layers of cloth held together in places by the transferred warp threads.

Textiles were coloured either by *dyeing in the piece* after weaving (p. 161) or by using threads *dyed in the hank*. *Stripes* and *bands* were produced by using groups of differently coloured threads in either the warp or the weft, some writers distinguishing between bands as colour divisions in the weft, and stripes as divisions in the warp, but this is not a universally accepted distinction. Where groups of coloured threads of equal numbers were used in both weft and warp *checks* were formed, while if groups of coloured threads of unequal numbers were woven in the same sequence in both warp and weft *tartans*, sometimes wrongly called *plaids*, resulted.

More complex coloured designs were usually produced either by tapestry weaving or by brocading. In *tapestry weaving* a tabby weave was used, the wefts generally being thicker and having a higher count than the warp, the design normally being in the weft. Since the threads of the weft, according to the line of the design, might not run from selvage to selvage, the differently coloured threads of the weft were often doubled back within the line, with the result that gaps appeared in any line of weft wherever there was a change of colour. *Darned tapestry* differs from this in as much as a cloth was woven first, without coloured design, in plain tabby weave. From this threads were drawn, and coloured threads darned in their place. Normally, of course, the original weft was the final background colour and these threads were left undrawn in the finished design.

Brocade differs from tapestry in two essential features. The coloured threads of the weft were allowed to float over the warp, and when not required in the design were allowed to float behind the warp. Generally, but not invariably, thinner binder threads in tabby weave were used in the weft, alternately with the coloured threads, to give strength to the fabric. Where the design would demand long lines in the weft of the same colour, the coloured threads were often held at intervals by single warp threads to eliminate excessively long floating threads.

FINISHING

A number of finishing processes were commonly carried out after weaving. Woollen cloth in particular often underwent quite a number of treatments. After picking out any remaining knots or particles left in the fabric, *burling*, woollen textiles were often felted. The primitive method was to *scour* the cloth in hot soapy water, followed by *walking* (*waulking*) in which the material was laid out on an even surface and pounded under foot. As a result of this treatment woollen cloth might shrink up to two-thirds of its original length and to half its original width. *Fulling* was equally a cleaning and felting process. The cleaning was done with fuller's earth, a fine marly clay which absorbed much of the oil from the wool, while after the introduction of water-power hammers were commonly used for the final felting. Finally, the clean felted cloth was often brushed with teazles (*teazling, rowing*) to raise a nap of fine hairs on the surface which were then *sheared* to an even length with shears often of formidable size.

Both woollen and linen cloths were frequently *bleached*, the usual process being to expose the materials to the effects of sunshine and rain. Decoctions of fuller's herb or soapwort (*Saponaria officinalis*) in western Europe, and *Gypsophila struthium* in southern Europe, were believed to bleach the cloth. In fact the extracts from these plants are most efficient soaps, and although they clean the cloth, they do not bleach. Traditionally in Europe linen, after bleaching, was washed in buttermilk.

Silk when thrown has a sticky surface, and before silk cloth could be used it had to be *degummed*. This was normally done by boiling in a weak soap solution after weaving, although wild silk was often degummed before spinning.

WOVEN BASKETRY

The materials from which woven baskets were made were generally stiffer than those used in coil-work, and the great majority of the materials were derived from the young straight shoots of trees and shrubs. Many basket-makers distinguished between *rods*, the single year's growth; *sticks* which are of two or more years' growth; and *skeins*, or young growths split longitudinally. Cleft larger timbers were also used for basket-making, and here again the distinction is often made between *clefts* (*spelks, spales, swills, laths*) which have been split radially from the timber, and *chips* which have been split along the annual growth rings.

Most baskets were made by first weaving a base, although solid wooden bases drilled to take the uprights, or *stakes*, were occasionally used. The woven base began with the making of a *slath* in which the stakes were laid cross-wise, bound, spread out like the spokes of a wheel, and then woven into this position by a spiral of rods, canes or clefts. When the base was sufficiently large the stakes were bent upwards and weaving continued. The simplest weave, *randing*, was done with a single rod passed behind one stake and in front of the next, and thus corresponds in effect to tabby weave. *Slewing* (*sluing*) is similar to randing, save that two or more rods were woven at the same time. Both slewing and randing require an odd number of stakes to avoid the rods making the same passage in each row as in the previous one. Since the slath will normally provide an even number of stakes, an additional stake may have been added at the base. Failing this, each rod had to be cut after making one complete turn of the basket, and a fresh rod used for the next row. *Pairing* was done with two rods woven simultaneously so that they crossed between the stakes to produce an effect similar to twined weave; while in *chain pairing* two rows of pairing were worked, the crossing of the rods being in opposite directions in each row. Where three rods were used simultaneously with a crossing, each rod passing in front of two stakes and behind the third, the weave is referred to as *waling* (*wailing*); while two rows of waling with the twist in opposite directions is called *chain waling*. Waling was frequently used at the base of baskets in order to hold the upright stakes securely in position, in which case it is often referred to as *upsetting*.

The borders of baskets were generally made by bending the stakes and weaving them into the basket. In the *trac border* one stake at a time was bent and woven in completely before the next stake was bent and woven; while in the *plain border* each bent stake was held in position by bending down another stake over it further round the rim. Thus the first stake bent down might be held by the fourth, the second by the fifth, the third by the sixth and so on. In a *wrapped border* the stakes were bent and wrapped around one another spirally, while in a *plaited border* the stakes were bent and plaited.

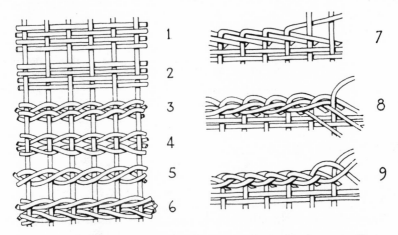

FIG. 38   BASKET WEAVES AND BORDERS. RANDING (1). SLEWING (2). PAIRING (3). CHAIN PAIRING (4). WALING (5). CHAIN WALING (6). TRAC BORDER (7). PLAIN BORDER (8). PLAITED BORDER (9).

If the stakes were not long enough to produce the whole side of the basket, additional bye-stakes might be woven in alongside them part of the way through the work, while if a flairing shape of basket was required it was necessary to insert an additional set of stakes between the original ones at some stage. Loop handles were either plaited, wrapped or twisted, and for strength some of the rods from which the handles were to be made were commonly inserted alongside a stake well below the border during weaving. Openwork areas of bare stakes without woven rods are often referred to as *fitching*.

The basket-maker's tools were few and simple and are unlikely to be recognized as such from antiquity. A sharp knife and a heavy rod, today called a *driving-iron*, used for beating down the weave, were all that were required.

Chapter Eleven

HIDES AND LEATHER

SYNOPSIS

Skins and Hides: Scudding · Fleshing · Sweating · Liming. *Dressing:* Smoking · Oil dressing · Tawing · Tanning · Plumping · Tannins. *Leathers:* Grain · Rawhide · Parchment. *Shaping and Decoration:* Cutting · Sewing · *Cuir bouilli* · Engraving · Stamping · Embossing.

Skins and Hides

THE SKIN OF any mammal is composed of three layers. The thin outer layer, or epidermis, is made up of scale-like cells which, when dead, peel away as scurf. Functionally the epidermis acts as a protective coating to the thick inner skin or corium. This is chiefly composed of a fine fibrous material, collagen, and it is this that gives the skin its characteristic elasticity. The corium also contains sweat glands; hair follicles, from which the hairs grow; sebaceous glands, the secretions from which lubricate the hair; and small blood vessels and nerves. The third layer, the subcutaneous fatty tissue, is made up chiefly of bands of connective tissue and globules of fat, larger blood vessels than in the corium, and nerves. While the fat of this layer acts as an insulator against cold and as a reserve supply of food in the living animal, once removed from the dead beast it will soon begin to putrify and the bacteria will spread to cause the decay of the entire skin. The first stage in the preparation of skins, or *hides* as they are generally called once taken from the carcass, must be the removal of the subcutaneous fatty layer. This is generally done by scraping the fat away, and many of the stone tools of early man seem excellently suited to this purpose. With the introduction of metal and especially steel tools, this could be done more quickly with a large, two-handled knife, similar to a drawknife, known as a *scudding, fleshing, beaming* or *paring knife*. For this purpose the hide was normally placed over a bench or beam. The process of scudding could be made simpler by soaking the hide in water, followed by a thorough pounding, but this could only be done if the hair was ultimately to be removed from the hide.

A number of processes were evolved in antiquity for the removal of the hair and epidermis. This might be done simply by scraping in the same manner in which the hide was scudded. By *sweating* the hide, usually by placing it in urine, which becomes strongly alkaline in time, decay took place, and the hair and epidermis became loose enough to allow their removal, a tool with teeth set in a circle, the *currier's comb*, generally being used for this purpose. The chemical decay of the hair and epidermis was sometimes achieved by *liming*. Quicklime or fresh wood ashes were rubbed into the moistened surface, the alkalis so produced attacking the epidermis and hair. These were removed with the currier's comb and the hide washed to prevent further chemical attack.

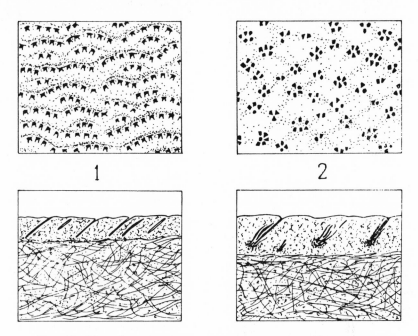

FIG. 39 'GRAIN' AND SECTIONS THROUGH LEATHERS. THE CHARAC-
TERISTIC ARRANGEMENT OF SINGLE HAIR FOLLICLES IN OXHIDE (1).
THE HAIR FOLLICLES ARE ARRANGED IN GROUPS IN CAMELHIDE (2).

DRESSING

The hide from which the fat and hair has been removed, or *pelt* as it is usually called, will become stiff and open to further bacterial decay unless treated to prevent this happening. One of the simpler means of preserving hides was by *smoking*, in which they were suspended over a slow-burning wood fire, or in a specially constructed chamber. During this treatment the hides absorbed a wide variety of resinous materials (p. 164), but the active preservatives appear to have been a mixture of aldehydes formed during the burning, or more precisely the partial dis-tillation of the wood. Hides were sometimes given an *oil-dressing* or *chamoising*. A great variety of oils, or oil-containing materials, were used for this purpose—tallow, yolk of egg, the brains of cattle—being rubbed into the hide by hand. Chemically speaking, only those fats which will oxidize on exposure to the air will serve, but doubtless early man discovered which materials were suitable by trial and error. *Dubbin,* a mixture of cod-liver oil and tallow, still used extensively today, is of considerable antiquity.

Two mineral preservatives were used extensively in antiquity, salt and potash alum. In both *salt-dressing* and *alum-dressing,* or *tawing,* the dry materials were rubbed into the surface of the hides. The resulting leather was generally very pale as a result of this treatment, as for example the Roman *aluta.* In areas where neither salt nor alum was readily available, spent wood ash may have been used as a preservative although it was far less effective.

The methods of dressing so far described had little permanent chemical effect on the hide and the preservatives could for the most part be removed or rendered less effective by prolonged soaking in water, with the result that the leather became prone to decay. This was more particularly true of smoked and oil-dressed leathers and because the preservatives could be readily removed these methods of leather-dressing are spoken of as reversible. *Tanning,* on the other hand, is an irreversible process, the functional ingredients of the tan bath, the *tannins,* forming a chemical combination with the materials of the hide.

Before tanning it was an advantage, but not essential, to make the hides swell. This process of *plumping, bating* or *puering,* was essentially one of partial putrefaction for which the necessary bacteria could most easily be provided by making an infusion of dung, the excreta of dogs being especially suitable. The hides were suspended in this mixture until sufficiently flabby, and then transferred to the tan-bath.

Tannins were obtained from a very wide variety of trees and shrubs. The term tannin in fact covers a large number of complex chemical compounds, but these may be classified according to two broad chemical groups which can be distinguished by analysis (p. 227). One group of tannins, the *pyrogallol* or *hydrolysable* group (chemically formed by esterification) could be obtained by infusing the woods of oak, chestnut, the leaves of sumac, valonea acorns or the fruit of the myrobalan, to mention only the main sources. Leathers tanned in these infusions tended to be rather pale. The second group of tannins, the *catechol* or *condensed* group (chemical formed as condensation products) were obtained from such sources as the woods of mimosa, mangrove, babool or cutch, and the bark of the larch. Leathers tanned in these infusions tended to be dark and red. Infusions of the North American hemlock and of oak bark contain tannins of both groups.

Leather might, of course, undergo more than one preservative process. It was, and still is, a common practice to give leather an oil-dressing after tanning, since tanned leather becomes stiff and liable to crack on drying. Equally, Cordova leather was tawed after tanning in an infusion of sumac.

All these methods of dressing were obviously not applicable to fur pelts. After scudding the pelts were sometimes salt- or alum-dressed, and usually stretched in the sun to dry thoroughly. As a result the pelts would become hard and stiff. This defect might be alleviated by oil-dressing, but amongst some primitive peoples the inner surface of the pelt was thoroughly chewed. The effect of this treatment seems to have

been threefold. The pelt was made supple; the saliva had a limited preservative action; and the operator tended to ingest any residual fatty
matter that might have acted as the seat of further decay.

Leathers

Amongst preliterate people the skins of few animals, wild or domesticated,
were discarded; some animals were hunted only for their pelts. The
skins of the fur-bearing animals were generally not converted into hides,
but used as fur pelts for rugs and clothing. Despite the various treatments which they may have undergone, however, most leathers have a
characteristic *grain* due to the different arrangement of hair follicles and
sweat glands, as well as varying degrees of coarseness and arrangement
of the collagen fibres. If leather is not too far decayed it is usually
possible to determine the genera of animal from which the skin came, if
not the precise species.

Today, leathers are generally classified either by the type of animals
from which the skins came, or by the nature of the treatment they have
undergone. This terminology can, however, be confusing. The terms
'kidskin' and 'chamois' should imply the use of the skins of kids and
chamois, but today they are frequently used to describe lambskins that
have undergone different treatments. Equally, the term 'Morocco' should
mean a goatskin, sumac-tanned and dyed red; 'Cordova' indicates
horsehide, sumac-tanned and tawed, and 'Russian leather' calfskin
dressed with birch oil. Due to modern imitations in lamb- and sheepskin,
these terms have, however, lost their precise meaning, and when describing leathers from antiquity it would seem advisable to state both
the animal from which the skin came and its treatment.

In general the finer leathers came from the smaller animals—goats,
sheep and the small deer—or from the young of the larger animals, as did
calfskin. The coarser hides, if left untanned, became very hard and in-
flexible. *Rawhide* was used where these properties were of value. The
thickness of leather is, however, no guide to its source, for thick leathers
could be put across the currier's beam and split to produce several sheets
of thin leather. *Parchment* or *vellum* was made in this way, calfskin
being split into thin sheets or *skivers*. For writing purposes the calfskin
was normally tawed, and then pounced with chalk or talc, while as a
window-covering an oil-dressing was given to make the parchment
translucent.

Shaping and Decoration

The ordinary pointed knife blade is of little use for cutting leather, since
the point soon loses its edge. Thus, for most purposes the leather-
worker's cutting tool was a crescentic-bladed knife, or *half-moon*. Small
knives of this shape are known from the early metal ages (often classified
as chisels, or even turf-cutters!) but this exact shape is difficult to
produce in flint or similar stones. Nevertheless it would seem that some
round-ended flint tools, generally described as scrapers, would have been
more effective for cutting leather than for any other purpose.

Most articles made of more than a single piece of leather were sewn, with either thong or thread. In anything but the softest of leather, bone and early metal needles would have been of little use alone; the leather would have required piercing first with an *awl*. In later periods leather was, however, also joined by riveting, usually with copper rivets. This method was adopted chiefly for the making of vessels, which were, incidentally, commonly lined with pitch (p. 165) both to preserve the leather and to make the vessels water-tight.

While most leather objects were made by cutting and sewing, rawhide and leather that had not been oil-dressed were sometimes shaped by scalding in near-boiling water, followed by pressing into a form or die, commonly of wood. The product of this treatment, *cuir bouilli*, was exceptionally hard, and retained its shape well unless subjected to prolonged soaking in water, a mishap that could be guarded against by dressing with wax, resin or pitch.

Apart from dyeing, painting and gilding, leather was frequently decorated by tooling. The term *engraving* is often applied to a form of linear decoration, but this is something of a misnomer since the blunt tool used for the purpose more commonly than not compressed a line on the surface rather than cut through it. The technique was, in fact, more akin to tracer-work (p. 78) than to engraving. *Stamping* with specially designed steel punches was used either as a backgrounding or to produce repetitive designs. Thin leather may also have been embossed from the reverse side, a technique strictly comparable to repoussé work (p. 78). *Incised* decoration, since it weakened the leather, was generally reserved for strictly ornamental leather. Designs worked by burning with a hot metal rod or needle (*poker work*) are quite commonly executed by preliterate people, but there seems to be little record of this type of work in antiquity.

Chapter Twelve

ANTLER, BONE, HORN AND IVORY

SYNOPSIS

Structure and Composition: Bone · Antler · Horn · Ivory.   *Shaping:* Carving.

STRUCTURE AND COMPOSITION

FOR MOST PURPOSES the only bones used for making artifacts were the *long bones* from the legs of the larger animals, since only from these could sufficiently large pieces of compact bone be obtained. Anatomically the long bones are little more than long cylinders of compact bone, with a central cavity containing marrow, and two ends composed of spongy (cancellous) bone. Since the marrow cavity is an essential organ for the formation of blood, the outer compact layer is perforated at intervals for the passage of blood vessels and nerves. Save for those places where the muscles are attached, the outer surface of the bone is smooth and although to the naked eye bone may appear to be a fairly homogeneous material, under the microscope it may be seen to be made up of many minute canals, around which the hard material of the bone is laid down in concentric lamellae. The bones of the human skull were occasionally used for making small, flat objects. Unlike the long bones, the hard bony inner and outer layers are thin, the space between being filled with cancellous bone.

Antlers, which are shed annually, are an outgrowth of the bones of the skull. Generally only the males of the various species of deer grow antlers, but the female reindeer and caribou are exceptions to this rule. Initially the antlers are covered with skin (velvet) which is shed when the antlers are fully grown. The outer surface of the antler then appears rough, very largely due to the fact that the surface is channelled to take the numerous blood-vessels necessary to supply such a rapidly growing organ. Structurally antler is somewhat similar to a long bone. There is an outer cortex of compact, bone-like material, although the inner cavity is not marrow-filled, but instead is a spongy structure rather similar to cancellous bone. While the proportions of cortex and cancellous antler vary considerably between one species of deer and another, it is seldom a simple matter to determine beyond question from what species a small antler artifact may have come.

Horns, unlike antlers, are an outgrowth of the skin, and are not normally shed. The fibrous material of which horns are composed, keratin, is chemically identical to that of which claws and hooves are made, and is incidentally a major constituent of the epidermis of the skin (p. 148). Growth takes place by the laying down of layers of keratin over the horn-cores—protuberances of cancellous bone projecting from the skull. This growth is often interrupted during lean seasons. Horn is thus a fibrous material, often laminated, the layers tending to exfoliate if the horn is partially decayed. Horns of this type are carried by cattle, sheep, goats, and antelopes, but the horn of the rhinoceros does not develop on a horn-core; it is simply an outgrowth of the skin.

The term *ivory* should, strictly speaking, be applied only to the tusks of the elephants, but other materials somewhat similar in character are often described as ivory. Ivory tusks are the upper incisors of the elephant, but unlike other teeth they are not covered with enamel, save for the tips when the tusks are very young. The tusk is thus composed almost entirely of dentine, with a relatively small pulp-cavity at the base. Growth occurs by the laying down of layers of dentine, and as with horn the development of the tusk is normally seasonal. While the lamellae cannot be seen in fresh ivory, when the material begins to decay it will usually exfoliate as concentric layers. In fresh ivory, when polished, crossing arcs of areas of light and dark material can often be seen, a pattern somewhat similar to 'engine turning' on the back of many stainless steel watch-cases.

Walrus ivory was often used in antiquity, especially in areas in which the importation of true ivory would have been prohibitive. The tusks, the upper canines of the walrus, are without enamel, but the dentine is laid down in two distinct layers. The outer dentine is homogeneous, but the inner secondary dentine has a marbled, and at times almost crystalline, appearance and is translucent. Normally the inner dentine was avoided.

Both the canines and incisors of the *hippopotamus* were sometimes used in place of ivory. These teeth have large pulp cavities, and the dentine is always banded, the bands running straight down the outer dentine, and as wavy lines through the inner dentine. In the decayed state fracture follows the line of the banding.

SHAPING

All these materials were most commonly shaped by carving with either stone or metal tools, but in the working of ivory, which is quite the hardest, the drill in one form or another was frequently used, especially to remove large areas of the material. Antlers, on the other hand, could be made relatively soft by prolonged soaking in water, after which its carving became a comparatively simple matter.

The choice of these materials for different purposes, apart from availability, depended on their particular qualities. The great virtues of ivory, at least to the artisan, were its strength and homogeneous nature; the lack of grain allowed free carving without any danger of running into unforeseen difficulties, while its hardness allowed intricate and delicate work. Although the colour of ivory is normally appreciated for its own worth today, it was in antiquity commonly gilded; while in the Far East ivory was occasionally stained in imitation of jade.

Horn, by contrast, is relatively soft, fibrous and flexible. This flexibility was sometimes put to use as, for example, when used as a component of composite archers' bows. If horn is soaked and then boiled in water it can readily be split into thin sheets which are translucent. These sheets were often used as window panes, or for making lanterns. Horn sheets can, at a slightly higher temperature, be pressed into a die, but this technique does not appear to have been used in antiquity.

Although shed antlers are hard, and those cut from the freshly slaughtered beast rapidly become so, the material can be temporarily softened by soaking in water. To stone-using societies antler was a valuable hard material that presented few difficulties in its working, save that its normally small diameter limited severely the size of object that could be made from it. Perhaps for this reason antler was seldom used by more sophisticated people.

Larger objects could be made of bone rather than of antler, and to many people it was obviously a more accessible material. Its strength and hardness made it suitable for an almost unlimited number of purposes, more particularly in those instances where a wooden object would have proved too fragile in service.

Chapter Thirteen

DYES, PIGMENTS AND PAINTS

SYNOPSIS

General: Pigments · Dyes · Paints · Media · Mordants.   *Pigments:* Ochre · Amber · Sienna · Orpiment · Realgar · Cinnabar · Terra verde · Malachite · Azurite · Lapis lazuli · White lead · Carbon black · Red lead · Vermilion · Naples yellow · Copper resinate · Massicot · Egyptian blue · Smalt · Gamboge · Sepia · Bistre.   *Dyes:* Kermes · Lac · Cochineal · Madder · Brazil · Safflower · Weld · Saffron · Iris green · Sap green · Woad · Indigo · Tyrrhian purple.   *Painting:* Fresco · Tempera · Oil-paints · Inks. *Dyeing.*

GENERAL

PIGMENTS ARE COLOURED materials, insoluble in water, applied generally in powdered form to the surface of objects; and since they have no adhesive qualities they require some vehicle or *medium* to hold them in place. *Paints* are thus mixtures of pigments and media. *Dyes* on the other hand are soluble in water, combine, often chemically, with the materials to which they are applied, and so require no media. Most pigments used in antiquity were naturally occurring minerals, artificially produced inorganic compounds, or easily obtained organic materials. Occasionally, however, a satisfactory colour could not be obtained from these sources, and the pigment might then be produced by dyeing a white material to provide a *lake*. The white materials used for this purpose, *mordants*, might be chalk or kaolin, but where available potash alum was often used. While many dyes will combine directly with most materials, others will not, and in these cases potash alum, which acts as a 'link' between the dye and the material, is used as a mordant. The former type of dye is sometimes described as *substantive*, the latter as *adjective*.

PIGMENTS

Those pigments that occur as natural minerals or deposits must be ground into a very fine powder before they can be used. This was normally done by hand using a pestle and mortar, while for the better quality paints the finer fraction only was separated by elutriation (p. 20).

A number of naturally occurring deposits could be used as white pigments, for example, chalk, lime, gypsum and china clay. The natural earth pigments—*ochres, umbers* and *siennas*—are earthy deposits containing ferric oxide as a colourant. In its hydrated form ferric oxide, limonite, is yellow, but it is easily dehydrated by heating to form the red oxide, haematite. The more or less pure iron minerals, ochres, might be used as pigments, but both the umbers and siennas contain small proportions of black manganese dioxide and thus give rather browner colours. Sienna is the more yellow as it occurs naturally, becoming red when burnt; umber is naturally brown, turning red-brown when burnt. Black was most commonly some form of charcoal, technically an artificial pigment, but both bitumen (p. 165) and graphite were also occasionally used. Their occurrence is, however, very limited. Both *orpiment* and *realgar* (sulphides of arsenic) give clearer yellows than ochres. The two minerals are often found closely associated and were ground together to provide a yellow pigment. The mineral *cinnabar* (mercuric sulphide) is vermilion. This pigment, however, was also produced artificially (see below). Green pigments might be obtained from *terra verde* or from *malachite*. The first of these, originally deposited as a marine clay, contains the green minerals glauconite and celadonite both containing iron in the ferrous form; the second is a basic carbonate of copper and is a less yellow shade of green. The mineral *azurite*, another basic copper carbonate, was used as a blue pigment, while the semi-precious stone *lapis lazuli* was also ground down to give a blue.

Many inorganic pigments were artificially produced. *White lead* (basic lead carbonate) was produced by exposing metallic lead to the action of the fumes of organic acids such as those given off by vinegar or oak-bark. *Carbon black* was often nothing more complicated than charcoal, although lampblack was produced by burning organic matter and allowing the soot from the flame to collect on a cool surface. Bone and ivory were also burnt to provide fine quality black pigments. *Red lead* or *minium*, often mistaken for vermilion, was produced by heating lead carbonate at a low temperature (about 400°C.). True *vermilion*, on the other hand, was made by heating a mixture of mercury and sulphur. *Naples yellow*, lead antimoniate, was of rare occurrence in antiquity, and the precise method by which it was manufactured is unknown.* Yellow lead monoxide, *massicot*, was more commonly used; it was made by gently heating white lead. No artificial inorganic green pigments were produced in antiquity, but a metallo-organic material, *copper resinate*, was made by dissolving a copper salt, such as copper acetate, in a resin (p. 164). Both massicot and copper resinate discolour rapidly. Two blue pigments were made by first producing vitreous materials, and then converting them into frits (p. 46). *Egyptian blue* was made by fusing lime and silica with copper as a colourant (p. 49). The material usually contained traces of calcite and quartz as impurities. *Smalt* was most commonly a soda-lime glass with cobalt oxide as the colourant.

The majority of organic colourants are dyes, but a few pigments of organic origin were used in antiquity. The yellow pigment *gamboge* is the

---

* The pigment may have been prepared by heating antimony with potassium nitrate to give potassium antimoniate. If a solution of this is added to one of a soluble lead salt, such as lead acetate, the lead antimoniate would be precipitated from the solution.

resin of a tree of the genus *Garcinia*, native to South-east Asia. It can also be dissolved in alcohol and used as a lacquer (p. 165).

Sepia, obtained by pulverizing the dried ink-sac of the cuttle-fish and boiling in an alkaline solution, really only became popular in the late eighteenth century and its use in antiquity is doubtful. Another brown pigment, *bistre*, was made by burning peach-stones or a resinous wood. The pigment is rather tarry and could only be used in thin washes. Two dyes, the yellow *saffron*, and the blue *woad* (below), were quite commonly used as pigments without a mordant.

Dyes

An enormous number of dyes has been extracted from different plant and animal sources in various parts of the world throughout antiquity. It would be impossible to mention them all here. In any event a large proportion of them was quite unstable, and would not normally have survived today. Instead, a few of the more stable dyes, all of which have at some time been used for the preparation of lakes, are discussed.

Three red dyes were obtained from insects of the genus *Coccus:* kermes, lac and cochineal. The dye *kermes* was obtained from the insect *C. ilicis* found in galls of the oak *Quercus coccifera*, which is native to many parts of southern Europe. *Lac*, from which the word 'lake' is derived, was obtained as a by-product in the manufacture of lac, (p. 163), while *cochineal* came from the insect *C. cacti*, native to Central and South America. The cochineal insect lives on various cactus plants, and the dye, although it has ten times the tinctorial power of kermes, is unusual in that alum makes an unsatisfactory mordant, and thus tin oxide was used as a mordant for cochineal from the middle of the seventeenth century onwards. A few plants produce satisfactory red dyes. *Madder* was prepared from the root of the plant *Rubia tinctorium*, indigenous to south-east Europe. This extract is in fact a composite dye containing the two components purpurin and alizarin. The latter was isolated from the extract in 1826, and synthesized half a century later (see below). *Brazil* or *logwood* was extracted from the wood of trees of the genus *Caesalpina*, different species of which are found native in Ceylon and in Brazil and Jamaica.

Yellow dyes were generally of plant origin. *Safflower* was prepared from the dried leaves of the Dyer's Thistle, *Carthanus tinctorius*, native to eastern Asia and southern Europe, while *weld* was obtained from a species of wild mignonette, *Reseda luteola*, indigenous to southern Europe, and later cultivated for the dye. *Saffron* was obtained from the dried stigmas of the Autumn crocus, *Crocus sativus*, native to countries of the Near East.

There are very few satisfactory green dyes that can be obtained naturally since they nearly all fade rapidly. *Iris green* was extracted from the leaves of iris plants, and *sap green* from the ripe berries of the buckthorn.

The two most common blue dyes used in antiquity were indigo and woad. Both colours are similar since the dye material, indigotin, is present in both preparations. *Woad,* extracted from the plant *Isatis tinctoria,* is native to southern Europe, while *indigo,* as the name implies, is indigenous to India, the dye being extracted from the plant *Indigofera tinctorium.* The dye was formed by allowing the plant extracts to ferment, and being insoluble in water it had to be dissolved in a dilute acid before it could be used.

The only satisfactory purple dye from antiquity was *Tyrrhian purple,* and even this tended to be on the crimson side. The dye was extracted from the *Purpura* shell-fish and the *Murex* snail by the removal of a small sac containing a white fluid which turned purple by photochemical reaction when exposed to the sun. The dye was manufactured in the Near East, and in Mexico, where a snail similar to *Murex* is indigenous.

The following pigments and dyes have been artificially prepared since 1700. Their presence on an antiquity of greater age should thus be of great concern: Prussian blue (1704), Barium yellow (*c.* 1810), Emerald green (1814), Ultramarine (1828), Zinc white (1834), Cadmium red and Cadmium yellow (1846), Chrome green, Chrome yellow and Cobalt violet (1859), Cerulean blue (1860), Cobalt yellow (1861), Synthetic alizarin (1868), Titanium white (1920) and Monastral blue (1935). Blue verditer, a synthetic basic copper carbonate generally made by mixing a soluble copper salt with an alkali and ammonium chloride, was in use as a substitute for azurite by the eighteenth century, but the precise date of its initial synthesis is unknown. The first aniline dye, a shade of mauve, synthesized from a distillate of coal tar, was produced in 1856. Other aniline colours followed soon afterwards.

PAINTING

Unfortunately the term 'painting' can be used to describe both the use of a material and a technique. One may speak of a 'painted panel', implying that it has been decorated with paint, or of 'painted pottery' meaning that coloured slips have been applied by brush. As a result, many artifacts that have never been given a coat of paint are often described as 'painted' and the reader may be left to discover, if he can, what precisely is meant. Thus a wooden artifact may be coloured by applying dyes to different areas with a brush. Such an object would be better described as 'stained', or even 'dyed', rather than 'painted', unless a complete account of the method of colouring is given. In many cases the word 'coloured' is preferable to 'painted' since it is non-committal.

The colouring of a wall, for example, may be done in a variety of different ways. In the first place, the pigments may be applied dry and rubbed into the surface, or put on as a suspension in water, and left without further treatment. Colours applied in this way are, of course, not stable and tend to rub off, but their instability should not be exaggerated. In practice it takes a great deal of soap, water and scrubbing to remove haematite from a porous surface; the surface itself is very likely to become damaged long before all traces of the pigment are eliminated. A second method of colouring that has been advanced involved covering the surface with the medium and blowing the dry pigment on to this

This technique has been suggested as the means of executing some European palaeolithic cave designs, but evidence that this was the method used is totally lacking. The fact that the pictures in some caves have remained in such a good state of preservation is probably due more to the formation of a deposit of dripstone over their surfaces than to the use of any medium in the first instance. Pigments applied dry, or as a suspension, might have been bound to a degree by covering with a lacquer (p. 164), but clear gums and resins suitable for this purpose were not everywhere easily available.

The two most common techniques for colouring walls developed in antiquity were tempera and fresco. In the *fresco* technique the pigments were applied as a suspension in water to the surface of fresh lime plaster, and as a result of chemical changes taking place in the plaster (p. 171) the pigments in time became fixed and would not easily rub off. Unhappily the term fresco is used by some writers to describe walls decorated in a particular style, or the word may even be used as a synonym for mural painting. This can be confusing, apart from being erroneous. *Tempera* painting was done by making a paint in which the medium was not an oil. In practice this almost invariably meant the use of egg-yolk or size as a medium in the Western World. In Eastern Asia the same kind of work was often executed using various gums (p. 164) as the vehicle. The introduction of oils which set hard on exposure to the atmosphere, the so-called *drying oils* such as linseed, as a medium in the making of paint appears to have been a relatively late innovation.

The essential qualities for a medium, good adhesion and stability without discoloration on ageing, are less common amongst the adhesives discussed below (p. 162) than might be imagined. In some parts of the world wax was used as a medium for fine painting. The paint naturally had to be used warm. Difficult as this technique must have been and fragile as the paint surfaces were, work carried out using this medium retained its freshness to a quite remarkable degree.

Inks may be essentially either paints or dyes. A black ink, for example, may be either a suspension of lampblack in a water-miscible adhesive, or a dye that will produce a black or other coloration. Many early black inks were simple mixtures of lampblack and animal glue. Of the staining type of inks, black was commonly a mixture of a soluble ferrous salt, such as ferrous sulphate, and an extract of tannins (p. 150). This gave a black stain composed of tannates of iron. Sometimes the two types of ink were mixed. Sepia inks were normally of the stain type. They might be true sepia, obtained from the ink-sac of the cuttle fish, but quite commonly the juice of the ripe walnut husk was extracted and used as an ink. Red inks might be made from kermes, lac or cochineal. Quite commonly a little gum was added to increase the viscosity of staining inks, and the presence of an adhesive is thus not in itself evidence that the ink was of the paint type.

DYEING

Dyes will combine with a wide variety of organic materials—wood, bone, ivory, leather, and plant fibres. As a means of colouring, dyes were commonly used on these materials rather than paints, often because they were less liable to damage in service. Amongst the more sophisticated people, dyes were sometimes used to imitate other materials; ivory was dyed to imitate jade or bone and wood stained to give the impression of ebony, for example.

The dyeing of woven fabrics might be carried out either in the hank, when the thread was dyed before being woven, or in the cloth, after weaving. In cases where a mordant was being used, it was normal to dip the hanks or cloth in a solution of the mordant first and then transfer the material to the dye-vat. To ensure even dyeing it was usual to pummel the material thoroughly, either by hand or by treading under foot.

Pattern dyeing of cloth and similar fabrics demanded a different technique. The material might be laid flat or stretched on a frame and the dyes applied by brush, to give the so-called *painted fabrics*. Alternatively, areas might be protected by a screen that was non-absorbent, usually made so by waxing, and the uncovered areas were then dyed by brushing. This was, of course, a stencilling process. More even dyeing in pattern, however, was achieved by the *wax resist* or *batik* method. In this, areas were reserved by covering with wax. The material was then dip-dyed in the first colour, washed and boiled to remove the wax. The dyed areas were then stopped off in wax, and the material dip-dyed in the second colour. For this type of dyeing a great many colours could be used, each colour demanding a separate stopping-off with wax of the areas not to be dyed in that colour. An alternative, and rather cruder form of resist dyeing was that known as *tie-dyeing*. The areas to be left undyed were tied off or bound with a wax- or oil-impregnated cord. For obvious reasons only simple figures could be produced in this way— normally circles, squares or stars, depending on how the cloth was folded. Printed dyeing, in which dyes thickened with a gum were applied by means of wooden printing blocks, was a relatively late introduction.

In nearly all areas the number of colours available for dyeing was rather limited in antiquity but the range of colours could be extended by over-dyeing. Thus an orange could be produced by dyeing first in a yellow and then in a red dye. In the Old World, for example, Tyrrhian purple was most expensive, and not particularly satisfactory, but a purple could be achieved by over-dyeing red with blue, although unless very carefully manipulated the end product would be black. In fact, nearly all early black dyeing was done by heavy dyeing of one colour over another, commonly red and blue. Because of the instability of most green dyes, yellow was often overdyed with blue to give green, weld and woad being a typical combination.

Chapter Fourteen

ADHESIVES

SYNOPSIS

Animal waxes: Beeswax · Wool wax · Chinese insect wax.   *Glues:* Gelatine · Size · Glue.   *Lac:* Shellac.   *Gums and Resins:* Tree and seed gums · Tar · Pitch · Turpentine · Rosin · Varnishes.   *Latex.*   *Bitumen.*

THE WORD ADHESIVE is taken here to cover a wide variety of more or less sticky materials used for a number of purposes, not all of which were simple adhesion. With age many of these materials have become considerably altered. Usually they have blackened and become brittle, and it is a very common mistake then to dismiss them as 'bitumen' without further thought. In fact, bitumen is a comparative rarity on antiquities, and although it is generally not possible to state what adhesive is present without chemical examination (p. 226), one should at least appreciate the other possibilities.

The overwhelming majority of adhesives were derived from either the animal or vegetable worlds. Many of these were obtainable with little effort, while others were prepared deliberately or as a by-product of some other process. The adhesives derived from animals were principally either waxes or glues, and from plants either gums or resins.

ANIMAL WAXES

Animal waxes are usually very impure substances and although they are chemically akin to fats they are non-greasy and solid when cold. Although they are soluble in some organic solvents, in antiquity waxes were used hot and hence set by cooling. *Beeswax*, derived from honeycombs, was probably the main source of wax, but it should not be forgotten that fleeces contain a high proportion of *wool-wax*, or *lanolin*, and that when the wool was scoured much of this would float to the surface of the water and could be collected. In Eastern Asia the Chinese wax insect (a species of *Coccus*) secretes a wax while in the larval stage on the twigs of trees on which it lives. This wax was collected and used presumably even in early antiquity. Although waxes lack strong adhesive qualities they were nevertheless useful as a medium for paints (p. 160) and for modelling, although other materials, such as tallow (below), could have been used for this purpose. Waxes were invaluable, however,

162

as a means of water-proofing porous surfaces and on some materials had a considerably hardening effect, as, for example, on leather.

GLUES

The glues, which include gelatin and size as well as animal glue, were prepared by the prolonged boiling of hides and bones to extract from them the gelatinous protein materials, collagen and ossein. In the living tissues these exist as fibres, but as a result of boiling they break down to become water-miscible. The gels so formed set by the evaporation of much of the water, although they also become partially solidified on cooling. The process of extraction was sometimes more efficiently carried out by initially breaking down the collagen or ossein in an acid or alkaline solution (p. 169), followed by neutralizing. The distinction between gelatin, glue and size is only in the degree of purity. The first extracts made were generally fairly free of extraneous matter and are designated *gelatin*; the final extracts are termed glue, when moderately pure, and *size* when less so. Animal glue was normally an extract prepared from the hides and bones of sheep and cattle, while fish glue was made from the skin, bones and offal of fish.

The use of *yolk of egg* as a medium for paint has already been referred to. This sets initially by evaporation of the water, although later chemical changes take place with the result that, unlike glues, the material becomes virtually insoluble in water. Before the introduction of domesticated fowl the eggs of many birds were used for this purpose, for example those of gulls and pigeons.

In theory many of the animal fats and oils could have been used as adhesives in the past although in the impure form they would have been prone to bacterial decay. Good quality *tallow*, which was mutton fat that had been purified by repeated extraction of extraneous matter in boiling water (*rendering*) however, would have been a reasonable substitute for waxes in many instances. Pork fat, on the other hand, would have been unsuitable since it is soft at normal temperatures. This difference between mutton and pork fats is due to the different proportions of stearin, which is normally hard, and olein, which is soft, both being mixed compounds of the fatty acids, stearic and oleic. There is, nevertheless, very little direct evidence for the use of fats as adhesives in antiquity.

LAC

One animal secretion, *lac*, resembles plant resins in many chemical and physical aspects. The lac insect, *Coccus lacca*, is indigenous to India. The larvae of the insects secrete the lac around themselves as a protective coating so that the whole twig on which the larvae have settled becomes covered with scales of the material. The twigs were gathered and the lac (*stick lac*) removed, to be purified by boiling in water. The lac itself is insoluble in water, although softened by it, but the red dye it contains is not and was thus easily extracted and later concentrated by evaporation. The purified lac might be either rolled into balls or stretched out into thin sheets which set hard on cooling. These sheets were broken up to provide a flaked material, *shellac*, which was more easily dissolved in alcohol than the lump. The lac, which might be pigmented, might either be applied or worked warm, or used as a solution in alcohol. In the latter form lac was introduced into Western Europe as the basis of French polish, although it had been put to similar use, often pigmented, in far greater antiquity in India. Some tree resins of Eastern Asia below, have properties so similar to those of lac that the two materials have often been confused.

Gums and Resins

Adhesives derived from plants were chiefly of two kinds—gums and resins. In everyday speech these two terms are used somewhat carelessly, but they are by no manner of means synonymous. While both are plant secretions, *gums*, on the one hand, are water miscible, or hydrophilic, to form colloidal mucilages or jellies. Chemically they are carbohydrates, being akin to sugars and starches, and are thus generally insoluble in organic solvents such as alcohol. *Resins*, however, are insoluble in water, or hydrophobic, and more or less soluble in organic solvents. Essentially they are aromatic substances normally exuded as solutions in essential oils, in which state they are referred to as *oleoresins*. Unlike the gums which set by evaporation of the water, resins set partly by evaporation of the essential oils, and partly as a result of chemical changes that take place in the presence of air. Gums and resins were thus put to quite different uses. It would clearly have been of no value to waterproof a porous pot with a gum, and equally a resin could not have been used as a medium for a water-based ink or paint.

Gums were derived from a wide range of sources. Some were tree exudations, such as *gum arabic*, tapped from a species of acacia, and *gum tragacanth*, derived from a shrub indigenous to Asia Minor. Seeds, such as those of the locust bean and quince, were other possible sources. Gums may also have been extracted from some algae and lichens although there is scant evidence that these sources were ever used in antiquity.

The resins commonly used in Europe were extracted from the pine, larch and fir, while in the Mediterranean area *sandarac* was tapped from the tear tree, native to North Africa, and *mastic* from a small evergreen shrub, fairly ubiquitous within the region. Asian sources include *damar*, from a small conifer native to the East Indies, and Japanese lacquer from the shrub *Rhus vernicifera*, a resin often mistaken for lac. In the New World both firs and spruces were tapped for resins; *Canada balsam*, for example, coming from a species of fir, the balm of Gilead.

Resins were not always obtained by tapping trees. A crude form of dry distillation was commonly used in Northern Europe to extract *wood tar*. Billets of resinous wood were burnt in a supply of air inadequate to allow complete combustion and the tar, oozing from the ends of the billets, was collected. This impure form of the resin, containing a considerable amount of free carbon and other impurities, might be used as it stood for waterproofing, 'Stockholm tar', but by further distillation it could be separated into two fractions; a distillate of creosote containing a proportion of organic acids, apparently not put to use in antiquity, and a residue of *wood pitch*. The latter, being more viscous than tar, and setting harder, was often of more value for waterproofing.

Tapped resins might also be distilled. Thus the resins from pine, larch, fir and spruce were distilled to give a distillate of *turpentine* and a residue of *rosin*, or *colophony*. In this case most of the essential oils present in the original oleo-resin were carried off in the turpentine, while the rosin was composed largely of the more resinous materials. The turpentine was used, amongst other things, for thinning oil-bound paints (p. 160), while rosin was employed as a waterproofing, especially for thread.

While in remote antiquity resins were used unadulterated as adhesives, many were used later as the bases of *varnishes*. Most resins are more or less soluble in a wide range of oils, and when mixed with *drying oils*, such as walnut, linseed or hempseed oil, they would provide *oil varnishes* that would set hard on drying. *Spirit varnishes*, on the other hand, were made by dissolving resins in alcohol.

All resins, of course, were not used as adhesives. The use of gamboge as a pigment has already been mentioned (p. 157). Frankincense, myrrh and hashish were used for cosmetic and medicinal purposes, while the resin of some trees, for example some species of maple, contained sufficient sugar to have made its extraction worthwhile. The fossilized resin, amber, is discussed later (p. 172).

LATEX

Rubber latex is neither a gum nor a resin. As tapped from the tree, *Hevea brasiliensis*, latex is a colloidal suspension of rubber as minute droplets in an aqueous solution. This sets by evaporation of the water and coagulation of the droplets to give soft rubber. The material appears to have been used over a considerable period in the pre-Columbian New World, as a waterproofing and for making rubber balls for games. True rubber can be tapped in usable quantities only from trees indigenous to the New World, but a somewhat similar material, *gutta-percha*, was obtained from the tree *Palaquium oblongifolia*, in South-east Asia. Although introduced into Europe only as late as the mid-eighteenth century, its use was known in China long before this. Waxes can also be extracted from many plants, but there seems to be no evidence that these waxes were used in antiquity.

BITUMEN

The only adhesive of mineral origin that appears to have been used in antiquity was *bitumen*. It was presumably gathered as the result of seepage from oil-wells, being a mixture of crude petroleum, mineral wax and many impurities. By itself bitumen is not sufficiently viscous to be of value as an adhesive, and requires a filler. Dry clay or some similar material may have been mixed with bitumen to provide an adhesive; on the other hand, *asphalt*, limestone impregnated with bitumen, occurs naturally, and was probably more commonly used.

Chapter Fifteen

SOME OTHER MATERIALS

SYNOPSIS

Fuels: Wood · Charcoal · Coal · Peat · Dung.　*Acids and Alkalis:* Soaps.　*Plaster:* Lime · Gypsum.　*Salt.　Shells.　Amber.*

FUELS

ALTHOUGH THE THREE most important fuels used in antiquity were unquestionably wood, charcoal and coal, it is important to remember that many dry vegetable materials other than wood may have been used. In some arid areas timber may not have been obtainable, and grasses or small shrubs may have been the only available fuels; while in some tropical regions, because of the high humidity, timber was not always satisfactory. Selection of fuel, however, depended not only upon availability, but also on the nature of the fire required. The finer types of vegetation, such as grass, while providing an immediate and very hot fire, soon burn away and if a long-burning fire that could be controlled was needed, some other form of fuel must have been sought. For this reason, as much as any other, cattle dung was collected and made into fuel cakes, so giving a slow burning and controllable fire, in which respect peat blocks have very similar properties.

When speaking of fuels, it is very important not to confuse measurements of temperature with those of the total quantity of heat available, or thermal capacity.* The thermal capacity of a fuel expresses the available quantity of heat on complete combustion and is thus largely determined by the chemical composition of the fuel. Thus dry wood, which is made up largely of cellulose and lignin, but nevertheless contains a fairly high proportion of water, has a relatively low thermal capacity, while coal, which contains a high proportion of free carbon, apart from other readily inflammable materials and less water, has a relatively high thermal capacity. Damp wood will, of course, give an even lower heat output since much of the available heat is dissipated in converting the water to steam before combustion can take place.

The maximum temperature that can be obtained from any fuel is largely determined by the size of the fuel particles and the shape of the furnace or other structure in which it is being burnt; both these factors,

---

* Thermal capacity is normally expressed either as calories or as British Thermal Units (BTU). Both are standards based on the amount of heat required to raise a stated volume of water through a stated temperature range.

in fact, influence the rate at which oxygen is available to cause combustion. Thus, a wood fire provided with inadequate draught cannot give a high temperature simply because the rate of combustion is too slow. If the draught is improved, the rate of combustion is raised and so is the maximum temperature, to a degree. In improving the draught, however, much of the available heat may be lost either in the escaping gases or due to poor insulation of the furnace, and the temperature need not, therefore, be raised proportionately as the draught is improved. Where the draught is poor a reasonably finely divided fuel, since it presents a large surface area to the unit of weight, will burn more rapidly than a coarse one and give, weight for weight, a higher temperature. Up to a point this is equally true of conditions in which draught is improved, but in practice a situation soon arises in which the rate of combustion of a finely divided fuel is so rapid that it becomes no longer physically possible to keep the fire stoked, and for this reason a coarser fuel must be used.

The design and function of a kiln or furnace can thus be accurately assessed only when one knows the precise nature of the fuel that was used. This is seldom appreciated by archaeologists who, while determining the species of plants represented by the charred remains, often fail to record the size range of the fragments. In parenthesis, the vegetable remains from such a site need not in any way be representative of the ecology of the region—a use to which they are too often put—since man was presumably highly selective in his choice of wood as fuel.

Wood

Because of their different structure and composition, different timbers have quite distinct characteristics as fuels. There can be little doubt that early man knew this perfectly well and although the traditional verse about English woods* may itself be relatively modern, it must embody a stock of knowledge common in very remote antiquity. What is true of Britain is, of course, equally true of other regions; in any woodland or forest region some trees provided better fuel than others and it is clearly important for those studying the history of technology to establish which they were. The differences are determined by such things as water content or the presence of resins, waxes and so on. In general, however, wood has the great single disadvantage of its high water content which in practice severely limits the highest temperature that can be obtained from it as a fuel. In an enclosed structure such as a kiln, temperatures in the vicinity of 1,200°C. were demonstrably obtained, since wasters (p. 41) resulting from the sagging of bodies with a melting point in this

* Beechwood fires burn bright and clear,
Hornbeam blazes too,
If the logs are kept a year,
To season through and through;
Oak logs will warm you well,
If they're old and dry,
Larch logs of resin smell,
But the sparks will fly,
Pine is good and so is yew,
To warm the winter days,
But poplar and willow, too,
Take long to dry or blaze.

Birch logs will burn too fast,
Alder scarce at all,
Chestnut logs are good to last,
Cut when the leaf's in fall,
Holly logs will burn like wax,
You should burn them green,
Elm burns like smouldering flax,
And no flame is seen,
But ash logs, all smooth and grey,
Burn them green or old,
So buy up all that come your way,
They're worth their weight in gold.

region are not uncommonly found on wood-fired kiln sites. It seems unlikely, however, that any such temperatures could be achieved using
wood fuel with open or smaller structures in which the heat loss would
have been proportionally greater. Thus, although it may have been
possible to melt copper in a wood fire—cases of copper implements that
had become molten during cremation have been reported—from a practical point of view, wood fuel was of little value for working copper since
the size of fire required would have made handling the molten metal
impossible.

Charcoal

As a fuel charcoal has two great advantages over wood. During its preparation water is removed as steam while at the same time the carbohydrates—cellulose and lignin—are converted into elemental carbon.
Hence when it is burnt no heat is wasted either eliminating the water or
converting the carbohydrates to readily combustible carbon. In its preparation charcoal required no specialized equipment. The wood was
stacked, covered with soil to prevent ready access of air and a small fire
was kindled at the base of the stack. During the 'burning' the fire con-
sumed only a small proportion of the wood, but generated sufficient heat
throughout the stack to ensure the physical and chemical changes
already mentioned. When this process had been completed the small vent
at the top of the stack was closed, so quenching the fire, and the whole
stack was allowed to cool. The site on which charcoal has been 'burnt'
thus leaves no very distinctive remains, and the use of charcoal as a fuel
in antiquity can only be inferred from the design and known function of
furnaces, smithies, bloomeries and so on. The presence of charcoal in a
hearth is clearly not evidence that charcoal was used for firing since it
could equally be derived from a wood fire.

Coal

Apart from free carbon most coals contain a small proportion of
volatile and highly inflammable materials, but they also contain variable
quantities of sulphur and phosphorus. While the latter have virtually no
effect on heat output their presence would have been fatal in the making of
many metals (pp. 81, 85) and glasses (p. 52), and it is probably partly
for this reason that many surface outcrops of coal were not used by early
man. On the other hand, the early appearance of iron-working in China
and Turkey, for example, cannot be totally dissociated from the presence
of ample outcrops of coal in these countries. In fact, the composition of
coals varies enormously. Today one normally speaks of lignites and
brown coals, bitumous coals, and anthracite. The lignites and brown
coals contain a relatively high proportion of carbohydrates, such as
cellulose, and water; bitumous coals less of each; while anthracites have
a low carbohydrate and water content. This means, of course, that the
anthracites have the highest thermal capacity; but simply for providing
heat any of these coals would have been perfectly adequate for the
normal early furnace processes, and it would perhaps be more rewarding
to examine the nature of impurities such as sulphur and phosphorus in
many regions rather than the thermal capacity of coals.

The thermal capacity of most coals is certainly not greater than that of charcoal and the advantage of coal over charcoal as a fuel was a physical rather than a chemical one. Charcoal is very easily crushed and in a tall furnace the weight of the whole charge might have been so great that the charcoal at the bottom readily became compacted, so inhibiting an adequate draught up the furnace. The greater resistance to crushing of coal prevented this cutting down of the draught. The comparatively late introduction of coal distillation, by which the majority of the detrimental impurities were removed, gave a material, *coke*, which while retaining much of the physical strength of coal allowed it to be used in most furnace processes.

Peat

In recent times peat has come to be looked upon as a fuel typical of regions in which wood is scarce or lacking. This is largely true of the ecology of Europe today but was not necessarily always so. Apart from being an excellent fuel for such operations as the smoking of hides, peat has the advantage of providing a low but steady temperature. Furthermore, some peat deposits have a surprisingly high thermal capacity due to the presence of plant waxes. Very little is known about the use of peat as a fuel in antiquity, but it is possible that some of the better quality deposits may have been used at least for such things as iron forging, if not for smelting.

Dung

Dung fuel, like peat, is also often looked upon as a fuel typical of treeless regions, but this is far from true even today. The particular advantage of dung fuel over wood is that it can act both as a fuel and as a temporary dome to a kiln. Today cakes of fuel may be laid over a stack of pottery and not allowed to burn out until the very end of the firing. Such a fire, although generically a bonfire, behaves in fact as a kiln. The fuel is used widely in Southern Asia and Africa today and there seems little doubt that it was used in these regions in antiquity also.

ACIDS AND ALKALIS

Many processes already described demand the use of either acids or alkalis, both of which would have to be prepared in or near the workshop. The acids used in antiquity were of organic origin, and hence weaker than many of the mineral acids used by chemists today, but they were not difficult to prepare since purity was normally not required. The juices of most fruits, especially when unripe, are sufficiently acid to etch steel lightly or to alter the plasticity of clay, while the juice of citrus fruits, even when ripe, are always acidic. Perhaps the strongest organic acid available to early man was acetic acid, obtained in the impure form as vinegar. This was a by-product of the fermentation either of grape-skins or of malt-husks and was thus unlikely to have been used before the introduction of alcoholic drinks. Acetic acid is also an ingredient of the distillate of wood tar, but to what extent it was derived from this source in antiquity is a matter of conjecture.

Alkalis, on the other hand, were less easily obtainable directly from the plant kingdom, although extracts of some plants are sufficiently alkaline to have served as soaps (p. 146). Wood and plant ashes, on the other hand, are quite rich in alkalis, and since they are highly soluble in water the alkalis were easily separated from the other ingredients of the ash by adding water, stirring, allowing the solids to settle, and decanting the fluid, which might then be concentrated by evaporation. In the majority of regions this was the only manner in which alkalis could be obtained, but in a few favoured areas deposits of sodium and potassium salts could be utilized. The carbonates of these metals are sufficiently alkaline to be used in solution without further treatment, but the carbonate of calcium, being virtually insoluble in water, would have required calcining first in order to convert it into the oxide below. If kept for a fairly long period, urine becomes strongly alkaline, owing to the formation of ammonia through the bacterial decomposition of urea and other nitrogenous substances. Impure ammonia derived in this manner was used in the sweating of hides (p. 148) and may well have been used for other purposes.

Most *soaps* used in antiquity were compounds of fats and alkalis. The fats might be either vegetable oils or of animal origin, while the alkalis were commonly the soluble fraction of wood ash—*lye*. In function the alkalis reacted with the weak acids of the fats to form soluble organic compounds that, by freeing the alkalis on wetting, lowered the surface tension of adhering particles of dirt, and so helped the cleaning process.

PLASTER

The terms plaster, mortar and cement are generally much abused by archaeologists and although the identification of these materials in the field is not particularly difficult, it is seldom undertaken. Before the introduction of cements, the basic material for consolidating and surfacing walls might be one of three things; mud or clay, lime plaster or gypsum plaster. *Lime plaster* was obtained by calcining more or less pure lime, so converting the calcium carbonate to calcium oxide, or *quicklime*. This was then mixed with water to provide calcium hydroxide, or *slaked lime*, which set partly by the evaporation of the excess water, and partly by the slow conversion of the calcium hydroxide to calcium carbonate by reaction with the carbon dioxide in the atmosphere. Lime plaster alone has very little strength and it is not uncommon to find either fibrous plant materials or coarse animal hairs mixed in with it to give it greater strength. *Lime mortar*, on the other hand, was made by adding sand to the lime before slaking, the end-product thus being a sand concreted by slaked lime or calcium carbonate. *Gypsum plaster* was made by calcining hydrated calcium sulphate, or gypsum, to drive off some of the water of chemical combination. The anhydrous form, *plaster of Paris*, was then mixed with water, and this set by reconversion to the hydrated form. The time required for setting is far less for gypsum plaster than for lime plaster. In some regions sand was mixed with plaster of Paris to provide a gypsum mortar.

Both these materials—lime and gypsum plasters—were prepared from more or less pure minerals, although under primitive conditions one must expect to find a fairly high proportion of extraneous matter, especially clay minerals, in the final product. Unfortunately, however, in many areas the naturally occurring clays may contain quite a considerable contamination of either lime or gypsum, and unless testing is carried out with considerable care, simple clay or mud 'plasters' may be falsely recorded as being of lime or gypsum. Furthermore, a gypsum plaster may contain an appreciable quantity of lime as an impurity, and if the only test carried out in the field is the application of a drop of dilute acid (p. 193), the impression may easily be gained that one has a lime plaster. In effect, it is essential to carry out a semi-quantitative examination by digesting all the calcium salts in a small sample in a surplus of nitric acid, followed by assessing the ratio of the insoluble residue of clay to the size of the initial sample. A high ratio of clay would suggest that one is dealing with a calcareous mud or clay 'plaster'; a low clay ratio would indicate the presence of a true plaster. It is also worth remembering that early lime and gypsum plasters were prepared in rather crude kilns and that a certain admixture of charcoal was unavoidable. Small flecks of carbon are thus a common feature of most early plasters.

In order to give ornamental plaster and fine facing plaster additional strength, adhesive materials such as size or yolk of egg were sometimes added, so that in effect the plaster work was a type of gesso (p. 121). Over the years a number of very complex chemical changes take place within this type of plaster, with the result that an exceptionally hard and durable material is formed.

Cements are chemically more complex than plasters. In their preparation both lime and clay are calcined together, either as a deliberate mixture or as a naturally occurring rock, cement stone, but the end-product would be a mixture of different aluminates and silicates of calcium. On adding water, these set by the hydration of the silicates, followed in time by other complex changes. Apart from the fact that cements are far harder than plasters, the silicates are not readily soluble in dilute acids.

SALT

Common salt, apart from its use as a preservative and flavouring for foods, was required as a raw material in many processes (p. 49). In a small number of regions salt could be deep mined, but they were very limited, and one must conclude that much of the salt used in antiquity was obtained by the evaporation of sea water. In warm climatic regions this obviously presented no problem, a shallow tank being the only equipment required; but in more temperate areas other means had to be found to recover the salt. Broadly speaking, one of two expedients might be followed. In the one, brine was heated in shallow vessels; in the other it was sprinkled on to a heated surface. The first of these methods is essentially a domestic one and since it could have been carried out in any cooking-pot there is no way of saying when or where it was done in antiquity. The second method is rather more sophisticated and is suggestive of specialization. A wide variety of stone and clay structures—salinières—were used for this purpose, but most of them were essentially devices with a flat surface under which a fire could be kept burning and on to which the brine could be sprinkled.

SHELLS

The shells of many fresh- and salt-water molluscs were used in antiquity, chiefly for personal adornment, and the recovery of shells in regions with an environment completely alien to the living mollusc has often thrown interesting light on the trade or movements of early communities. It must be confessed, however, that the working of shell, perhaps because of its normally fragile nature, is seldom of great interest. Frequently little more was done than drilling a hole to allow the shell to be threaded. Large shells, such as the chank (*Xancus pyrum*), were sometimes sawn into segments to provide bangles, while the oyster and similar large flat shells provided mother-of-pearl, often used for making buttons or for wood inlay. Perhaps the most elaborate technique for the working of shell was the cutting of false cameos from variegated species, but on the whole the means employed were only those used in stone-working, and no tools appear to have been developed specifically for dealing with this material. Of the egg-shells of birds only those of the ostrich were sufficiently strong to be of any use, and the material was commonly used for making beads.

The identification of the species of mollusc from the shell is a matter for the specialist, but shell fragments may be too small or too decayed to permit any such identification. Indeed, when badly decayed, it is often difficult to distinguish between shell and bone without examination under the microscope.

AMBER

Amber is included in this section only because, being a fossilized tree resin, it is variously described as a mineral or as a resin. The material shares with many other non-conductors of electricity the property of becoming charged with static electricity by rubbing against wool, fur or similar materials. In this charged state it will attract small, light particles to it, and to the primitive mind this may have seemed a magical property. Although amber was traded over wide areas—it has often been found far from any possible source—it is a difficult material to allocate to one particular deposit since even within a fairly small region the chemical composition of different samples of amber is apt to vary considerably. True amber, however, is largely derived from the resin of the now extinct species of pine, *Pinus succinifera*, and contains a small proportion of succinic acid, one of the fermentation products of higher sugars. Some amber deposits appear to contain a higher proportion of succinic acid than others, and it is chiefly through the proportion of this acid that ambers have been allocated to different sources. Some amber-like fossil resins contain little or no succinic acid, for example the fossil damar of the East Indies, but without chemical examination it would seem to be impossible to attribute amber and amber-like materials to their source.

Most amber artifacts are rather small and the material was used chiefly for the making of beads and similar objects, although larger pieces are known from periods as remote as the European palaeolithic. In its working the techniques were precisely those used to shape the softer stones.

PART II:

THE EXAMINATION OF ARTIFACTS

Chapter Sixteen

GENERAL PRINCIPLES

SYNOPSIS

General: Qualitative and quantitative limitations · Sample size · Corrosion and decay · Experience.   *Physical Examination:* Colour · Hardness · Specific gravity · Infra-red · X-ray · Microscopic examination.   *Chemical Examination:* Specific tests · Qualitative analyses · Quantitative analyses · Spectrometry · X-ray diffraction.

THE FOLLOWING CHAPTERS deal briefly with the examination of artifacts with the aim of determining their composition and the methods used in their making. This work must often be carried out by scientists with specialist training in particular techniques, and while a detailed account of their methods cannot be given here an attempt will be made to show the purposes for which various techniques of examination can, and cannot, be profitably used. Every method of examination has, in fact, its own limitations: often one analytical method must be employed to examine one group of phenomena, and a second quite distinct method to examine other aspects of the same artifact. Various analytical methods, their limitations and uses will be discussed later.

It is important to understand, however, why in his final report a scientist, after carrying out a detailed examination, may be unable to provide a simple unqualified statement. To begin with there are the known qualitative limitations of the methods themselves. To give a simple example, fibres from a piece of fabric may be identified as being of bast. While the cells may be of a size which precludes the possibility of the fibres being derived from many species of plant, one may be able to do no more than attribute the fibres to a wide range of possible species all of which have bast cells of much the same size and characteristics as the sample. On the other hand it may be possible to narrow the field to three possible species, only one of which is indigenous to the region from which the sample came. It is clearly probable that the fibres were derived from the indigenous species; it is equally clear that the qualitative limitations of the method are such that one can only demonstrate that any one of three species of plant has provided the fibre. A statement to the effect that the fibre was probably derived from the indigenous plant is a conjecture, and although perfectly legitimate as such, must never be treated as a statement of fact.

Whenever an analysis aims at measuring the relative proportions of the constituents of an object, it must be remembered that most methods used have their own quantitative limitations. This is true not only of all forms of chemical analysis (below) but also of measurements of specific gravity and indeed any method that relies upon inference rather than upon a direct count. Because of the cumulative effect of a number of very minor experimental variations, few measurements other than direct counts can in fact be absolute. Thus, in counting the number of threads in the warp of a textile, there should be no experimental error; but in determining the specific gravity of an alloy two weighings must be made. Using the normal laboratory balance neither weighing will be precise, and the cumulative effect of both errors in weighing will provide a specific gravity that only approximates to that of the object. For most purposes this approximate figure will suffice, provided that one knows how great are the likely experimental variations. The likely variations can, of course, be determined by making repeated measurements of the same sample. Let us say that in the analysis of an alloy containing tin repeated measurements of the same sample gave values ranging from 7·8 % to 8·2 % of tin. Clearly, for the whole sample the experimental variation will not allow an estimate of tin more precisely than within 0·4 %. Using the same method of analysis an alloy may have a measured tin content of 6·1 %, whereas in fact the actual tin content may lie anywhere between 5·9 % and 6·3 %. For many purposes this may be a perfectly adequate measurement, but when comparing a series of analyses it is not possible, for example, to take one specific percentage of tin as a line of division between one group of alloys and another. In this case, were such a division to be made, two figures at an interval of at least 0·4 % would need to be stated, below and above which measured percentages of tin must fall. In most analytical reports the experimental error to which the results are subject is stated and during interpretation must be taken into account.

Apart from methodological limitations, however, the size and condition of the sample must be taken into consideration. It is axiomatic in all analytical work that a sample must be of a size sufficiently large to be representative of the whole. Again, to use a simple example, one fibre removed from a thread in a piece of fabric may be shown to be of sheep's wool. This, however, does not mean that the whole cloth is made of wool, for the sample—a single thread—is far and away too small. Further examination may show pure sheep's wool only in the weft, and a mixture of wool and camel-hair in the warp. Only when warp and weft have been examined in sufficient quantity can one show the composition of the fabric. The same principles apply when sampling for chemical analysis.

Few ancient objects are of identical chemical composition throughout and it may be essential to take a large sample, or number of smaller samples, before an accurate picture of the composition of an artifact may be drawn. Unfortunately, few archaeologists seem to have grasped this principle, many actually believing that the smaller the sample so much the better, since less damage is thereby done to the artifact! There is, of course, no doubt that using modern equipment an accurate analysis can be made of very small samples indeed, but it is equally true that by over-emphasis on minimizing the damage done to an artifact the size of sample may become so small that it is no longer representative of the whole artifact, so that the analysis itself no longer reflects the true composition of the object. Where there is any doubt whether the sampling method is representative or not, a number of samples may be taken from different parts of an artifact, either randomly or selectively, and the results of the examinations compared. If there is any significant difference between the various analyses, then it is clear that too small a sample is being used or that the composition of the object is not uniform, and larger samples must be taken to determine which is the case. This applies, of course, to all forms of examination and not only to sampling for chemical analysis. When it comes to excavation most archaeologists are, in fact, well aware of this principle. Any excavator would be deeply and rightly offended were he asked to interpret the whole of a large and complex habitation site on the basis of a single small cutting made at its periphery, but far too often when a scientific examination is called for he is apt to make the proviso that the artifact must not be noticeably damaged. In the face of such illogicality the scientist cannot be blamed if he gives up in despair.

The corrosion or decay of an object may be so far advanced that many forms of examination are impossible, or may be severely limited. That an object has deteriorated to a point where examination becomes exceptionally difficult is not always immediately apparent. A small fragment of cloth adhering to an iron object may, for example, have become largely mineralized, the original organic materials having been replaced by compounds of iron. To the naked eye there may seem little wrong with the fabric, but at the same time, because the fibres cannot be separated, it may be impossible to identify them. The corrosion of metal objects may, equally, have gone so far that all the original metal has become mineralized, although outwardly the object may seem to be tolerably sound. Under these circumstances, of course, a chemical analysis would be pointless save to provide a very rough idea of the nature of the original alloy. Even, however, where decay has not gone to these extremes the micro-structure of an object may be so badly damaged that identification of the precise nature of the material is impossible. This is particularly true of organic materials and under these circumstances the archaeologist must accept identification only within broad categories.

In the overall examination of artifacts there is no substitute for experience. Familiarity with techniques and materials can only be gained by studying a wide range of objects, and by learning what is and what is not significant. It is perfectly understandable that many archaeologists, art historians and ethnographers, when given an artifact to examine, will begin by noting morphological and stylistic details, and from there will go on to make mental comparisons between the object and others of the same class known to them. Necessary as these observations are, while making stylistic comparisons it is unlikely that one is at the same time making technological observations. Experience of the kind required can, thus, only be attained by examining artifacts with the single purpose of deciding how and of what they were made, uninfluenced, at least at the time, by any other considerations. This does not deny the fact that some people have an almost uncanny gift for making perfectly correct observations about materials or techniques by the 'look' or 'feel' of things. Such an ability is usually completely subjective and those who have it are frequently incapable of putting into words the criteria on which their judgment is based; others may make perfectly pertinent observations about materials or techniques without realizing their physical implications. One archaeologist claimed, quite correctly, to be able to distinguish between two outwardly very similar types of pottery by crumbling them, one being more gritty than the other, without apparently realizing that one type was sand-filled and the other grog-filled. Accurate as these subjective observations may be, skill in making them cannot be communicated. The noting of relevant detail and its logical significance has the virtue that it can be understood and learnt by others.

First-hand experience in the working of materials may also help very considerably when it comes to examining artifacts from the point of view of methods of manufacture. Many crafts, such as metal-working, pottery-making or glass-working, can only with great difficulty be understood fully without practising them. Some raw materials have 'wills of their own'—characteristic properties which quite literally force those who are working them to take specific lines of action if they are to get reasonable results—which although they may be gathered from written sources are more easily grasped at first hand.

Physical Examination

The use of subjective terms to describe colours, hardness and specific gravity is notoriously variable and other means must be used to give precision and uniformity to such observations. Two observers may record the same green as 'olive' and as 'sage', the same red as 'light red' or as 'red-buff'. Differences of this kind can, to some extent, be overcome by making reference to some standard and widely used colour chart such as the Stanley Gibbons Colour Chart used by stamp-collectors. A colour chart of this kind, however, although eliminating differences of terminology still tells one very little about the colour itself. The *Munsell Colour Chart*, on the other hand, takes into account a number of factors which allow one to see what has determined the colour. These factors are the *hue*, the pure spectral colours present; the *value*, the concentration of the spectral colours; and the *chroma*, the degree of purity or absence of shade. The hue, value and chroma may all be expressed quantitatively by reference to the matching samples on the chart. The Munsell system is of particular value in the examination of pottery (p. 196) and should be used whenever colour differences are felt to be important.

Different observers also have conflicting ideas about hardness. The same ceramic body may be described as 'soft' and as 'moderately hard' by different people. In cases where hardness is of importance, therefore, a scale of hardness using standards for comparison must be used. For minerals and similar materials, such as glasses, the *Moh Scale* is generally sufficiently accurate. In this, specific minerals are numbered in order of hardness.

10 Diamond	5 Apatite
9 Corundum	4 Fluorspar
8 Topaz	3 Calcite
7 Quartz	2 Gypsum
6 Felspar	1 Talc

If one of the scale-minerals will scratch the material, then it is clearly softer than that mineral and *vice versa*.

For metals, however, the Moh Scale is not sufficiently precise and a different type of hardness test is used. A commonly applied test is that yielding a *Brinell Hardness* figure. In this a small hardened steel ball of selected diameter is forced for a standard time under a standard pressure into the surface of the metal, which is supported on a hard anvil, the diameter of the depression left in the face of the metal after the operation being measured with a micrometer. Obviously, the softer the metal, the greater the diameter of the depression. Some Moh and Brinell hardness numbers are given for the purpose of very rough comparison since the two methods measure, in fact, different properties.

Moh Number	Brinell Number	Moh Number	Brinell Number
8·0	627	6·0	302
7·5	555	5·5	248
7·0	444	5·0	192
6·5	375	4·5	149

There are many other methods of testing the hardness of metals, for example that giving a Vicker's Pyramid number (V.P.N.), but normally hardness is stated as a Brinell number.

The weight of a material relative to an equal volume of water, its *specific gravity*, can only be guessed within very broad limits. The method generally applied to measure specific gravity is to weigh the object on a balance in the normal way, and then to weigh it again suspended in water, for which purpose many balances are fitted with a specially designed arm. The original weight is divided by the weight difference to provide the specific gravity. This method can, obviously, be applied only to materials that are not porous and are not soluble in or adversely affected by water, although in the latter case some other fluid of known specific gravity may be used instead of water. Equally the materials must be homogeneous, there being no point, for example, in determining a 'specific gravity' for an object clearly made by joining parts of two distinct metals. The specific gravity of most pure substances in various physical conditions is known, so that its determination can often suggest identification of the material. Equally, in instances where the material of which an artifact is made is known, the determination of specific gravity will show whether the object is solid or hollow.

Infra-red and X-ray examination

Radiation of wavelengths lying beyond the visible spectrum can often be used to record details of structure and composition invisible to the naked eye. This is possible because radiation with a wave-length slightly longer than the red of visible light—infra-red—has the ability to pass through certain materials which are opaque to visible light, such as ebonite or leather, or more simply a layer of dirt, to be reflected by the relatively denser surface of the solid object beneath. For this purpose a photograph may be made using film specially prepared so as to be sensitive to infra-red rays. Alternatively one may use an infra-red viewer, a device developed during the war for penetrating fog although this gives lower contrast and poorer resolution than the film. The painted surface of pottery that has become obscured by a layer of calcareous matter or dirt may be studied in this way without running the risk of removing brush-marks or similar details by cleaning.

Infra-red radiation is normally employed to penetrate very thin films, and where examination is required in depth the radiation of very short wave-lengths, X-rays, are used. The heavier elements, such as silver and lead, absorb X-rays powerfully with the result that when X-rays pass through an object and impinge on a sensitized photographic plate areas in which these metals are present are less well exposed. When one examines a radiograph, therefore, one has to make allowances not only for the varying composition of the object but also for the varying thicknesses of the object itself, since a material less dense to X-rays in great thickness may give the same degree of absorption as a more dense material present only as a thin layer.

Another difficulty often encountered in interpreting radiographs lies in the fact that one is viewing a three-dimensional structure projected as a shadow on to a two-dimensional surface, all depths of the object normally contributing to the shadow. One thus has no indication from the radiograph at what depth in the object any feature may lie, while several features may cross one another within the material without any indication which are nearer to or which further from the face of the object. Difficulties of this nature can often be resolved by the simple expedient of making a further exposure at an oblique angle, when the relative change in position of two or more features will indicate their relationship within the object. For very complex structures, however, it may be advisable to make left and right oblique exposures and to study them simultaneously through a stereo-viewer.

Microscopic Examination

Probably the most useful single piece of equipment for the examination of artifacts is the low-magnification binocular microscope. A magnification up to 20 diameters allows a reasonable depth of focus and hence three-dimensional vision. It is almost impossible to list all the uses of this instrument. It is invaluable in the examination of every kind of surface marking, and without its aid it is often quite impossible to determine the true significance of tool marks. In the study of ceramics, however, it is quite essential. Mineral particles, barely visible to the naked eye, and seen only as distinct grains under a hand-lens may, with experience, be identified under the binocular microscope. Much past confusion could have been avoided by its use. Seemingly dissimilar ceramic bodies that might otherwise be classified as distinct wares, may be seen to be identical save in the degree or nature of firing they have undergone;

while on the other hand apparently identical bodies may be seen to be of completely different composition.

The use of higher powered microscopes normally demands some training in specialized techniques. Broadly speaking, in both biological and petrological work it is usual to prepare thin-sections of the material being examined, and to study these using transmitted light; while in

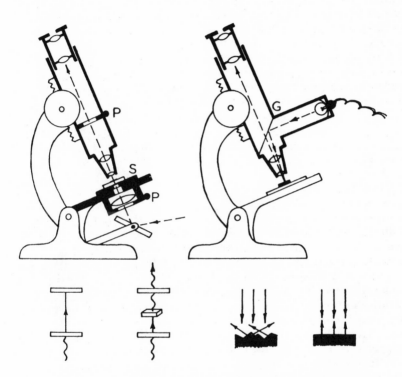

FIG. 40 'PETROLOGICAL' MICROSCOPE (*left*) WITH POLARIZERS (P) AND REVOLVING STAGE (S). *Below:* LIGHT POLARIZED BY THE LOWER POLAR-IZER CANNOT PASS THROUGH THE UPPER UNLESS ROTATED BY A CRYSTAL ON THE STAGE. 'METALLURGICAL' MICROSCOPE (*right*). THE LIGHT IS REFLECTED BY THE GLASS (G) DOWN ON TO THE OBJECT. *Below:* AN OBJECT WITH A BROKEN SURFACE SCATTERS THE LIGHT AND SO APPEARS DARK. A SMOOTH SURFACE REFLECTS THE LIGHT AND APPEARS LIGHT.

metallurgical examination the material is normally polished to give a flat mirror-like surface, which is then etched and studied by reflected light. This is not to say that biologists never use reflected light. It is often necessary, for example, to use reflected light when studying the bracts on the surface of hairs, especially where heavy pigmentation may obscure surface detail. The techniques used in preparing sections and the methods of adapting the high-powered microscope for particular purposes will be discussed in the appropriate chapters below.

CHEMICAL EXAMINATION

Specific Tests

For many purposes it is not essential to have a detailed chemical analysis of an object, but only to know its chemical nature within broad limits. Information of this kind can usually be gained by testing for a single chemical element or an association of elements called a radicle. Thus, a white material used as a pigment is likely to be either gypsum (calcium sulphate) or chalk (calcium carbonate). A drop of dilute acid applied to the material will show an effervescence due to the formation of carbon dioxide gas if it is chalk. This is a specific test for the presence of the carbonate radicle; the presence of calcium can be verified by a further test for that metal. There is a great number of such spot-tests, many of which can be carried out on minute samples observed under a microscope—microchemical tests. While these tests establish the presence or absence of elements or radicles, they do not show, save in a very broad sense, what proportion of the sample is made up of those elements or radicles, nor do they show, of course, what other elements may be present.

Qualitative Analyses

A more precise picture of the nature of a material may be gained by carrying out a more exhaustive series of such specific tests. A piece of white metal, for example, may be dissolved in a suitable acid, the solution being tested for the presence of silver, tin and copper. All three elements may be shown to be present, but the relative proportions of each remain unknown; the material might be basically a bronze containing a little silver, or it might be a silver alloy containing relatively small quantities of copper and tin. Furthermore, it is important to appreciate that such an analysis will show the presence only of those elements that are sought deliberately. In the presentation of his results the analyst will say what elements were in fact looked for, and whether or not they were found to be present. It must never be assumed that an unsought element was absent from the sample.

Quantitative Analyses

Quantitative analyses, which aim at determining the proportions of the elements present in the sample, may be carried out by 'wet' methods fundamentally similar to those described above, save that the weights of all the reagents used are estimated so that the quantity of the elements present, if great enough, can thereby be calculated. This is generally a very time-consuming business and where very small quantities are concerned may not be sufficiently accurate.

Today analyses are more commonly made by spectrometry. The basis of emission spectrometry lies in the fact that the atoms of all elements when sufficiently heated will emit light rays of specific wavelengths, and these narrow bands of light in the spectrum may be recorded photographically. Briefly, a sample of the material being examined is volatilized in an electric arc and the light emitted by the atoms in the vapour is diffracted in order to produce a series of lines on a photographic plate, each line representing a single wavelength characteristic of a certain element. The greater the amount of any element present, the greater will be the intensity of exposure on the negative of the lines character- istic of the element, and from the degree of exposure the relative quantity of the element can be calculated, for which purpose the images of the lines are normally examined with a densiometer. From this state- ment it might seem that the spectrograph is some kind of machine into which one feeds samples at one end and pulls out the answers from the other. This is only true of industrial practice in which very expensive equipment is set up to produce results from an enormous number of samples from a limited range of material. This is far from being the case when archaeological materials are being examined. In the first place, the apparatus has to be calibrated against samples of known composition and this calibration must be done over the whole range of the expected

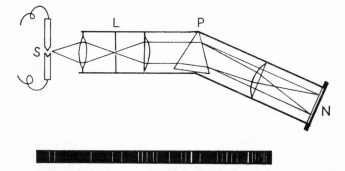

FIG. 41 SCHEMATIC DIAGRAM TO SHOW THE FUNCTION OF THE SPECTRO- SCOPE. LIGHT FROM THE SAMPLE (S) IS FOCUSED THROUGH THE SLIT (L) ON TO THE PRISM (P). THE SPECTRUM IS THEN FOCUSED ON TO THE PHOTOGRAPHIC PLATE (N). BELOW, THE SPECTROGRAPH OF COPPER.

magnitudes. This will provide a calibration curve for each element showing the relationship between the intensity of its characteristic line and the percentage of that element present in the sample. Furthermore, calibration must be done using a material very similar in composition to that about to be examined, since the presence of one particular element may often make the detection of another more difficult or may modify its calibration curve. Finally, experimental conditions must be kept constant; the preparation of the sample, the time of arcing, the photo- graphic plate, developer and so on, must not vary from those used during calibration.

In most cases the major part of any analysis will be made up of relatively few elements. Thus a glass may contain 25 % silicon, 40 % oxygen, 27 % sodium and 6 % calcium,* while a bronze might contain 86 % copper, 5 % tin and 7 % lead. In both instances it will be seen that 98 % of the sample is made up of three or four elements. These are the

* The analysis of a glass is, however, more commonly expressed as percentages of the oxides present (p. 43).

major constituents representing the 'ideal' glass or alloy. In both these cases, however, the remaining 2 % of the sample will be made up of a number of other elements, the *minor constituents*, the presence of which may be significant. They may have been present originally in the raw materials or they may have been introduced as the result of some process during manufacture. There is, of course, no fixed and unalterable percentage below which an element must be considered as a minor constituent. A large number of analyses of glass objects may show, for example, a variable but low percentage of lead in the majority, while a minority may contain a very much higher and rather less variable quantity of lead. The lead in the former cases might be looked upon as a minor constituent, probably unknowingly introduced, while that in the latter it might be regarded as a major constituent, perhaps deliberately added.

It is usual to estimate the quantities of elements in the sample present above 0·0001 % spectrographically. These are termed *traces*, but here again, there is no fixed point below which an element becomes quantitatively unmeasurable, although there may be theoretically definable limits for a selected method. Some elements are more readily detected and measured than others, while equipment and methods vary considerably in degree of sensitivity. Thus, before comparing analyses from different sources, it is essential to know the precision which can reasonably be expected from the method of analysis employed. From this point of view analyses presented in the form of a series of symbols denoting major and minor constituents, trace elements and elements not detected, without further comment, are not very illuminating.

Where a number of analyses is being compared it is often initially difficult to see what elements are, and what are not, significant. Furthermore it is frequently necessary to know if there is a definite relationship between one element and another. Both these problems of interpretation can be overcome by plotting the percentages of elements in pairs on graph paper. Thus, in a series of analyses both cobalt and manganese may be present in apparently widely different quantities. If a graph is prepared relating the percentage of one of these two elements to the percentage of the other the points may cluster about a line running obliquely across the graph showing that the two are, in fact, connected and that as the quantity of one increases, so does the quantity of the other. The points may, however, form two distinct groups on the graph suggesting perhaps two different sources of raw materials or two different formulations of the material. If the points lie scattered all over the graph, then there is clearly no connection between the two elements and the presence of one, or both, of them is of no significance in this context. Further plotting may show, however, that there is a definite relationship between cobalt and, say, nickel, while manganese, when plotted against each of the other elements in the analyses, may still fail to provide a pattern having any meaning.

Quantitative analyses may be provided by means other than emission spectrometry. In X-ray fluorescent spectrometry the material being examined is irradiated with X-rays, and as a result the atoms of each element emit a characteristic radiation of a particular wavelength. The emitted radiations are then separated by a diffraction crystal and can be detected and measured either by a photographic plate or by a geiger counter. The actual technique is, in principle, very similar to that of emission spectrometry save that one employs X-rays rather than light rays as a means of detecting those elements present. As might be expected, many of the same precautions apply, but it is important to appreciate that while in X-ray fluorescence spectrometry there is no need to remove a sample from the specimen, the results obtained will then be an analysis of the surface only. Thus the corroded surface of a metal object will give a result quite different from the metal itself, and it is thus often advisable to work with drillings from the uncorroded core of an object.

X-ray diffraction

X-ray diffraction analysis is of a nature completely different from that just described. In fact, this form of examination can be used only on crystalline materials—glass, for example, will not give a diffraction pattern—since it depends on the diffraction of an X-ray beam from the planes of atoms within a crystalline structure. For every crystalline

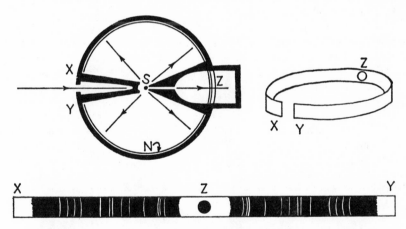

FIG. 42 THE X-RAY DIFFRACTION CAMERA. X-RAYS ARE FOCUSED ON TO THE SAMPLE (S) AND DIFFRACTED ON TO THE PHOTOGRAPHIC FILM (N). RIGHT, THE FILM REMOVED FROM THE CAMERA. BELOW, DIFFRACTION PATTERN OF ZINC.

substance the pattern of diffraction is characteristic and differs from that of other substances. Thus, while using normal spectrometric methods gypsum would give typical spectrum lines for all the elements present— calcium, sulphur, hydrogen and oxygen—using X-ray diffraction the material would be identified from a single diffraction pattern, and the variously hydrated forms of gypsum would yield slightly different patterns.

X-ray diffraction normally requires a very small sample, of a few milli-grams only, scratched from the object. The method is most useful when

EXAMINATION OF ARTIFACTS: SUMMARY OF METHODS USED

PHYSICAL EXAMINATION	MINERALS AND ROCKS	CERAMICS	VITREOUS MATERIALS	METALS	ORGANIC MATERIALS
1. Colour	* Other optical properties often more important.	* Munsell Chart. Determination of firing conditions.	* Can be misleading.	* Can be misleading, especially corrosion products.	
2. Hardness	‡ Mohs' Scale.		* Often misleading.	* Brinell.	
3. Specific Gravity	† Cannot be used with porous materials.			* Of limited use.	
4. Radiography		† Examination of structure.		† Examination of composite structures.	
5. Microscopy	‡ Powder and thin sections. Determination of minerals.	‡ Thin sections. Determination of minerals and structure.		‡ Metallography. Examination of grain structure.	‡ Often stained. Examination of cellular structures.
6. Other Methods	† Separation of heavy minerals.	† Refiring of sherds.			† Solubilities in various solvents.
CHEMICAL EXAMINATION					
1. Spot Tests	† Identification of some minerals.			† To establish presence of metals only.	For the examination of non-cellular materials a wide variety of analytical methods is used. Amongst these methods chromatography is particularly valuable.
2. 'Wet' Analysis	† Chiefly examination of ores.			† For single analyses.	
3. Spectrometry	† Seldom required save for ores.	† Examination of homogeneous bodies.	† To establish composition.	‡ To establish composition.	
4. X-ray Diffraction	† Examination of crystalline minerals.	† Examination of clay minerals.		† Examination of crystalline state.	
5. Other Methods			B-scatter eta-ray back		

* Methods of value only when other data are taken into consideration.
† Methods of limited value applicable only to specific cases.
‡ Methods applicable to most cases.

dealing with mixtures of crystalline substances—clay minerals, pigments, and so on—although it may be applied to other less obviously crystalline materials such as metals. As will be discussed later (p. 220), an alloy that contains a fixed proportion of elements may exist as different distinct crystalline structures. By an adaptation of the normal X-ray diffraction equipment, using the whole sample rather than a powder sample, it is possible to show which crystalline structure is present.

X-ray diffraction patterns may also be used semi-quantitatively. Much as the strength of spectral lines may be measured using a photometer, so may the intensity of the X-ray diffraction patterns be used to establish the approximate proportions of the crystalline materials present, but it must be appreciated that the method as yet lacks the precision possible with spectrometry.

Chapter Seventeen

EXAMINATION OF STONE ARTIFACTS

SYNOPSIS

Minerals · Rocks · Colour · Streak · Hardness · Specific gravity · Crystal shape · Microscopy · Thin-sections · Refractive index · Cleavage · Pleochroism · Isotropism · Twinning · Chemical analyses · X-ray diffraction · Sources of rocks and minerals.

SO MUCH ARCHAEOLOGICAL method depends upon principles that are shared with geological studies that as a rule archaeologists are more familiar with geological methods of examination and interpretation than they are with other techniques to be discussed in later chapters. For this reason, only a brief resumé will be given here, chiefly to illustrate the difficulties of applying established mineralogical and petrological methods of study to archaeological materials.

Minerals, although often of highly complex molecular structure, are more or less pure chemical compounds, and thus each mineral contains a number of chemical elements in fixed, or within limited, proportions. Furthermore, the majority of minerals are crystalline: that is to say, the atoms of the chemical elements present are arranged in an orderly manner to form a three-dimensional lattice in which there is a regular repetition of structural units throughout the material (Fig. 4). This orderliness at the molecular level is reflected in the typical geometric shapes of the crystals, seen either by the naked eye or under the microscope. As a corollary of a lattice structure, however, there exist a number of planes throughout the crystal at which radiations, such as visible light and X-rays, may become modified. It is very largely due to these two phenomena—crystal shape and the modifying effects of crystalline materials on different types of radiation—that minerals are identified.

Rocks are aggregates of mineral particles, frequently of several different kinds. In some cases the particles are large enough to be identified with ease: the quartz, felspar and mica grains in a granite, for example, seldom require much magnification to be seen clearly. By contrast the grains of the typical clay minerals are usually so small that they cannot be resolved even under the highest magnification of the optical microscope. The classification of a rock, however, depends not only upon being able to identify the minerals present, but also upon the sizes and shapes of the particles, and their relationship to one another. The same factors—specifically, the minerals present, the sizes of the particles, and the degree of cohesion between them—give each rock its own particular working properties. Thus, before the methods employed to shape a rock can be usefully discussed it is essential to define at least its main characteristics, if not to identify it exactly.

Colour

Two precautions are particularly important when making observations about the colour of minerals in artifacts. In many cases it will be found that conditions of burial have caused surface alterations, such as weathering and staining. Wherever possible, therefore, the colour of minerals should be observed from fresh breaks. Many minerals have a fairly narrow colour range to which the majority of specimens will belong, but due to small differences in chemical composition, many minerals can also show very wide variations of colour. Olivine, for example, is typically a drab green, but white, yellow, brown and black olivines are also found. Bearing in mind that abnormally coloured materials are precisely those that are most likely to have attracted early man, at least for decorative purposes, one must expect to come across a high proportion of unusually coloured minerals amongst his artifacts. Apart from noting the colour of minerals it is always advisable to record the colour of a *streak* made either by scratching the surface of the mineral or by rubbing it against a piece of unglazed porcelain. In the case of olivine, just mentioned, the streak will be white no matter what colour the mineral is in the mass. The streak colour can thus often be a useful corrective to false impressions gained by noting colour only.* Other optical properties may be as important, or even more important than colour. The iridescence of mica and the metallic lustre of pyrites or galena are phenomena of far greater value in their identification than their colours.

Hardness

The hardness of a mineral is normally determined by reference to the Mohs' Scale (p. 179). As in the case of colour observation, in applying the Moh tests one must be certain that the surface of the object has not undergone any change that would give a lower hardness reading than would a fresh break; and ideally, of course, the test should be carried out on a fresh break. Apart from helping the identification of the material, the Moh hardness is of great importance when discussing working methods, especially those involving the use of abrasives or cutting tools (p. 105). As a general rule it may be said that since the majority of naturally occurring sands contain quartz, minerals with a hardness of 7·0 or less could have been abraded with sand, but for those that are harder some other abrasive must have been used. Similarly, work-hardened bronze has a Moh hardness of about 4·0, while a low carbon steel when quenched has a Moh hardness in the region of 7·0. Minerals harder than these metals, if engraved at all, must have been worked with a yet harder mineral in antiquity.†

---

* It would be of great help if the streak colour of stone artifacts were given in catalogues and museum accession-books, especially where the minerals have not been identified with certainty.

† Moh hardness, like streak colour, should ideally be given when recording stone artifacts of unidentified rocks.

Specific Gravity

Owing to their somewhat variable chemical composition, and because the same minerals may be laid down under different geological conditions, the specific gravity of any single mineral tends to have a fairly wide range. As a general rule, therefore, the specific gravity of an artifact is only useful as a rough guide to its composition. Thus, many ores, such as galena and tinstone, have an appreciably higher specific gravity than the more common minerals, and may be recognized on this basis. Attempts to distinguish minerals on the criteria of specific gravity alone are, however, usually unsatisfactory. The two common jadestones (p. 98), nephrite and jadeite, have ranges of specific gravity of the order 2·9-3·2 and 3·3-3·35, respectively. Clearly, a jade object with a specific gravity of 2·9 is likely to be of nephrite, and one with a specific gravity of 3·35 is equally probably of jadeite; but when allowance has been made for probable error (p. 176) one cannot be altogether certain that a jade object with an estimated specific gravity of 3·2 is of nephrite, for the figure is too close to the lowest possibility for jadeite. In order to use specific gravities in this way exceptionally accurate determinations must be made (p. 208).

The fact that some minerals have unusually high specific gravities can be put to use when examining rocks of sedimentary origin. If, for example, a piece of sandstone is pulverized the heavier minerals may be separated from the lighter ones by flotation in a dense fluid such as bromoform (S.G. 2·9) in which the lighter particles will float and the heavier sink to the bottom. This allows one to make a concentration of the heavier minerals, and an examination of these may in turn permit one to suggest a source of origin of the rock.

Crystal Shape

Although most minerals are crystalline it is often very difficult to observe the shapes of the crystals in artifacts for many reasons other than that of smallness of size. The effect of surface weathering has already been mentioned, but where an artifact has been thoroughly polished not a single crystal face may be left exposed. In normal petrological practice this would present no problem since the hand-specimen could be broken time and time again to observe crystal shape. This is very seldom the case with archaeological materials, and far too often the mineralogist has to work at the best with a single small fracture in which a particular mineral may be present as a few crystals only. This may severely limit the possibility of identification.

Microscopy

Much may be learnt about the coarser-grained rocks by examination under the binocular microscope, but for finer-grained and complex materials it is always advisable to prepare a *thin-section*. Usually a thin slice is cut from the artifact, sufficiently large to be a representative sample (p. 176). One face of this slice is polished with progressively finer grades of abrasive until perfectly flat and mirror-smooth. The polished face is then stuck to a glass slide with a suitable adhesive, and the other

face is gradually abraded away and polished until the slice is about
20/1,000 mm. thick (20 μ). Where, for one reason or another, a slice may
not be taken it is sometimes possible to work from surface scrapings.
These may be mounted in a block of some suitable plastic material which
is then treated as though it were a slice. The method is very seldom satisfactory and should be avoided whenever possible. The sample is usually
too small to be representative; the relationship between adjacent mineral
particles has of necessity been destroyed; and very often the scrapings
include materials acquired during burial or, due to surface weathering,
minerals present in the rock are totally absent or altered to a point
where they can no longer be identified.

Seen under the microscope by ordinary transmitted light most
common minerals are translucent, but the common ores are not and thus
appear black. A few of the latter, however, show characteristic colour

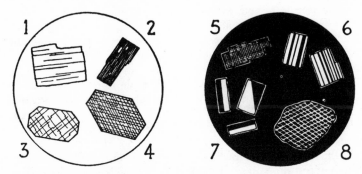

FIG. 43   MINERALS IN THIN SECTION. MUSCOVITE (1), BIOTITE (2),
AUGITE (3) AND HORNBLENDE (4) IN ORDINARY LIGHT SHOWING TYPICAL
CLEAVAGE. MICROLINE (5), PLAGIOCLASE (6), ORTHOCLASE (7) AND
CALCITE (8) UNDER CROSSED NICOLS SHOWING CHARACTERISTIC TWIN-
NING.

under reflected light, as for example haematite; but as a rule, ores are
better examined by chemical means. Of the translucent minerals, most
are colourless by ordinary light, but a few are characteristically coloured.
Some minerals have a *refractive index* similar to that of the glass slide and
mounting medium with the result that they will appear to merge with
the media: others with refractive indices different from the glass will
appear to stand out in relief.

Crystal shapes can be determined by ordinary light only if there are
sufficient crystals present in the section. Since the section may have cut
through a crystal in any plane, it is not always, however, an easy matter
to determine crystal shapes when a mineral is poorly represented. In
nearly all crystalline materials there exist planes of weakness along
which the crystal is liable to cleave. Some minerals are more prone to
cleavage than others, the *cleavage planes* being at characteristic angles to
the crystal faces or, where there is more than a single cleavage plane, at
characteristic angles to one another. In thin section the lines of cleavage
appear as striae crossing the crystals.

Other optical properties of minerals can be observed by modifying the nature of the light passing through the microscope. If a polarizing prism or a piece of polaroid glass is placed between the source of light and the stage on which the thin section is set, the light passing through the microscope will vibrate only in a single vertical plane. Some minerals viewed in polarized light will show a diagnostic colour, or *pleochroism*, changing as the stage is rotated.

If a second polarizer is placed between the eye and the stage, orientated at right angles to the first—an optical arrangement known as '*crossed nicols*'—no light will be seen, since the upper polarizer will not allow the passage of light vibrating in a different plane from that in which it is itself polarized. A glass slide placed on the stage will not alter this effect, for glass, being non-crystalline, will have no modifying effect on the polarized light. A number of naturally occurring minerals, notably glasses, opals and spinels, behave optically in the same manner, and are said to be *isotropic*, and will thus always appear as dark, or extinct, areas under crossed nicols. Most crystalline minerals, however, will under certain orientations so rotate the beam of light that it may be seen through the eye-piece, while at other orientations the light will not be refracted in the plane of the upper polarizer, and the minerals will become extinct. Thus, by rotating the stage, isotropic minerals will remain extinct throughout while anisotropic minerals will become alternatively luminous and extinct. Some anistropic minerals, however, appear to be made up of parallel bands which alternately become luminous and extinct as the stage is rotated. This phenomenon, known as *twinning*, is due to a crystalline structure formed as a series of mirror images on either side of a number of common planes, and is highly characteristic of some minerals, such as the felspars.

The identification of the actual minerals is, of course, only one aspect of microscopic examination, for the rock itself must be classified. Where the minerals are few, and clearly defined, this is normally a simple matter. In many rocks, however, this is not the case, and this is unfortunately true of many of the tough, fine-grained rocks that early man found so suitable for the making of axes and other stone tools. Not only may the minerals be difficult to identify with certainty, but their arrangement may be highly complex. Thus, the distinction between one rock and another may lie only in a different arrangement of the same minerals; or aggregates in which the arrangement is very similar may have slightly different mineral contents. In normal petrological work repeated sections may be made in order to sort out such difficulties of classification, but with archaeological materials this is normally impossible, and one can hope only that the single section will be sufficiently informative to allow one to classify the rock.

Apart from the mineral content and its arrangement, some rocks have other characteristic features, for example inclusions of foraminifera, which may allow one to trace the material to a particular source.

Chemical Analyses

A few spot tests are particularly valuable by way of making a preliminary examination of rocks. A great deal of past confusion could have been avoided had the tests for carbonate and sulphate radicles been carried out on materials variously described as marble, alabaster, calcite, limestone and gypsum. These cases apart, however, spot tests are really only of use when making a preliminary examination of ores.

It is seldom worth while making a complete chemical analysis—qualitative or quantitative—of rocks, save in the case of ores. These are, of course, a special case. One's interest in ores lies not only in their source, but also in the metals produced from them. Since individual ore deposits may have characteristic impurities, it is advisable to make a complete quantitative analysis either by 'wet' or by spectrographic means. The interpretation of this kind of analysis is considered later (p. 221).

X-ray Diffraction

Every crystalline mineral will give a distinctive diffraction pattern, and it would thus seem that X-ray diffraction is a method ideally suitable to the examination of antiquities that may not be sampled in quantity. In many cases this is certainly so, but the limitations already mentioned —sample size, weathering of the surface—must be kept in mind. Furthermore, the diffraction pattern cannot show the relationship between one mineral and another, but can only show what minerals are present. X-ray diffraction may thus be looked upon as a very valuable tool, but it cannot be used entirely as an alternative to thin-sectioning.

Sources of Rocks and Minerals

It is one thing to make an adequate description of a mineral or rock; it is quite a different matter to be able to show exactly whence it came. It is unreasonable to suppose that because a specimen has been identified, therefore the source can be pin-pointed. In the first place, many rocks are so ubiquitous and so similar in composition that the possible sources are innumerable. This is true of many flints and sandstones. As a general rule different deposits of flint show a remarkably uniform composition, although there are exceptions, and it seems unlikely that a satisfactory method of distinguishing between flints from the majority of sources can ever be hoped for. The same is true of many sandstones, particularly quartz sandstones; for although the heavy mineral content may be quite distinctive of a particular deposit, the deposit itself may be so widespread that the possibility of giving a precise source is out of the question.

On the other hand the examination of an artifact may show that the rock is very distinctive, and it may yet be impossible to show its origin. This may be because the geology of the region is inadequately understood, through a lack of detailed field survey. In other cases it may be possible to suggest the type of formation from which a rock came, and yet one may be unable to match the material in the field. This may be simply because the initial deposit was extremely small and has been worked out, or destroyed in later years; or the deposit may have become covered by solifluction, peat growth or forest, or even submerged under a lake or the sea. In cases of this kind it may, nevertheless, be possible to describe a circle of fairly small radius from within which the material must have come, and this alone may often be sufficiently precise to be of value.

Chapter Eighteen

EXAMINATION OF POTTERY AND GLASSES

SYNOPSIS

Pottery: Colour · Hardness · Microscopy · Thin-sections · Radiography · Re-firing · Chemical analyses · Spectrometry · X-ray diffraction. *Glasses:* Colour, Hardness and Specific Gravity · Radiography · Microscopy · Stones · Chemical analyses · Beta-ray back-scatter. *Moulds, Crucibles and Slags.*

POTTERY

THE EXAMINATION OF pottery, with the aim of discovering the methods employed in its manufacture, is far more difficult than is sometimes supposed, and all too often it may be impossible to put forward sufficient evidence to allow any positive statement. Indeed outward appearances may be most misleading, and the acceptance of any single group of phenomena as indicative of a method of forming, without further study, may lead to totally false assumptions. Thus coil or ring-built pottery quite frequently cracks or fractures along the join of successive rings, but not inevitably, and the absence of any signs of such fractures cannot be taken as proof that the pottery was built by some other method. Similarly, the presence of rilling lines, far from being clear-cut evidence that pottery was wheel thrown, may not indicate that it was made on any form of wheel. The same effect can be produced by rotating pottery on a mat while finishing, or even on a flat surface liberally coated with slurry.

Even more dangerous is the type or argument often put forward by those working in regions that are, today, somewhat backward, and in which traditional hand-made pottery is still being produced. The assumption is not uncommonly made that, because the pottery of today and of antiquity bear strong resemblances, therefore the methods of today's potters are identical to those of antiquity. Probable as it may seem, this need not be the case, and in fact such a continuum of tradition can be argued only after the pottery of antiquity has been studied alone and on its own internal evidence has shown this to be the case. It is, after all, the business of archaeology to show that a continuum of this kind exists, and not uncritically to accept the possibility as a fact.

It is perhaps inevitable that certain characteristic methods of decoration should be given descriptive terms that bear little or no relationship to the actual methods used in antiquity. Thus, an impressed decoration may appear to have been made with something resembling a short length of barbed-wire, and this observation may in turn give rise to 'barbed-wire decoration' as a term. This can hardly be said to be misleading since no one supposes the use of barbed-wire in antiquity, although when the term is used to describe wares there is always the danger that the same type of decoration may have been applied to different bodies. Not all descriptive terms are, however, quite so harmless. A surface may have the black, lustrous look of graphite and hence be called 'graphitic'. In fact such a surface is far more likely to be due to the presence of magnetite formed under reducing conditions, but once the term 'graphitic' has been used and become accepted it may be very difficult for the student to discover, especially from literary sources, whether the actual use of graphite for surfacing is meant, or whether the term is, after all, purely descriptive.

Within broad limits the surface treatments given to pottery are not difficult to distinguish. The matt surface of an unaltered slip and the high shine of a burnish can hardly be confused, but within each major group of surface treatments the finer distinctions are less easily made. A wet-hand finish, an all-over slip applied by painting, and a slip applied by dipping may appear identical, although technologically speaking they are poles apart. There are, of course, many small details for which to look. An even slip and the presence of finger marks near the base of the pot would suggest dipping; while brush or wiping marks would indicate painting; but unless the sample is adequately large these criteria alone may not be adequate to allow anything but tentative conclusions to be drawn. The same kind of difficulty may be met with when examining burnished surfaces. In crudely burnished wares the individual burnishing strokes may be clearly visible, but when pottery has been burnished on a wheel, if the body is sufficiently fine, it may be quite impossible to distinguish the treatment from turning in which, of course, the surface also tends to become slightly burnished. Here, again, is a fundamental technological difference that cannot be easily demonstrated from the material itself. The problem may be even more difficult to resolve when a pigment has been applied to the surface followed by burnishing. Apart from identifying the pigment, one may want to know whether it was applied dry; as a wet-hand process; painted on as a water suspension; painted on as a coloured slip; or applied by dipping. Depending on how meticulously the work was done, it may be quite impossible to distinguish between any of these processes by visual inspection, and it may be necessary to resort to a thin section (p. 198) to provide the answer.

Colour

Observations about the colour of pottery can be most misleading if not made with great caution. The same red clay may be fired to an enormous variety of colours—black, greys, browns and reds—depending upon the treatment the clay has been given during preparation and manufacture, and upon the conditions during firing. Many different colours are often to be seen on the same pot, although it may be of fairly homogeneous composition, while pots fired in different parts of the same kiln, although of identical body, may be of totally different colours. Thus identical vessels fired in the same kiln might have a red body with a pale cream slip, or a black body with a white slip, depending on the local oxidizing or reducing conditions in the kiln. Under these circumstances there is, of course, no possible justification for classifying the two kinds of pottery as distinct wares. Before differently coloured vessels of identical composition and technique of manufacture can be accepted as distinct wares, it is essential first to demonstrate that the different colours were deliberately and not accidentally achieved. In this case, were one type of design found only on the red-and-cream vessels, and a different type of decoration found only on the black-and-white, then the distinction might be considered as valid, although it should be noted that the potters of antiquity, if aware of the peculiarities of their kilns, could still have produced both wares at the same firing.

Colour readings using the Munsell Chart are, perhaps, most useful when considering the variation of firing conditions in a large sample of sherds of similar composition. In the case of terracotta wares, fired under more-or-less oxidizing conditions, it will generally be found that the reading for the 'chroma' will remain unaltered over a wide temperature range, the 'chroma' varying only when the clay minerals have broken down, usually at about 850°C. In the same way, variations in the 'value' reading normally reflect differences of free carbon content in the sherds, while differences in 'hue'—from predominantly yellow to predominantly red—usually indicate the degree to which limonite has been dehydrated to give haematite. Different clays will, of course, give very different readings, and the use of colour changes as a means of examining firing conditions can, therefore, only be used when it is known that all the sherds are of the same fabric. It is also generally impossible to make satisfactory readings from fractures or grossly unevenly coloured surfaces. A group of 108 sherds, for example, might give the following readings.

Value	No. sherds	Chroma	No. sherds	Hue Y/R	No. sherds
6	2	6	2	10	—
5	28	5	5	7·5	3
4	37	4	101	5	25
3	41	3	—	2·5	80

From these readings it is clear that the majority of the sherds have been fired under similar conditions, although the variable 'value' readings would suggest rather different quantities of carbon present, and hence different degrees of oxidation. That only seven sherds have a high 'chroma' reading would suggest that they are abnormal, and that most of the pottery was fired to a rather low temperature; whilst the fact that only three sherds have a high yellow/red 'hue' equally indicates that the pottery was not normally underfired.

Where there is any doubt about the meaning of colour readings, it is often possible to check the effects of different firing conditions on the sample by re-firing (p. 200) under controlled conditions.

Hardness

Although it is common to speak about 'hard-fired' and 'soft-fired' wares, these terms appear usually to refer not to hardness but to strength.

It is doubtful whether hardness in this sense is a useful criterion when examining pottery that has been buried, for under unfavourable conditions even the toughest pottery may become friable. This is especially true where the ground-water contains a high percentage of soluble salts, and where the conditions of burial have allowed the pottery to become alternately damp and dry; for the repeated solution and recrystallization of the soluble salts within the pottery has the physical effect of making it disintegrate. Unless, therefore, the conditions of burial have been studied from this point of view, observations about the strength of pottery can be most misleading.

Microscopy

The body composition of pottery and other clay objects can initially best be examined from fresh breaks. If the material has been carefully excavated these should not exist, and it may be necessary to break a few sherds for this purpose. Old fractures may be most misleading when examined, for coarse inclusions, if not removed by weathering, easily become detached during cleaning, so giving the impression that the ware contains less filler than indeed it does. Apart from this, a thin film of dirt is often left over the face of the break and effectively prevents detailed study of the material. While it may be possible to determine the size, shape and nature of the larger particles with the naked eye or with a hand lens, for the smaller inclusions a binocular microscope is essential. The sizes and shapes of the particles should be noted, and their orientation, if any. It should also be possible at this stage to identify many of the minerals present. When dealing with finer wares this preliminary examination may be quite unrewarding, little of significance being observable; but when looking at coarser pottery it should already give one a very clear indication of the nature of the material.

A careful study of the orientation of the larger particles and lacunae, where the body is coarse enough to allow it, may be most informative. Generally, in wheel-thrown pottery particles and air spaces tend to become orientated with their long axes parallel to the plane of the wheel-head; in coil- or ring-built wares this orientation is far more haphazard; while in pottery that has been drawn up with the rib the orientation tends to be vertical to the base.

Where there is residual free carbon visible in the fracture it is also possible to make broad generalizations about the firing conditions. Under conditions of slow carbon burn-out, that is to say where the firing temperature was low and the flame somewhat sooty, the carbon will be diffused throughout the thickness of the sherd, becoming more intense at the middle; under conditions of rapid burn-out of short duration, as when a fire is allowed to flare up quickly and die down again quickly, the residual carbon may present a sharp line of demarcation at some little depth below the surface, and to the naked eye the burnt-out surface may even look deceptively like a slip. The rate at which carbon burns out depends, of course, not only on the nature of the firing conditions, but also on the porosity of the body, and due allowance must be made for this. It is, in fact, seldom possible to say more than that the burn-out of carbon has been rapid, slow or of medium rate, but this in itself can be

very valuable when other information about firing conditions is not to
be had.

Examination under the binocular microscope may also show whether
one is dealing with a naturally occurring clay or with a clay to which has
been added a filler. In the first case, although varying considerably in
size, the non-plastic inclusions should show the same variety of composition, and have the same physical shape, whether they are large or small.
Thus one may notice in a sherd that the smaller inclusions are all of
quartz, while the larger inclusions are of some other mineral. Under
these circumstances one would naturally infer that one is not dealing
with a naturally occurring clay, but with a body made by adding mineral
fillers to a clay that already contained grains of quartz. Equally, one may
observe in another sherd that the finer grains are all rounded, while the
larger grains are all angular, although both types may be of the same
mineral. Here again one would infer that the coarser material had been
added to a naturally sandy clay. Even, however, where the inclusions are
of the same mineral and of the same shape, there may be an appreciable
gap in particle size between the finer and the coarser grains, again suggesting the addition of a coarse filler to a fine sandy clay.

Thin-sections

The technique of preparing thin-sections of pottery is identical to that
used in petrological work (p. 190) save that in some instances it may be
necessary to impregnate the sherds with a plastic material to prevent
the pottery crumbling away during polishing. The examination of
thin-sections of pottery is, however, rather different from that of rocks
in that one can, apart from identifying the minerals present, also study
the structures of the pottery.

One's first concern on examining a thin-section is normally to define
the nature of the body, and to decide whether one is dealing with a
naturally occurring clay or with a composite body. To this end precisely
the same criteria are used as under binocular examination. The shapes
of the finer and coarser grains are compared as well as the mineral content, or a definite particle-size hiatus normally indicating a composite
body. Where grogs have been used these may be studied separately as
though they were a distinct body, but where vegetable fillers have been
used it will normally be found that they have burnt out, leaving lacunae,
and it is thus often impossible to determine their original nature.

Identification of the minerals present will sometimes allow attribution
of the material to a definite source. Thus, for example, if pottery
excavated from a loess region is found to contain large unweathered
grains of quartzite and felspar, one can be quite certain that the material
was not gathered in that region, and this in itself may be significant.
A more detailed examination of the mineral present may, of course,
allow one to attribute the material to a specific region, but this can only
be done in those areas in which the sedimentary petrology has been given
detailed study.

Since many clay minerals break down at about 850°C. to produce
spinels and glasses, in wares fired to this temperature, or above, the
clay material will become isotropic (p. 192), while at even higher

temperatures, of course, partial fusion may take place between the clay material and the particles, or between adjacent particles of filler. The change of clay minerals to isotropic materials is very useful when assessing the maximum temperature attained in the firing of terracotta wares, but the degree of fusion is useful only when the maturing temperature of the body is already known.

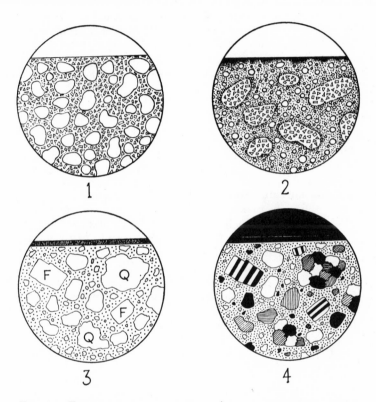

FIG. 44 THIN-SECTIONS OF POTTERY. A CLAY CONTAINING SMALL, WELL-SORTED, SHARP GRAINS FILLED WITH LARGER, WELL-SORTED, ROUNDED GRAINS (1). GROGS CONTAINING SMALL ANGULAR GRAINS IN A CLAY CONTAINING SMALL ROUNDED GRAINS (2), THE SURFACE HAVING A FINGER-APPLIED MINERAL COATING. SLIPPED POTTERY UNDER ORDINARY (3) AND CROSSED NICOL ILLUMINATION (4). UNDER CROSSED NICOLS THE QUARTZITE GRAINS (Q) SHOW DIFFERENT DEGREES OF BRIGHTNESS, AND THE FELSPARS (F) SHOW TWINNING. THE SLIPPED SURFACE HAS BECOME ISOTROPIC.

In highly ferruginous bodies it is often difficult under the binocular microscope to assess the quantity of carbon present in a clean fracture because of the iron colouring. In thin-section this is less difficult, and the distribution of carbon within the body can be seen more clearly. Equally, it is usually simpler to study the orientation of particles and lacunae in thin-section, it being possible to cut both vertical and horizontal sections from a sherd in order to compare orientations.

Thin-sections are exceptionally valuable when examining surfaces. A slip, unlike a wet-hand finish, will invariably show a distinct line of demarcation from the body, while a thin-section is virtually the only way of determining whether a single or multiple slip has been applied. Pigments added to the slip can, of course, be identified in thin-section.

Radiography

It is seldom necessary to use X-rays in the examination of pottery, although radiographs can be used to study the orientation of particles and lacunae in the body of pottery, and to examine joins. It must, however, be emphasized that not all joins made during manufacture will show up on a radiograph, just as they cannot always be detected in thin-section.

Re-firing Experiments

The re-firing of sherds may be carried out with the aim of learning more about initial firing conditions. The work is normally done in a thermostatically controlled electric or gas-fired muffle kiln into which must be fed organic matter, for example damp sawdust, whenever sooty or reducing conditions are required. The method is of most value when one wishes to establish the maximum temperature to which wares have been fired, or whether sherds which are seemingly dissimilar are in fact identical save in the nature of the firing they underwent. In the first case a group of sherds may be re-fired within, and at temperatures above, the probable range of the initial firing, a sherd being withdrawn from the kiln at regular temperature intervals and compared, after cooling, with the original material. Any sherds showing radical differences from the original, such as a change of colour, or shrinkage, will obviously have been fired at a higher temperature than initially, and thus the upper possible temperature limit can be established. Care must be taken, however, that the atmospheric conditions are identical to those of antiquity, and in fact this is often so restricting that, practically, the method can be used confidently only with wares that were initially completely oxidized.

The second type of re-firing experiment aims at deliberately altering the firing conditions from those initially used. Thus, it may be suspected that black pottery is a variant of a red ware, produced by firing under reducing conditions. Under these circumstances a sherd of the black ware can be re-fired under oxidizing conditions, and on cooling may be compared with the red.

In cases where the original clay source has been definitely established re-firing experiments can be carried out with the accompanying production of test sherds. Using fresh clay, test sherds may be made of the same thickness as the wares being studied, and these test sherds may be fired under known conditions, later being compared with the original wares. Depending upon what aspect of the wares is being studied, a series of test sherds may be fired at varying firing rates, maximum temperatures or under different atmospheric conditions as a means of establishing the actual conditions of firing in antiquity.

Chemical Analyses

Spot tests are used in the examination of ceramics chiefly to establish the nature of one of the fillers, but not for the study of the clay minerals. Thus, a white filler may be thought to be either lime or gypsum and a small sample may be removed and tested to determine if the filler is either of these materials. It is also often possible to show whether black particles are of carbon or of magnetite by soaking a small sherd in a suitable concentrated acid in which the iron oxide will dissolve but the carbon will not. Tests of this kind are, however, of very limited application and will not normally give an adequate picture of the nature of the whole body.

Analyses of ceramic materials carried out by 'wet' methods are difficult and excessively laborious, and while quantitative analyses can be provided by these means, spectrographic methods are on the whole more satisfactory.

Spectrometry

Normally, quantitative analyses of ceramic bodies are made by removing a suitable sample from a sherd, or the whole pot, with a fine drill. The sample is then ground to a very small particle size to ensure an even mixture of the various component minerals, and this powder is arced in the case of emission spectrometry, or irradiated in the case of X-ray fluorescent spectrometry. Clearly, sampling is of the utmost importance where this technique is being used since an unduly large proportion of any one mineral in the sample will give totally atypical results. For this reason it is probably not a satisfactory means of examining very coarse wares unless a large number of samples are taken from each sherd and the analyses compared for conformity of results. Fine wares, however, especially those produced under industrial or semi-industrial conditions, will provide perfectly adequate analyses.

Analyses produced by spectrometric methods will, of course, give no indication of the minerals in the body, save in the broadest possible sense, but a list of the chemical elements present in their proportions. Since it is not practicable to seek more than, say, a dozen elements, it is usual to look only for those known to be present in the various minerals making up the body. In practice, therefore, it is normal to determine the proportions of silicon, iron, the alkalis, the alkaline earths and a few of the lighter metals.

Spectrographic analyses of ceramic bodies are especially valuable in distinguishing between wares that under the microscope appear to be identical. It is not uncommon to find clay deposits which, although widely separated geographically, cannot be distinguished in thin section simply because the non-plastic inclusions are the same in each case. The differences in composition lie, in fact, in the proportions of the clay minerals and other minute particles present, and it is exactly differences of this kind that spectrometry is most suited to detect.

X-ray Diffraction

Sampling for examination by X-ray diffraction is carried out in the same manner as for spectrometry, and the same precautions must be taken to ensure that the sample is truly representative. The diffraction pattern produced from a sample of this kind will be the sum of the patterns of all the crystalline minerals present in large enough quantities to be detected. Obviously, the simpler the composition of the pottery the easier it will be to distinguish the various component minerals from this palimpsest, and where the ceramic body is highly complex, sorting out the different minerals may become very difficult. If, however, one merely wishes to know whether two bodies are identical, there is strictly speaking no need to distinguish any of the components, since identical samples will give identical diffraction patterns, and in this case one need only compare the patterns to have the answer.

GLASSES

Transparent or semi-transparent glasses are not difficult to study from a structural point of view since any joins made during manufacture will be clearly visible, while bubbles due to gases becoming trapped in the glass metal will also be quite obvious. Bubbles in a glass may be spherical, but more commonly they are elliptical, indicating the direction in which the glass metal has been stretched during forming, and hence they can give valuable information about methods of manufacture. The more opaque glasses can often be examined for this kind of detail in front of an exceptionally strong light, but if a glass is so dense that this fails, it may be necessary to make a radiograph in order to be sure of the method of manufacture.

The manner in which glazes have been applied to pottery is also usually self-evident, for it is almost inevitable that when a glaze has been applied by brush, some trace of brush-marks will remain. It may be more difficult to say whether the glaze was applied raw or as a frit, but on the whole raw glazes are more blotchy than those applied as frits. Furthermore, if the glass-modifying material of a raw glaze has not been particularly well ground, the coarser particles, combining with silica present in the underlying body, may etch small pits in the surface which become filled with glaze. This kind of irregularity is commonly to be seen where a raw lead glaze has been used. It is also normally quite easy to see the order in which differently coloured glazes have been applied to the same body—whether as under-, in- or over-glaze colours. Where there is any doubt, and a sherd can be spared, one can make a polished face at an oblique angle to the surface using a fine abrasive as in the preparation of mineral sections. A taper section of this kind will give an exaggerated depth to the glaze layers, and allow the order in which they have been applied to be seen quite clearly.

Colour, Hardness and Specific Gravity

Although the glass-colourants used in antiquity were on the whole few and simple, one should be very careful not to make the mistake of assuming that because a glass is of a particular colour, the colourant is therefore known, for not all colours are due to the presence in the glass of simple oxides. A number of complex molecular structures may on occasions have been produced, either accidentally or by design, which gave colours very similar to those of the metallic oxides. Thus, while one may suppose that a purple is due to the presence of manganese dioxide, it is important to appreciate that one of the complex molecular structures containing iron can also give a purple colour to glass. The accurate recording of colour is, of course, very necessary and while one may legitimately make the observation that a particular colour may be due to the presence of a particular glass-colourant, it is always advisable to seek analytical verification that this is the case.

Although glasses vary considerably in degrees of hardness, a hardness test such as that used with the Mohs' Scale is of little value in the examination of glass and glazes. Apart from the fact that either may have devitrified with age, the hardness of glasses can be greatly reduced if there are present any glass-modifiers or colourants that are not in chemical combination with the silica, and in practice it will be found that nearly all ancient glasses were so formulated that there was an excess of glass-modifiers in the metal. As a result nearly all glasses of antiquity are far softer than would be the case were all the glass-modifiers in chemical combination. The variation in hardness of glasses due to free glass modifiers is often greater than the variation in hardness that could be expected as a result of different deliberate formulations.

In theory the specific gravity of a glass could be used to show whether there were lead present in the glass or not, since lead, being denser than the other constituents of ancient glasses, would increase the specific gravity. It is very doubtful if the determination of specific gravity would normally be sufficiently accurate to indicate anything save the presence of large quantities of lead, however, and there are other simpler and more certain means of showing the presence of lead in glasses (p. 205).

Radiography

It is sometimes advisable to examine the structure of optically dense glassware by means of a radiograph since joins and gas bubbles may be shown up on a radiograph while being otherwise undetectable. Enamels are also best examined by means of X-rays, not so much for the enamels themselves as for the metal backing, as for example when one wishes to know whether the edges of champlevé fields have been undercut, or whether the backing has been roughened to help the enamels to adhere.

Radiographs will often show that the enamel being examined is unusually dense to X-rays, and may even be denser than the copper or bronze backing to which it has been applied. Density to X-rays in an enamel is generally taken to mean that it contains lead and there is little doubt that this is normally the case. Nevertheless it is advisable to verify the presence of lead by other analytical means since other heavy metals such as silver accidentally or deliberately introduced into the frit would also give abnormal density to the radiograph.

Microscopy

The microscope is less useful in the study of glasses than is the case of any other material used by early man, but even so the binocular microscope remains a valuable tool when studying details of decoration, especially abrasion marks made during cutting; while the nature of non-vitreous inclusions in glasses may sometimes be determined under the binocular microscope. It is seldom necessary to examine glass under high magnification but there are exceptions. *Stones*, which are small inclusions of non-vitreous matter in the glass, may often suggest a source of raw materials or a feature of the preparation of the metal. Usually stones are small particles present either in the raw materials or in the walls of the glass-pots that have not become dissolved in the metal, but under some circumstances they may be materials that have crystallized from the molten metal on cooling.

Chemical Analyses

For reasons already explained, the chemical analyses of glasses are normally expressed in the form of percentages of oxides present, rather than as a list of chemical elements in their proportions. Thus a glass might contain 25 % silica, 27 % sodium, 6 % calcium and 40 % oxygen, in which case the results would normally be expressed as 43·5 % silica, 36·3 % soda and 8·2 % lime. This method of recording the composition of a glass has the particular advantage that it enables one quickly to see how the material was formulated, an aspect that is not so easily appreciated from a list of single elements.

On the whole, while the chemical analyses of glasses provide a very clear picture of the type of glass being studied—potash-lime, soda-lime, and so on—analyses are less likely to be of much help in resolving problems of the provenance of the raw materials. There are exceptions to this generalization, to be discussed below, but normally the raw materials from which glasses were made—white sand, potash, lime, soda—were so ubiquitous and so varied in their composition that the presence of minor constituents is very unlikely ever to point to particular sources. It is thus quite common to find glasses which are known to have been manufactured in widely separated regions having very similar compositions, while the composition of glasses contemporaneously produced in a very limited region may vary just as much as that of glasses of the same period known to have been manufactured very much further afield. The analyses of glasses are hence more useful for determining changes in over-all formulation than for tracing down individual regional products.

Some of the glass colourants used in antiquity may, nevertheless, have been a source of minor constituents that can give a reasonably clear picture of the type of mineral deposit from which they were derived, if not the precise source. Thus if chromium were introduced as a colourant in the form of chromite (p. 45) the glass would almost certainly contain some iron, while if a chromate or bichromate were used the glass might contain no iron at all. Cobalt introduced as linnaeite (p. 45) might be quite free of manganese, while glasses coloured by the use of ashbolite would contain a relatively high proportion of manganese. If the analyses make it sufficiently clear that one particular type of ore was being used as a colourant in antiquity, one may then go on to examine the available ores, and thus to establish the probable provenance of the raw material.

Beta-ray Back-scatter

A relatively simple device for determining if lead is present in vitreous materials depends upon the back-scattering of beta-rays. Beta-rays, moving electrons emitted by a suitable radioactive isotope, are directed on to the surface of the glass being examined. Most of the normal constituents of glass, the chemical elements with low atomic numbers, will absorb the beta-rays but elements with high atomic numbers, such as lead, will back-scatter the rays, and by measuring the degree of back-scatter on a geiger-counter the quantity of lead present can be estimated.

MOULDS, CRUCIBLES AND SLAGS

Clay moulds used for casting metals, and crucibles no matter how heavily weathered they appear to be, will nearly always repay chemical analysis. During casting it is inevitable that some of the molten metal will become oxidized and that the oxides will be absorbed by the porous materials of the moulds and crucibles, much as happens during deliberate cupellation (p. 93). As a result very small proportions of the metals that have been cast will be found on, or just below, the surfaces of used moulds and crucibles. Analyses made of these surfaces will not, of course, reflect the proportional composition of the metals that have been cast, but may well give a clear indication of the type of metal being used. Thus, analyses from the surface of a mould for axes may show whether it was used for casting copper or bronze simply by the presence of copper and presence or absence of tin; in the same way, a mould for casting coin blanks might, on analysis, be shown to have been used for casting gold or silver.

Particles of slag adhering to crucibles, however, present a very different problem. The composition of a slag will not be a simple proportion-by-proportion reflection of the composition of the ore from which it was derived, less still of the metal cast from the crucible. In the first place, the slag will contain a high proportion of fluxes (glass modifiers) such as lime, soda and potash, as well as the more readily oxidized metals, all of which may be completely absent, or present only as traces, in the prepared metal. Equally, the slag may contain a far higher proportion of glass colourants, such as iron, than is present in the metal prepared in the crucible. Where a mixed ore, such as pyrites (p. 65), has been used, the prepared metal may be a relatively pure copper containing very little iron, while the slag may contain a great deal of iron and very little copper. In this case, an analysis of the slag alone might suggest to the unwary that iron was being worked—a conclusion that could be quite disastrous. Thus, if the detritus of a metal-workshop is being examined it is obviously preferable that both the slags and the porous surfaces of moulds and crucibles should be examined rather than either one or the other.

Chapter Nineteen

EXAMINATION OF METAL OBJECTS

SYNOPSIS

General: Corroded surfaces · Colour · Hardness · Specific gravity · Radiography. *Metallography:* Space lattice · Crystal habit · Dendrite · Grain · Chill casts · Slipping · Solid solution · Phase · Eutectoid · Copper alloys · Steels · Austenite · Ferrite · Pearlite · Cementite · Martensite · Troostite · Sorbite. *Chemical Analyses:* X-ray diffraction. Quantitative analyses.

GENERAL

IT IS IMPORTANT to appreciate that when one is superficially examining metal objects of any antiquity one is seldom looking at the original surface, but at a layer of corrosion products. The rate and nature of the corrosion of a metal depend very largely on its past environment. Where the environment has been most detrimental, and corrosion has been widespread and has eaten deeply into the metal, it is normally only too painfully obvious that the original surface has been destroyed. Quite frequently an excavated object, however, may seem to have undergone little change save for a superficial tarnish. This is often the case with bronze and copper artifacts, but a closer examination will commonly show that the surface, sometimes called a 'patina', amounts to little more than a compacted layer of dirt overlying a considerable depth of corrosion. One should, therefore, be very cautious about drawing conclusions from the examination of the surfaces of uncleaned corroded objects. Abrasion marks, for example, may belong not to the original surface at all, being only scratches made later in the corroded face.

The various forms of evidence of the techniques used to shape metals have already been described. Flashes, chaplets, centre-marks and the facets due to heavy hammering may have been left unobscured and thus clearly visible to the naked eye. On the other hand, all such traces may have been removed by later planishing and polishing, and it may be necessary to resort to other forms of physical examination before the technique of manufacture can be determined. It is, however, generally profitable to examine any metal artifact thoroughly under the binocular microscope before resorting to the more destructive methods of examination. A line that may seem to the naked eye, for example, to have been engraved, may under sufficient magnification be seen to be made up of a series of accurately punched tracer marks. Apart from this, tool-marks,

or other significant details, may often be left in the more awkward un-
polished corners of a metal object.

Colour

The colour of a metal artifact can be a very poor guide to its composition,
especially where the surface is covered with products of corrosion. A
silver-copper alloy, for example, may become completely covered with
green corrosion products of copper, so that it may seem to be of bronze,
while corroded lead may have become so stained with rust from an adjacent iron object that it, too, may appear to be of iron. Even in those
cases where corrosion does not obscure the surface, or the object has been
cleaned, colour alone remains a poor guide to composition in many cases.
It is often very difficult to say, for example, whether an object is made
of silver, tin or speculum without making additional tests (p. 182); brass
and a highly leaded tin-bronze also have a very similar appearance.

It is also important to realize that the process of corrosion may have
completely altered the composition of the surface of a metal object. An
extreme example of this process is frequently to be seen on bronze objects.
Under some conditions of burial metallic copper may become redeposited from the corrosion products and exposed by cleaning on the
surface of the bronze, and if only those areas in which this has taken
place are examined one may easily gain the impression that the object
is made of copper. It should be added also that in some of the older
methods employed in the chemical cleaning of bronze, the redeposition
of copper on the surface of the object often accidentally occurred or was
accepted as a penalty for the preservation of surface detail. Today the
possibility of this happening is generally appreciated by conservators,
who take steps to avoid it, but unfortunately there are still cases of
'copper' objects in collections which resulted from these rather uncritical methods of cleaning.

Hardness

The hardness of a metal (p. 179) can be a useful guide to what treatment
it has undergone, but generally only when the composition of the metal
is known. Cold-worked and fully annealed copper has a Brinell hardness
of about 50, while copper cold-drawn into wire, and left unannealed, has
a hardness of about 110. If one knows that one is examining objects of
reasonably pure copper, the Brinell hardness will allow one to distinguish
between metal that has been annealed and that which has been cold-
worked and left in that condition. However, a 70 : 30 brass will have a
hardness of 50 to 65 as cast, a hardness of 150 when fully cold worked,
and one of 60 when fully annealed. A 60 : 40 brass, on the other hand,
will have a hardness of 90 to 100 as cast, and a similar hardness when
both cold-worked and annealed. A hardness test will thus tell one little
about the working of a 60 : 40 brass, while a 70 : 30 brass that has been
cold-worked and not fully annealed could well have a hardness within the
range of that of a 60 : 40 brass and one cannot assume that a brass,
because it has a hardness of 90 to 100, is therefore of 60 : 40 composition.

The hardness of an alloy is not always a matter of simple progression,
the material becoming harder or softer with the increased proportion of

one of the alloyed metals. The hardness of quenched steel, for example,
varies greatly with small changes of carbon content:

% Carbon	0·1	0·3	0·5	0·7	0·9	1·2
Brinell hardness	155	500	670	710	680	685

In this case quenched steels having carbon contents of about 0·55 % and
1·2 % will both give a hardness of 685, and while this difference in composition may seem small, it is in fact very critical (p. 217). On the other
hand a hardness test will obviously distinguish between a steel that is
low in carbon (less than 0·5 %) and one containing a greater proportion,
if a suitable heat treatment can be applied to it first (p. 218).

Specific Gravity

The specific gravity of a metal may at times be a useful guide to its composition; but unless carried out with exceptional accuracy determinations of specific gravity may be totally misleading. Pure gold, for example,
has a specific gravity of 19·30, and if an object is shown to have a specific
gravity of 17·20, one can be quite certain that it is not of pure gold, but
an alloy. Furthermore, if the colour of the metal is rather red one may
assume that the composition is in the order of 80 % gold to 20 % copper.
However, an alloy of composition 79 % gold, 6 % silver and 15 % copper
will have a similar specific gravity, so that while a specific gravity determination may tell one whether or not a metal is pure, it cannot
provide any precise information about the composition. At times
specific gravity determinations may not even provide this information.
An alloy of 90 % copper, 6 % tin and 4 % lead will give a specific gravity
equivalent to that of pure copper. In such cases colour and hardness,
however, will usually correct the false impression that might be otherwise gained.

TABLE OF SPECIFIC GRAVITIES OF SOME COMMON METALS

Antimony	6·62	Lead	11·34
Arsenic	5·72	Nickel	8·80
Copper	8·93	Silver	10·50
Gold	19·30	Tin	7·28
Iron	7·86	Zinc	7·10

Slight experimental errors made during the estimation of specific
gravity are less misleading when the metals making up the alloy have
widely differing specific gravities than when the metals have specific
gravities that approach one another. Thus, if there is an error of 0·1 made
in the determination of the specific gravity of a gold-silver alloy, the
resulting error in computing the composition will be in the order of 1 %,
but if the same error is made in estimating the specific gravity of a
copper-tin alloy, the computed composition will show an error in the
order of 6 %. It might be thought that an error of 0·1 in the measurement of specific gravity is easily avoided, and this is so if the object is
sufficiently large. Nevertheless, if a coin, for example, weighs about 1
gram, an error of 0·002 grams made during weighing will give an error in

the order of 0·15 in the calculated specific gravity, which in turn will give an error of 9 % in estimating the composition of a copper-tin alloy. Since an error of ±0·001 grams at a single weighing is not easily avoided with an ordinary laboratory balance, one must assume that specific gravity determinations of very small objects are liable to be inaccurate, unless, of course, the degree of accuracy obtained during weighing is stated. If, on the other hand, a bronze object weighs 100 grams, an error of 0·002 grams made during weighing will result in an error of only 0·0015 in the determinations of its specific gravity, and the result of this error on the computed composition will be negligible.

The specific gravity of most metals varies slightly according to the modes of preparation they have received during shaping. The specific gravity of copper as cast, for example, may vary anywhere between 8·3 and 8·93, while cold-worked copper generally has a specific gravity of between 8·92 and 8·96. In cases where chemical analysis has already shown that an object is composed of pure copper it might be reasonable to assume that a low specific gravity indicates that the metal is in the as cast condition. On the other hand an object which has not been analysed chemically and has a low specific gravity, say, 8·40, might not be a pure copper, as cast, but a copper alloy with arsenic, for example, in the cold-worked condition.

Radiography

For the general structural examination of metal objects X-rays are invaluable, since a radiograph will reveal not only the presence of different metals, but also the presence of joins in the same metal. Inlays and solders will almost invariably show up quite distinctly, as lead and the precious metals are, to the X-rays, denser than the metals to which they were normally applied. While iron and steel have very similar X-ray densities, welded surfaces were seldom so free from oxidation products or included slag that they cannot be detected on a radiograph. For similar reasons the joins between cast-on parts of a bronze object are normally clearly visible on a radiograph.

METALLOGRAPHY

A far more complete picture of the composition and the past treatment of metals can be obtained by metallographic examination. Unfortunately this demands some destruction of the object, since to be of any real value a metallographic study must be carried out in depth. In practice small blocks of the metal are cut from the object and polished with progressively finer grades of abrasive, for which purpose very small fragments may be mounted in a plastic material. The polished surfaces are finally etched to reveal detail, and examined under the microscope. Perhaps because it is a partially destructive method of examination, metallography has been used less and is thus less completely understood by archaeologists, than it should be.

The basis of metallography lies in the fact that metals are crystalline substances. The atoms that make up a metal are not haphazardly arranged, but form an orderly *space lattice*, giving a regular repetition of pattern in three dimensions. The atoms making up a metal will thus normally be found to arrange themselves in regular geometric figures, of which the cube and hexagon are the most common; the precise figure which the atoms of each metal will adopt being known as the *crystal habit* of the metal. When a metal melts, however, this orderly lattice breaks down, and the arrangement of the atoms becomes haphazard.

As a *pure* molten metal cools, small crystals begin to form from nuclei throughout the liquid, and as cooling continues more and more atoms attach themselves to these nuclei in the arrangement of the crystal habit typical of the metal. One might expect metals of cubic habit to solidify ultimately in the form of cubes, but more often than not, since there is a greater dissipation of heat at the corners of cubes than elsewhere, there is a tendency for atoms to become attached preferentially

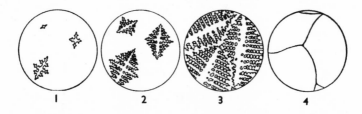

FIG. 45   DIAGRAM TO SHOW THE GROWTH OF DENDRITES (1, 2 AND 3) WITH ULTIMATE INFILLING TO GIVE POLYHEDRAL GRAINS (4).

to the corners of each cubic nucleus. As a result, radial arms form from the corners of the nuclei, and these in turn develop secondary arms, and so on until a crystal somewhat like a fir-tree, *a dendrite*, is formed. On yet further cooling these dendrites will grow until they come into contact with one another, so inhibiting any further outward growth, and at this point the remaining liquid metal between the branches of the dendrites will solidify to fill the spaces. Thus ultimately each dendrite will become a polyhedral crystal with its surfaces in contact with those of its neighbours. These crystals, which are irregular in boundary, are usually referred to as *grains*.

When a pure metal cools very slowly the nuclei will be more or less evenly distributed throughout the metal, with the result that the grains will be of approximately the same size and roughly equiaxial. If, however, cooling is rapid or uneven, as for example when molten metal is poured into too cold a mould, nuclei will appear first near the mould face, and the grains will grow rapidly until they come in contact with one another, when they will grow inwards. Thus in a *chill cast* metal it will be found that the grains near the surface are not equiaxial but elongated, their long axes being at right angles to the mould face.

The strength of a pure metal depends to a very large degree on the fact that the adjacent grain surfaces are cohesive and normally less liable to fracture than the grains themselves. Because the atoms of a metal are arranged in a regular lattice, it follows that there are planes of weakness running through the lattice. Thus, when a metal is hammered lightly whole volumes of lattice may become momentarily distorted, to return to their original position after each blow; but under heavier hammering these volumes of lattice may become permanently deformed, with the result that the crystal grain is given a new shape. This kind of distortion, known as *slipping*, will appear under the microscope on the etched metal as fine parallel lines traversing the grains of the metal. As a result of slipping, however, under severe hammering the grains themselves will become flattened.

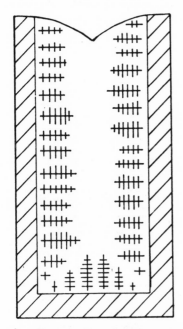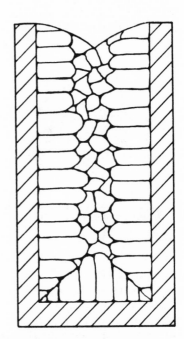

FIG. 46 DIAGRAM TO SHOW GROWTH OF DENDRITES FROM THE FACE OF A CHILL MOULD (*left*) TO PRODUCE COLUMNAR GRAINS (*right*). GRAINS IN THE CENTRE OF THE CASTING ARE EQUIAXIAL.

A cast or deformed metal if annealed may form a new grain structure. For this to happen there is no need for the metal to become molten again; heating to a temperature above what is called the recrystallization temperature being sufficient to allow the atoms to take on a new arrangement. The normal result of this treatment is to produce a coarser grain structure than initially, and because the new structure will thus have a smaller number of grain boundaries the metal will be softer and more ductile than before annealing.

When a molten alloy of two or more metals cools, a number of different things may happen, depending largely upon the sizes of the several varieties of atoms and crystal habits of the metals. In some cases the sizes of the atoms and the crystal habits of the metals may be so different that on cooling the metals separate completely. In some instances, for example when lead is mixed with copper, the one metal, lead, will separate out as globules within the grains of the other, copper, or at the grain boundary, and this can severely lessen the strength of the metal by preventing cohesion between adjacent grains.

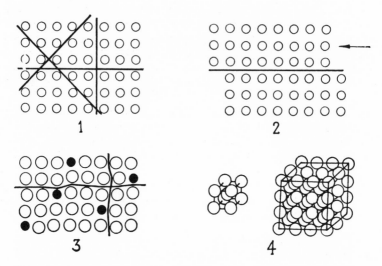

FIG. 47 DIAGRAM TO SHOW POSSIBLE SLIP PLANES THROUGH A CRYS-
TALLINE STRUCTURE (1) AND THE FORMATION OF A SLIP BAND (2).
ATOMS OF A DIFFERENT SIZE (BLACK) DISTORT THE LATTICE (3) AND
LESSEN SLIPPING. A UNIT AND A BLOCK OF BODY-CENTRED CUBIC HABIT
DRAWN ISOMETRICALLY (4).

On the other hand, the atom size and crystal habit of two metals may be sufficiently similar to permit the atoms of one metal to fit into the space lattice of the other. A structure of this kind may be referred to as a *solid solution* of one metal in another. Examples of this type of alloy are gold-silver, silver-platinum and copper-nickel mixtures. However, although the atoms of one metal may fit into the space lattice of another in any proportions, the lattice of the *solvent metal* is bound to be somewhat distorted by the presence of the *solute* atoms, since the atoms of no two metals are identical in size. As a result, the slip planes running through the lattice become, as it were, corrugated so that in effect the strength of the solvent metal is usually increased. It is for this reason that alloys are frequently stronger than either pure constituent metal.

Normally, when alloys of this type cool, the nuclei and the first branches of the dendrites contain a higher proportion of the higher melting metal than is present in the liquid. As the dendrites grow, the proportion of lower melting metal in the remaining molten material increases, so that the final infilling around the dendrites is proportionally far richer in the lower melting metal than are the dendrites themselves.

Were the metal allowed to cool exceedingly slowly this state of affairs would be rectified, atoms of the lower melting metal diffusing into the dendrites to give, finally, a more or less uniform structure. Under normal conditions, cooling is seldom sufficiently slow to allow this to happen, and on sectioning and etching one sees a *cored* structure of dendrites, the centres of which are rich in one metal, with an infilling rich in the other.

In many cases, instead of two metals being mutually soluble in one another, they will only dissolve in one another to a limited degree. As a result two or more types of grain may be formed in an alloy, each being a solution of one metal in the other. These different solid solutions are referred to as *phases*, and usually occur when metals of rather different atom size are alloyed. Bronzes and some brasses are typical of this kind of alloy.

Many alloys undergo structural changes on cooling after solidification. Thus some alloys will form one phase on solidification, which on further cooling will break down into other phases, usually with the result that some of the solute metal is ejected from the space lattice of the solvent metal. The ejected solute atoms may be precipitated as a nearly pure metal; they may form new solutions; but commonly a *eutectoid* is formed, often being composed of alternate thin layers of the metal and the solid solution. A eutectoid of this kind, pearlite (p. 216), is a constituent of many steels.

Copper Alloys

Dendrites are formed when *completely pure* copper first solidifies from the melt and on completion of solidification the infilling of equally pure copper results in the production of polyhedral grains, as described above, all trace of dendritic growth having by now been lost. On the other hand, when copper is alloyed with a *small* proportion of tin a solid solution of tin in copper, the α-phase, is formed on solidification. Initially at a certain temperature the dendrites will contain only a small proportion of tin, but as they grow the proportion of tin to copper in the remaining molten material now at a slightly lower temperature will increase, so that further outgrowths of the dendrites will contain increasingly larger proportions of tin, while the final infilling will contain an even higher proportion still. As cooling in antiquity was always fairly rapid, as-cast low tin bronzes always appear in cross-section as cored structures of copper-rich dendrites with an infilling of tin-rich material.

When copper-tin alloys containing more than 13·2% tin solidify, α-phase solid solutions are first formed, but the remaining molten material finally contains such a high proportion of tin that a new, β-phase, solid solution is produced. This, however, is only an intermediate solid solution, and on further cooling it breaks down to give a eutectoid—a mixture of α-phase solid solution with a pale blue, very hard, brittle, copper-tin compound called an intermetallic compound. The structure of a medium tin bronze is thus one of dendrites with an infilling of this eutectoid. In practice, cooling was generally so rapid that even in bronzes containing 7% tin and upwards one will normally find that during cooling the residual molten material became so tin-rich that a certain amount of the eutectoid was formed.

In the cases of copper-tin alloys containing more than 32 % tin—speculum—a number of intermetallic compounds of copper and tin are formed, so that finally the structure will be one of crystals of one inter-metallic compound in a background of a eutectoid of tin and other inter-metallic compounds. These intermetallic compounds become increasingly harder and more brittle as the proportion of tin rises. Speculum is thus hard and brittle while a low tin bronze, containing no intermetallic compounds, is relatively soft and ductile.

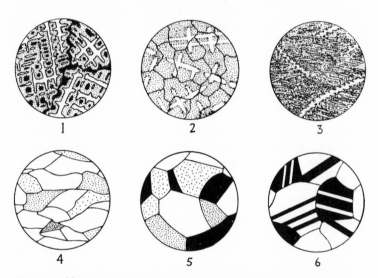

FIG. 48 METALLOGRAPHIC SECTIONS OF BRONZES. CORED 4 % TIN-BRONZE (1). 'SHADOW' OF CORING AND FORMATION OF FRESH GRAIN STRUCTURE DUE TO ANNEALING (2). DISTORTED DENDRITES DUE TO COLD WORKING (3). DISTORTED POLYHEDRAL GRAINS (4). POLYHEDRAL GRAINS OF 8 % TIN-BRONZE (5). TWINNED GRAINS (6).

When a cored bronze is annealed the dendritic structure gradually dis-appears as the copper-rich dendrites absorb tin from the infilling and a completely homogeneous structure of polyhedral grains is eventually formed. At an intermediary point, however, in which this change has only gone part of the way, one may see a 'shadow' of the original den-drites upon which is superimposed the new grain structure. If, on the other hand, a cored bronze is cold hammered or drawn and left in this condition, the dendrites will be seen to be distorted. Simple annealing of such a bronze will result in the production of a fresh grain structure, finer than that resulting simply from the annealing of a cast and un-worked bronze. It is generally true that the more a bronze has been cold-worked and annealed, the finer will be the grain structure. Additionally, *twinned* grains will appear. These are pairs of identical grains whose lattice structures are mirror images of each other formed each side of a common plane.

In summary, a prepared section of bronze may show a number of quite distinct features that will allow one to draw conclusions about its past treatment.

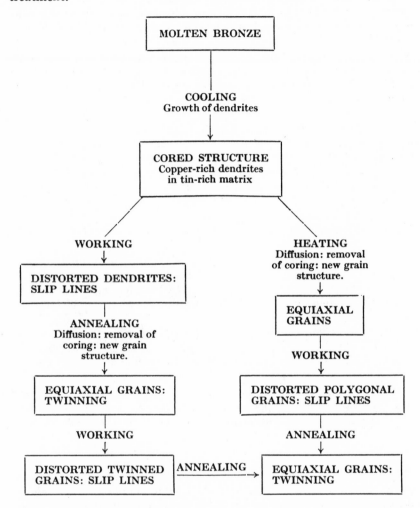

The metallography of the brasses is in many ways very similar to that of the bronzes. In brasses containing less than 36 % zinc a solid solution, the α-phase, is formed in which the zinc atoms enter the space lattice of the copper. On cooling from the melt, as with bronze, coring takes place so that the final appearance is one of copper-rich dendrites in a zinc-rich infilling. When the proportion of zinc rises above 36 % a new phase is formed on cooling, the β-phase, and the resulting material is thus one of copper-rich dendrites with a eutectoid infilling. When the proportion of zinc rises above 42 % other changes in composition take place, but brasses of this nature do not occur in antiquity. The results of the cold-working and annealing of brass are similar to those described in the working of bronze.

Copper-silver alloys differ from brasses and bronzes in that no intermediate phases are formed on cooling from the melt, the two metals being mutually soluble in one another in definite proportions. Thus on cooling from the melt cored dendrites are formed on solidification, the infilling being a eutectic of the two solid solutions, copper in silver and silver in copper. Very slow cooling would result in the gradual breakdown of the cored structure to give a material made up largely of this eutectoid. Cooling in antiquity was seldom slow enough to allow this to happen, and in practice as-cast copper-silver alloys will be found to be cored. The effects of cold working and annealing on copper-silver alloys are similar to those on bronze.

Although lead was quite commonly added to bronzes and brasses to form ternary alloys, the metal does not enter into solid solution with copper, and on cooling may be seen dispersed throughout the alloy as minute globules. Nickel, on the other hand, forms a solid solution with copper in all proportions and its presence in small quantities cannot, therefore, be detected in prepared sections. Arsenic also forms a solid solution with copper, but if oxygen is present arsenic will form the compound copper arsenite which, being insoluble in copper, forms minute globules throughout the alloy.

Apart from these metals, and others which behave in a similar manner, such as antimony and bismuth, the balance of oxygen and hydrogen present in the molten metal had a considerable effect on the soundness of a copper casting. Oxygen will combine with copper to give cuprous oxide, and on cooling this forms a eutectic with copper, appearing as globules throughout the metal, severely lowering its toughness. To overcome this defect copper was generally poled (p. 70) to reduce the cuprous oxide to metallic copper. If, however, poling was overdone the molten metal would absorb hydrogen from the furnace gases and at the moment of solidification this would react with any cuprous oxide present to form steam which, trapped in the solid metal, formed blowholes, so weakening the casting. This sequence of events may be expressed as a reversible reaction:

$$Cu_2O + H_2 \rightleftharpoons H_2O + 2Cu.$$

Clearly the art of sound casting was to produce a compromise by correctly judged poling in which both the production of cuprous oxide on the one hand and of steam on the other were kept to a minimum.

Steels

If a molten alloy of iron and carbon, containing less than 0.85% carbon, is allowed to cool slowly, it will solidify at a relatively high temperature to form an intermediate solid solution of carbon in iron, called *austenite*.* On further cooling the carbon is ejected from the space lattice of the iron, grains of pure iron, *ferrite*, being formed. The ejected carbon combines chemically with some of the iron to form iron carbide, and this is distributed in the ferrite as a more or less finely laminated eutectoid

---

* This term was derived from the name of the celebrated metallurgist Austen. Other metallurgists, Martens, Troost, Sorby—have given their names to different grain structures in steels.

infilling known as *pearlite*. If the original alloy contains exactly 0·85 %
carbon, no grains of ferrite will be formed, but instead the whole material
will be composed of pearlite. When the mixture contains above 0·85 %,
but less than 1·8 % carbon, grains of iron carbide, *cementite*, will be
formed with an infilling of the pearlite eutectoid. A prepared section of a
low-carbon steel that has been cooled slowly will thus allow a reasonably
accurate estimate of the quantity of carbon present.

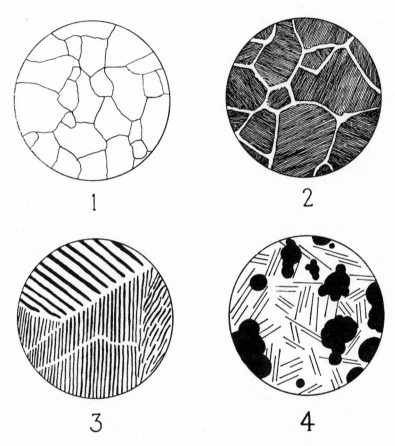

FIG. 49 METALLOGRAPHIC SECTIONS OF IRON AND STEEL. PURE FERRITE (1).
PEARLITE GRAINS IN A FERRITE MATRIX OF A 0·5 % CARBON STEEL (2).
PEARLITE GRAINS AT A HIGHER MAGNIFICATION SHOWING LAMINAE OF
CEMENTITE IN FERRITE (3). NEEDLES OF MARTENSITE (4).

The end-products that result when steel is cooled rapidly, as when it is
quenched, are very different, for the sudden cooling does not give time
for the complete rearrangement from the austenite solid solution.
Commonly, a material composed of fine, needle-like crystals, *martensite*,
was produced by quenching in water. This is believed to be a super-
saturated solid solution of carbon in iron, the presence of carbon atoms

greatly distorting the iron space lattice. Because of this distortion the material is exceptionally hard and will scratch glass—the hardest constituent of steel, in fact. A slightly slower rate of cooling achieved by quenching in oil produces a structure of finely laminated ferrite and cementite, known as *troostite*, which differs essentially from pearlite only in the degree of fineness of lamellae. The structure of troostite is generally too fine to be resolved under normal magnifications.

These products of quenching—martensite and troostite—are formed only when the steel has been heated sufficiently to allow the carbon to enter the space lattice of the iron, that is to say to a temperature above that at which austenite is formed. This temperature varies with the carbon content, but it is generally above 720°C.—a good red heat. Quenching of a given steel from below this critical temperature will not produce these constituents.

Steels containing martensite and troostite are hard but brittle. Some of this brittleness can be relieved, at some expense of hardness, by tempering (p. 84). The effect of gently heating a quenched steel is that at low temperatures any martensite present forms troostite, while at higher temperatures (above 450°C.) a new constituent, *sorbite*, is produced. This is a fine dispersion of cementite in ferrite in which, unlike troostite, the components can be clearly defined under normal magnification.

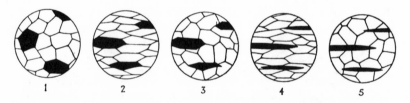

FIG. 50   DIAGRAM TO SHOW FORMATION OF SLAG STRINGERS. SLAG PARTICLES IN FERRITE (1) PROGRESSIVELY FLATTENED BY FORGING (2 AND 4), UNALTERED BY ANNEALING (3 AND 5).

Since carbon can only actually dissolve in austenite, case-hardening (p. 83) was carried out above 720°C. If allowed to cool slowly after case-hardening, a wrought iron object will show a core of ferrite and pearlite with a cementite and pearlite case of a thickness determined by the duration of the process of case-hardening.

A common feature of wrought iron and steels produced from wrought iron is the inclusion of stringers or fibres of slag (p. 83). During the process of forging these become flattened and elongated and their presence gives the metal its characteristic fibrous appearance, while in suitable cross-sections the slag inclusions may be rendered clearly visible. Other common impurities are sulphur and phosphorus. Sulphur will combine with the iron to form ferrous sulphide, a brittle, yellow-brown material that becomes deposited at the grain boundaries, so causing 'shortness' (p. 85). Phosphorus, on the other hand, although forming ferrous phosphide, which is to an extent soluble in iron, seriously affects the resistance of iron to shock, while in high carbon steels and cast iron ferrous phosphide forms a brittle eutectic, so that in either case the metal is again 'short' (p. 85).

It will now be appreciated that the changes that take place in the grain structure of steels, apart from those caused by working or annealing as described earlier, depend largely upon three factors:

1. The quantity of carbon present in the steel.

2. The temperature to which the steel is raised.

3. The rate at which the steel cools.

The products of the various heat treatments may be briefly summarized:

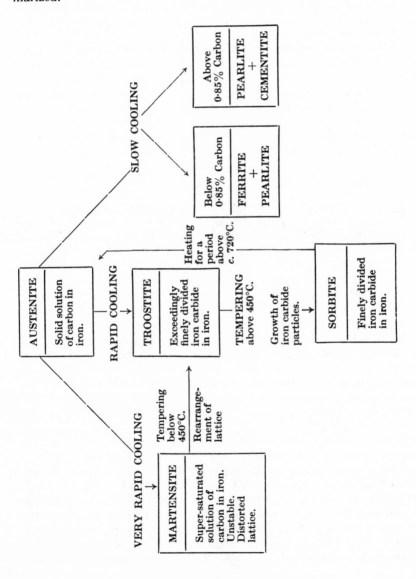

CHEMICAL ANALYSES

X-ray Diffraction

X-ray diffraction methods are of particular value in determining the lattice structure of metals, and hence in showing to what working methods or heat treatments the objects under study may have been subjected. Since this type of analysis depends upon the diffraction of X-rays at the planes between atoms, the diffraction pattern will show whether or not the space lattice of one metal has been distorted by the intrusion of atoms of another metal. Thus, for example, a cored bronze and one that has been fully annealed will give distinctive diffraction patterns. This method of examination is obviously of great value in cases where the object under study may not be damaged, but it is important to appreciate that under these circumstances the diffraction pattern will apply only to the surface of the object, and the structure at depth will remain unknown. While X-ray diffraction methods may be used in favourable circumstances to distinguish between cast and struck coins, striking causing grain distortion and hence a distinct diffraction pattern, care is needed in the interpretation of these results. In this instance, had both cast and struck coins been fully annealed after manufacture a new equiaxial grain structure would have been formed; and it might be impossible to distinguish between the two initial means of fabrication.

Quantitative Analyses

The interpretation of the results of the quantitative analyses of metals is by no means a simple matter, although the major constituents normally present few difficulties of interpretation, save where one of the metals is present only in relatively small quantities, when its deliberate inclusion in the alloy may be in question. Where sufficient analyses are available, plotting graphically may help resolve problems of this nature, but it might equally be essential to have analyses of the ores available in antiquity before a final answer can be given. The presence of a small amount of arsenic in early copper tools might, for example, result either from the use of a copper ore containing some arsenic, such as enargite, or from deliberate alloying with arsenic during smelting. Where the arsenic content proves to be consistently low and relatively invariable, one might suspect that arsenic entered the alloy as an 'impurity' in the ore; but where the content is high and tends to be variable, one might equally suppose deliberate alloying. All too commonly, however, the results of analyses will be found to fall between these two extremes, and if the source of the original ores remains unknown it may be quite impossible to say whether the alloy was accidental or deliberate.

When dealing with an unalloyed metal the nature and proportions of the minor constituents may be a useful pointer to the source of ores, methods of extraction and of working: but when one is examining objects made of remelted alloys, often scrap metal derived from many sources, the minor constituents are less likely to be of value in interpretation. Even the metal derived from a single ore will not give on analysis a proportion-by-proportion reflection of the metals present as minor constituents in the ore, for during roasting, smelting, refining and casting there may be considerable losses of some elements. Many metals are liable to volatilize or to oxidize and thus become lost to the alloy during any process involving excessive heat. This is especially true of arsenic and antimony and, at rather higher temperatures, lead and zinc. Other metals, especially iron and lead, may enter the slag and be lost in this way, while others may be absorbed by the ash of the furnace during smelting or by the crucible during melting, if oxidizing conditions are allowed to develop, as happens during deliberate cupellation (p. 93). Furthermore, some metals initially present in the ore may never enter the smelt at all: ores of manganese and cobalt, for example, may remain unreduced if the conditions in the furnace are not exactly right. When one makes allowances for the variable working conditions probable in antiquity, it seems likely that the same craftsman may have produced metals of very different composition in successive smelts, although using the identical ore. One must, therefore, expect the results of chemical analyses to reflect the vagaries of primitive working methods.

As far as the analyses of unalloyed copper objects are concerned, one can anticipate that the results should suggest the use of one of three broad categories of ore. Since native copper is generally remarkably pure, it is usually assumed that copper objects with few minor constituents were made from native copper. While this is undoubtedly often so, this line of reasoning should not be stretched unduly, for a few remarkably pure ores are known and the metal that can be derived from them is not, on analysis, necessarily very different from native copper. Copper derived from most 'oxide' ores, however, normally has a rather greater proportion and range of minor constituents than native copper, though a large part of these constituents originally present in the ore will have been weathered away from the 'oxide' ores and have been redeposited in the underlying sulphide ores—a process known as secondary enrichment of these underlying ores. Copper produced from sulphide ores, therefore, may be expected to have a relatively high proportion of minor constituents, especially of metals that form readily weathered minerals, such as iron. The same mineral deposit is likely, therefore, to provide very different qualities of copper, depending upon what level of the ore was being worked.

The analyses of unalloyed silver objects might also be expected to betray the source of the metal—native silver, silver recovered from electrum, or produced as the result of cupelling lead ores. In the last instance one would expect some lead to be present as a minor constituent, while silver recovered from the refining of electrum should be relatively pure. Native silver normally contains a rather high percentage of copper, but since copper was also deliberately alloyed with silver in order to make it harder, and thus more durable, it may be impossible to say whether or not the metal was native or alloyed.

The tracing of unalloyed metals to a particular source of ore must depend ultimately on the fact that some ore deposits contain peculiarly large quantities of one or more other metals. Many deposits are not sufficiently distinctive in this way and in some regions widely separated deposits have a content of other metals that differs less from one ore to another than the variation that may be anticipated due to the uneven quality of primitive smelting techniques. Clearly, tracing a metal to one such source would be a hopeless task. On the other hand, some ore deposits do have a disproportionately high or low content of other metals. One might thus, for example, find that in one region copper ores contain little arsenic while having a high content of nickel, and that in an adjacent area the position is reversed. In such a case it might be possible to allocate copper objects to approximate sources on the basis of analyses provided that the differences in composition are really adequately pronounced.

The interpretation of the analyses of alloys is an even more difficult matter. Even when one sets aside the problem of whether or not an alloy contains re-used scrap metal, one has to allow that minor constituents may enter the alloy through any of the major constituents. In the case of a bronze containing both tin and lead, for example, silver could enter the alloy with any of the three constituents, copper, tin or lead, as too might arsenic or antimony. Under these circumstances the alloy may well be a chemical palimpsest that will simply not allow one to trace any of the constituents to their sources. At the best one may hope to isolate a number of groups of alloys the compositions of which are significantly different, without necessarily being able to say how or why these differences came about. An impasse of this nature is not inevitable, especially when other data can be taken into consideration. If, for example, one can demonstrate that in a particular region the composition of a binary alloy remained relatively stable over a long period, and that at a particular point in time a consistent change in composition took place, one can reasonably infer that the source of one or both of the raw materials also changed, and by examining possible sources it may be demonstrable how the change came about.

The use of scrap metal in antiquity must necessarily complicate interpretation even further, especially in those areas where trade with adjacent regions was easily conducted. In geographically isolated areas, of course, newly smelted alloys and scrap metal would both have tended to have a very similar composition as long as the sources of raw materials remained unaltered; but in readily accessible regions the sources of scrap metal may well have been so varied that chemical analyses reflect nothing save the fact that the metal was derived from such a multitude of sources.

To recapitulate, differences in the chemical composition of metals may result from a number of factors, all of which must be taken into consideration when analyses are being compared:

(1) Differences due to the working of different ore deposits.

(2) Differences due to working different levels of the same ore deposits.

(3) Differences due to the use of scrap metal.

(4) Differences due to different methods or degrees of efficiency in the preparation and smelting of ores.

Chapter Twenty

EXAMINATION OF ORGANIC MATERIALS

SYNOPSIS

General: Cellular and non-cellular · Decay. *Microscopy:* Sections · Selective staining
· Fibres · Plant tissues · Animal tissues. *Chemical Analyses:* Chromatography.

GENERAL

ORGANIC MATERIALS USED by early man may be divided broadly into
two main classes. There are those materials that are cellular, or are made
up of a number of cells, and there are those materials that are non-
cellular, usually either secretions derived from living organisms or
extracts made from dead tissues. The *non-cellular* materials usually
cannot be studied under the microscope since they are optically amor-
phous, although some may contain inclusions that can indicate their
source. Beeswax, for example, commonly contains the shed wing-cases of
the insects hatched from the honeycomb, and the species of bee which
produced the wax can be identified from these inclusions. *Cellular*
materials are, on the other hand, most easily identified by examination
under the microscope. They may be made up of only one basic type of
cell, or part of a cell, as is commonly so with fibres used for textiles; or
they may be tissues containing a number of different types of cell, in
which case the shapes, sizes and arrangements of the different cells are
the criteria by which the material may be identified. On the whole, therefore, it is usually essential to work with a rather larger sample of whole
tissues than is so with materials composed of only a single type of cell.
Very few fibres, for example, need be teased from the edge of a piece of
cloth in order to identify the fibres from which it was made, although it is
risky to take too small a sample (p. 176). On the other hand, to establish
the species of plant or animal from which wood or leather were derived
may require a far larger sample than the layman imagines, simply
because a small sample may not contain any cellular structures that are
typical of one particular species.

Decay

Unlike the inorganic materials used by early man, organic materials are
subject not only to chemical corrosion but to the effects of bacterial
decay and the ravages of fungi and insects. As a result of the last the
cellular structure of many organic substances may be completely

223

destroyed, or so damaged that identification is no longer possible; while chemical and bacterial attack may result in the formation of a totally different series of chemical compounds from those initially present in the material under study. As a rule, the majority of organic materials will, therefore, survive only under exceptionally favourable conditions—water-logging, high salinity, or extreme desiccation—and even then the materials may become greatly changed before they establish a state of equilibrium with their environment. It thus quite commonly happens that while organic substances appear to be in tolerably sound condition, decay has in fact gone so far that precise identification becomes impossible. A wooden object, for example, may when first buried have been attacked by lignin-destroying bacteria. Due to changes in atmospheric or other environmental conditions the decay may have stopped short of the total destruction of all the lignin. In these circumstances the wood might not appear to be in too appalling a condition, but under the microscope it would be almost impossible to identify even its broad characteristics, let along the species of tree from which it came. In short, one should not be too optimistic about the possibility of identifying organic materials, no matter how sound they may appear superficially.

MICROSCOPY

Although a great deal of the preliminary examination of cellular materials can be done under the binocular microscope, in general it is necessary to make prepared *sections* or mounts of most of them before they can be completely identified. For example, it is usually quite simple to distinguish between hairs, cotton, and bast fibres under the binocular microscope; but to say from which species of plant or animal they came demands special techniques, and it will often be necessary to prepare sections of the materials in at least two planes before they can be identified. As a rule a fragment of the material under study is impregnated with wax to act as a support and prevent distortion during cutting. The required section is then cut from the sample, the wax removed, and the section mounted on a glass slide in some material with similar optical properties to those of glass.

Many cellular structures are transparent and colourless in thin section so that their identification under the microscope is impossible without further treatment. Many organic materials, however, have an affinity for particular dyestuffs, and it is possible to stain sections with selected dyes so that particular features will appear coloured under the microscope; while by the use of a number of different stains, different materials may be coloured in the same section. Because of decay, however, selective staining may be impossible with archaeological materials since the chemical components may have been destroyed or altered.

For the identification of *fibres* several commercial houses have developed 'blunderbuss' stains, composed of a number of dyes, that will colour virtually all the chemical components that are likely to be encountered in a particular type of sample. Hairs, however, seldom require staining, since their identification depends upon the configuration of the bracts on the surface, the relationship of the central medulla to the outer cortex, and the shape of the medulla itself. The medulla in natural hair is pigmented, save of course in white hairs, and may take on many shapes, each shape being more or less typical of a species of animal. The medulla may be a solid rod running down the centre of the hair, or a series of short rods, or even elaborate corkscrew or ladder-like shapes. A heavily pigmented medulla will, however, make it exceptionally difficult to observe the bracts on the surface of a hair by either transmitted or reflected light, and in such instances it may be necessary to prepare a

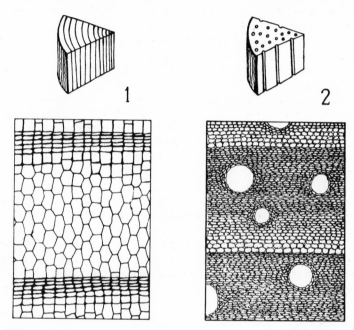

FIG. 51 HARDWOODS AND SOFTWOODS IN TRANSVERSE SECTION. SOFT-WOODS (1) HAVE NO VESSELS AND THE GROWTH RINGS ARE PRONOUNCED. IN HARDWOODS (2) THE GROWTH RINGS ARE LESS PRONOUNCED AND THE WOOD HAS TUBULAR VESSELS.

minute cast of the surface of the hair. This is generally done by making a thin film of some transparent plastic material on a slide, and laying the hair across the film before the plastic has set. The hair is then removed, leaving an impression of the surface in the plastic film. The shapes and relationships of the bracts are more or less typical for each species of animal, while the number of bracts to a unit of length normally varies with the age of the hair, or with the part of the body from which it came.

While cotton is not easily confused with any other fibre, bast fibres can be very difficult to identify. Often the distinction between bast fibres from different species of plant lies only in the comparative size, or in the presence of minute markings on the cell walls, so that decay often makes it quite impossible to distinguish between basically rather similar fibres. On the whole one must, therefore, expect less precise identification in the case of bast fibres than of other types.

15

The identification of whole *plant tissues* containing different types of cell, of which wood is probably the most important to archaeologists, is often difficult because cells performing the same function tend to look very much the same in many species of plant. Identification thus frequently hinges on minute differences of cell structure, cell arrangement and cell size. The broader categories of timber are not difficult to distinguish. Hardwoods for example are characterized by groups of specialized cells, known as vessels, running axially through the trunk, while in softwoods these are totally absent. When, however, identification of the species is required it is often difficult, and sometimes impossible, to distinguish between two timbers, although they come from trees which from the point of view of leaf and other general morphological characteristics are easily recognizable. Some species of oak for example cannot be distinguished by their woods, and the same is true of some species of beech.

The identification of other plant tissues, such as grasses and rushes used in the making of baskets, depends upon the same kinds of criteria, and thereby suffers from the same limitations. Generally, however, the identification of these materials is made on other considerations such as the shape of leaves, seed heads, and so on, with the result that identification to a species level is normally more possible.

As with plant tissues, the broad categories of animal tissues are easily distinguished. The cellular structures of sinews and hides are quite different and could hardly be confused, but to say from what species of animal either came can be a very difficult matter. Leathers, for example, must be identified by the shapes, sizes and relationships of such things as sebaceous glands and hair follicles. Dissimilar species often have hides that are virtually indistinguishable, and when allowance has been made for deterioration, there is all too often no possibility of identifying the animal from which the hides were derived.

CHEMICAL ANALYSES

Materials of organic origin are seldom pure substances, but are usually mixtures of complex organic compounds. A resin from one species of tree is, thus, not a single chemical substance but a mixture of a number of compounds, while a resin from a different species of plant might be a different mixture, or a mixture of the same compounds in different proportions. The problems of examining materials of this nature are, hence, twofold: first, it must be discovered to what general category the materials belong, and then the components of the mixture must be separated and classified. Only when this has been done is it possible to suggest an origin for the materials.

Where a very large sample can be spared there is, chemically speaking, little difficulty in deciding to what broad category an organic substance belongs, but when only a small sample may be used even this can be a complicated matter. As a rule, in order not to destroy the sample, preliminary examination is carried out by studying the solubility of the material in various solvents. For example, an adhesive may be thought to be either a glue or a resin. The former would be soluble in boiling water while the resin would not: equally the resin would be soluble in both alcohol and in essential oils. Thus, by conducting a series of such tests the general characteristics of the sample can be discovered without its destruction, since it can always be recovered from the solution.

Although it is impossible to give here even a brief outline of the methods of analysis applicable to organic compounds likely to be encountered in ancient artifacts, one type of examination should be mentioned, since it seems particularly suited to cases where only small samples can be spared, and this is *chromatography*. The basis of this form of analysis lies in the fact that any material in solution will be carried down an absorbent column by capillary action and that in any one solvent different materials may be carried at different rates. The absorbent column may be a glass tube carefully packed with an inert material such as alumina, or more simply a strip of specially prepared paper, rather like a very pure blotting paper. In practice a small spot of the material to be examined is placed at the top of the column, or strip of paper, and the solvent selected for the purpose is allowed to be absorbed under carefully controlled conditions of atmosphere and temperature. As the solvent front advances down the column, some materials present in the spot may be found to advance rapidly just behind the front, and are said to have a high *Rf value*: others will advance less rapidly so that ultimately all the materials in the mixture may become separated as distinct zones down the column or strip of paper. Using an identical solvent and identical experimental conditions the Rf value of any material will always be the same, so that once the equipment has been calibrated against standards of known composition it is possible, using the same procedure, to establish the unknown ingredients of a mixture. Many of the organic compounds being examined, of course, are naturally colourless and in order that they may be detected once the chromatograph has been made it is then necessary to treat it with a suitable reagent, or series of reagents, that will react with the colourless materials to give coloured areas.

In the examination of artifacts chromatography can be used to distinguish between pitch and bitumen, or between different types of resin, provided that they have not deteriorated with age; but the application of chromatography to determine whether egg, glue or oil was used as a medium in paints (p. 160) will be adequate to show the advantages and drawbacks of this method. Both egg and glue are essentially proteins, and are hence made up of large and complex molecules which, with age, oxidize and become insoluble. In this condition, however, they can be broken down by suitable dilute acids or alkalis to give a number of soluble organic materials which may be separated and identified by chromatography. One such compound, hydroxyproline, although present in glues, is absent from egg protein, and its presence or absence on the chromatograph will thus show which type of protein material has been used.

Oxidized oils, on the other hand, when broken down in a similar manner, give quite different end products to proteins, namely glycerol and a number of different organic acids. These ingredients can also be separated and identified by chromatography, but while all oils will provide glycerol in this way, different oils will produce varying proportions of different organic acids. These, in a small sample, can be very difficult to separate and identify and as a general rule it is doubtful whether the results would normally justify the effort of attempting to decide what oil was initially present. Any attempt to distinguish the source of protein in glues would be even less rewarding, for the composition of proteins from widely different animals and tissues is remarkably similar.

It is, in fact, fortunate that proteins and many oils are reasonably stable after oxidation, and thus endure longer and under less favourable conditions than might be expected. Other materials, and this is true of the resins, are less stable, and once oxidized it is virtually impossible to separate their ingredients by chromatography, and hence to demonstrate their source. In short, although it requires considerable skill and chemical knowledge, it is normally not difficult to distinguish between the major types of organic material—resin, wax, oil and so on—present in an artifact; but unless one is lucky, as in the case of egg and glue media just mentioned, there may be little or nothing present that will allow one to attempt further identification of the material.

BIBLIOGRAPHY

GENERAL

SINGER, C., HOLMYARD, E. J., and HALL, A. R. (Eds.), *A History of Technology*, Oxford, Vol. 1 (1954), Vol. 2 (1956), Vol. 3 (1957).

Only the first three volumes of this five-volume work fall within the scope of this book. Although the standard work on the subject, and likely to remain so for a long time, it is not without serious omissions—e.g. the spinning of sheet metal is not mentioned in Vol. 1, although practised widely under the Roman Empire. Recent work has made many of the contributions obsolete.

FORBES, R. J., *Studies in Ancient Technology*, Leiden, Vol. 1 (1955), Vol. 2 (1955), Vol. 3 (1955), Vol. 4 (1956), Vol. 5 (1957), Vol. 6 (1958), Vol. 7 (1963), Vol. 8 (1964), Vol. 9 (1964).

The following essays are relevant to this book: Vol. 1, Bitumen; Vol. 3, Paints and Pigments; Vol. 4, Fibres and Fabrics; Vol. 5, Leather and Glass; Vol. 6, Fuel; Vol. 7, Mining and Quarrying; Vol. 8, Metallurgy of Gold, Silver, Lead and Zinc; Vol. 9, Copper, Tin, Bronze and early Iron. The essays are particularly valuable for their wealth of historical references.

LUCAS, A., *Ancient Egyptian Materials and Techniques*, London (4th edn.), 1962.

The title is somewhat misleading since frequent reference is made to materials and techniques in other Near Eastern countries. An exceptionally valuable source book. One only wishes there were others like it dealing with, e.g. the Greek or Roman materials.

NEUBURGER, A., *The Technical Arts of the Ancients*, London, 1930.

Originally published in German in 1921, this work has recently been reprinted. Although the book contains a number of statements which in the light of more recent research are questionable, it remains an interesting account of Greek and Roman technology.

KLEMM, F., *A History of Western Technology*, London, 1959.

Essentially this is an annotated series of quotations from writers of antiquity to modern times. Its major value lies in the picture it gives of changing attitudes to technological development.

JENKINS, J. G., *Traditional Country Craftsmen*, London, 1965.
STOWE, E. J., *Crafts of the Countryside*, London, 1948.
ARNOLD, J., *The Countryman's Workshop*, London, 1953.
WYMER, N., *English Country Crafts*, London, 1946.

These four books all cover much the same ground—'traditional' rural crafts. Their particular value lies in the description of raw materials and tools, as well as the craft vocabularies. Similar territory is covered in the

New World under the heading of 'colonial' and 'pioneer' crafts in such books as:

TUNIS, E., *Colonial Craftsmen*, New York, 1965.

GUILLET, E. C., *Pioneer Arts and Crafts*, Toronto, 1968.

GRISWOLD, L. and K., *The New Handicraft Processes and Projects*, (10th edn.), New York, 1969.

The original edition of this book, published in 1925, was intended as a guide to home handicrafts such as pottery, weaving, basketry, woodworking and light metalworking. It contains a great deal of useful information about the manipulation of small tools and materials.

WULFF, H. E., *The Traditional Crafts of Persia*, Cambridge (Mass.), 1967.

The outcome of a recent survey of the modern craftsmen of Persia, this work includes useful historical introductions to each section.

HOMMEL, R. P., *China at Work*, Cambridge (Mass.), 1969.

This book, which covers a wide range of crafts, was also the result of a survey made between 1921 and 1930. While the work covers in detail the everyday crafts, it has little to say about the finer crafts such as jadeworking, lacquerwork and porcelain.

LEVEY, M., *Chemistry and Chemical Technology in Ancient Mesopotamia*, Amsterdam, 1954.

The text covers a rather wider field than the title might suggest. A useful account depending to a large degree on written sources.

STILLMAN, J. M., *The Story of Alchemy and Early Chemistry*, New York, 1960.

Originally published in 1924 under the title *The Story of Early Chemistry*, the initial chapters of this book give a lucid account of chemical and craft processes as understood by the ancients.

PARTINGTON, J. R., *A History of Chemistry*, Vol. 1 (to A.D. 1500), London, 1963.

This book is especially valuable for its account of early technological processes.

SPIER, R. F. (Ed.), *From the Hand of Man*, Boston (Mass.), 1970.

A valuable group of essays which consider primitive and pre-industrial technology from a number of very different standpoints.

DAVEY, N., *A History of Building Materials*, London, 1961.

A concise account of the preparation and use of stone, straw and reed, brick, plaster, mortars and cement, tiles and mosaic in the Old World.

ANCIENT TEXTS

Although often difficult to understand and frequently confusing the following ancient texts are invaluable as sources of information about ancient technology:

PLINIUS SECUNDUS, CAIUS (PLINY), *Historia Naturalis*. English editions by Bostock, J. and Riley, H. T., London, 1898 and Rackham, B. and Jones, W., London 1938.

A mine of information on subjects as diverse as metalworking, gemstones, glass and pigments in the ancient world.

VITRUVIUS, POLLIO, *Architectura*. English translation by Granger, London, 1956.
Like the work of Pliny the work contains a great deal of information on early technology throughout.

HERACLIUS (ERACLIUS), *De Artibus Romanorum*. English translation in Merifield, M. P., *Original treatises on the Art of Painting*, London, 1849, reprinted New York, 1969.
Written between the tenth and twelfth centuries A.D., the work describes the decorative arts of the period.

THEOPHILUS PRESBYTER (RUGERUS), *Schedula Diversarum Artium*. English translations by Hendrie, R., London, 1847, and Hawthorne, J. G. and Smith, C. S., Chicago, 1963.
A work similar in date and scope to that of Heraclius.

CELLINI, BENVENUTO, *Sopra l'Oreficeria e la Scultura*. English translation by Ashbee, C. R., London, 1888. Reprinted, 1967.

CENNINI, CENNIO, *Il Libro dell'Arte*. English translation by Thompson, D. V., Yale, 1933.

VASARI, GIORGIO, Introductory Chapters to his *Lives of the Artists*. English translation [*Vasari on Technique*] by Maclehose, L. and Brown, G. B., London, 1907.
Quite apart from the technology of painting, these three works cover a wide range of crafts as practised in the late Middle Ages and Renaissance. They are also valuable in the way they reflect the old craftsman's attitude to his work.

BIRINGUCCIO, VANNOCCIO, *De la Pirotechnia*, 1540. English translation by Smith, C. S. and Gnudi, M. T., New York, 1943.
Although concerned primarily with the mining, refining and shaping of metals, this work also contains sections on such topics as glass, minerals and gunpowder.

AGRICOLA, GEORG (BAUER), *De Re Metallica*, 1556. English translation by Hoover, H. C. and Hoover, L. H., New York, 1950.
A comprehensive treatise on mining, smelting and metalworking. The wood-cuts are most informative.

PICCOLOPASSO, CIPRIANO, *I Tre Libri dell'Arte del Vasajo*. English translation by Rackham, B. and Van de Put, A., London, 1934.
Unfortunately a limited edition and virtually unobtainable. Invaluable as an introduction to late Medieval and Renaissance pottery manufacture.

AMMAN, J. and SACHS, H., *Ständebuch*, 1568. Edited by Rifkin, B. A. [*Book of Trades*] New York, 1973.
A fascinating series of woodcuts by Amman depicting a wide range of medieval craftsmen at work.

ERCKER, L., *Allefürnemsten mineralischen Erzt und Berckwerksorten*, Prague, 1574. Translation by Sisco, A. G. and Serieter, C. S., *Treatise on Ores and Assaying*, Chicago, 1951.

This work covers much the same ground as the earlier book by Agricola.

DIDEROT, D., *Encyclopédie*, Paris, 1777.

The engravings have been republished as *A Diderot Pictorial Encyclopedia of Trades and Industry*, New York, 1962.

The pictures are invaluable as a source of information about eighteenth century technology.

PYNE, W. H., *Microcosm*, London, 1819. Reprinted, 1969.

The illustrations are particularly useful on the subject of rural crafts.

AUTOBIOGRAPHIES

The following modern autobiographies are of particular interest in that the authors are deeply concerned with the tools and materials of their various callings.

LEACH, B., *A Potter's Book*, London, 1940.

Contains a wealth of useful information about earthenware, simple glazes and wood-firing.

CARDEW, M., *Pioneer Pottery*, London, 1969.

An interesting approach to 'primitive' and studio pottery production.

STURT, G., *The Wheelwright's Shop*, Cambridge, 1934.

This book contains a most vivid account of blacksmithing, invaluable to those studying ironwork.

HULL, D. H., *Casting of Brass and Bronze*, Cleveland, 1950.

A useful account dealing with the vicissitudes of casting copper alloys. Very readable.

BENFIELD, F., *Purbeck Shop*, Cambridge, 1938.

Gives a vivid description of quarrying and masonry work.

ROSE, W., *The Village Carpenter*, Cambridge, 1938.

The descriptions of the uses of now obsolete tools such as the auger are most valuable.

CERAMICS, GLASS AND ENAMELS

SHEPARD, ANNA O., *Ceramics for the Archaeologist*, Washington, 1956.

This is the only book on the subject of pottery technology written specifically for archaeologists. Unfortunately the illustrative examples refer almost entirely to ceramics from the South-Western United States and Mexico, and to those not familiar with those wares this can make reading difficult. This tends to obscure the general excellence of the book. Glazes are not discussed.

FOSTER, G., *Contemporary Pottery Techniques in Southern and Central Mexico*, Tulane, 1955.

This is a regional study of simple pottery techniques based on very wide first-hand knowledge of the area. Its particular value lies in the unusually wide variety of technologies within the region and their interrelationship.

RIETH, A., *5,000 Jahre Topferscheibe*, Konstanz, 1960.
A profusely illustrated monograph on the development of the potters' wheel.

RIEGGAR, H., *Primitive Pottery*, New York, 1972.
This is an interesting, if somewhat personal, approach to a study of the problems that must have beset early man when making pottery.

KENNY, J. B., *The Complete Book of Pottery Making*, London, 1949.
A profusely illustrated and very clear account of the work of the studio potter.

RHODES, D., *Clay and Glazes for the Potter*, London, 1958.
Valuable for its description of the properties of clays and the simple explanation of the formulation of glazes.

RHODES, D., *Kilns*, Philadelphia, 1968.
A useful account of kiln construction and function written for the artist potter.

NORTON, F. H., *Ceramics for the Artist Potter*, 1956.
A clear account of the behaviour of clays and glazes during the process of firing.

NORTON, F. H., *Elements of Ceramics*, Reading (Mass.), 1974.
A scientifically orientated account of potter, glass and enamels.

RADO, P., *An Introduction to the Technology of Pottery*, London, 1969.
A lucid account of simple and industrial processes used in the manufacture of pottery.

CORNING MUSEUM OF GLASS, *Glass from the Ancient World*, Corning, 1957.
A beautifully illustrated description of early glass and the materials and processes used in its manufacture.

OPPENHEIM, A. L., BRILL, R. H., BARAG, D. and VON SALDERN, A., *Glass and Glassmaking in Ancient Mesopotamia*, Corning, 1970.
A valuable discussion of early glassmaking techniques.

NEUBURG, F., *Ancient Glass*, London, 1962.
FOSSING, P., *Glass Vessels before Glass-blowing*, Copenhagen, 1940.
Two short and useful accounts of the development of early glass manufacture from the manipulative point of view. Neither says much about the preparation of glass metal.

FLAVELL, R. and SMALE, C., *Studio Glassmaking*, New York, 1974.
An excellently illustrated account of glass manipulation and hand-forming techniques.

REYNTIENS, P., *The Technique of Stained Glass*, London, 1967.
Written primarily for the modern craftsman, this book contains a wealth of useful historical information.

BATES, K. F., *Enamelling: Principles and Practice*, New York, 1951.

UNTRACHT, O., *Enamelling on Metal*, London, 1958.
Two of a number of books on enamelling for the modern craftsman. Valuable particularly for the description of enamel formulation.

METALS

AITCHISON, L., *A History of Metals*, London, 1960.
A very readable and well-balanced account of the development of metallurgical techniques.

TYLECOTE, R. F., *Metallurgy in Archaeology*, London, 1962.
A most useful assessment of the present state of knowledge about early metallurgy in the British Isles derived from archaeological sources.

SCHUBERT, H. R., *History of the British Iron and Steel Industry*, London, 1957.
A clear, non-specialist account, with valuable chapters on the development of the foundry and forge.

OLDEBERG, A., *Metallteknik under Forhistorik Tid*, Lund, 1942.
A detailed account of metallurgy, particularly of bronze, in prehistoric northern Europe.

DRESCHER, H., *Der Uberfanggus*, Mainz, 1958.
A very valuable monograph on the technique of bronze casting-on in prehistoric Europe.

MARYON, H., *Metalworking and Enamelling*, London, (3rd edn.), 1954.
WILSON, H., *Silverwork and Jewellery*, London, (2nd edn.), 1951.
Both books were written by craftsmen of wide repute. In either case the subject of fine metalworking is clearly described.

UNTRACT, O., *Metal techniques for Craftsmen*, New York, 1968.
An exhaustive account of metalworking tools and techniques. Profusely illustrated with examples of both ancient and modern work.

SUTHERLAND, C. H. V., *Gold*, London, 1969.
The initial chapters of this book which cover the early mining and shaping of gold are particularly useful.

HOGG, G., Hammer and Tongs: *Blacksmithing Down the Ages*, London, 1964.
A historical account of iron-forging in which the chapters on decorative ironwork are very informative.

BEALER, A. W., *The Art of Blacksmithing*, New York, 1969.
This is perhaps the most profusely illustrated and exhaustive account of 'traditional' blacksmithing yet to be published.

STONE AND STONE-WORKING

HOLMES, W. H., *Handbook of Aboriginal American Antiquities*, Washington, 1919.
The title is misleading. The book gives a detailed account of stone-working techniques in pre-Columbian America. Applicable to a much wider field, this is the only general account of stone-working before steel tools.

ARKELL, W. J., *Oxford Stone*, Oxford, 1947.
A very readable account of quarrying and building in the Oxford region. Written for the non-specialist.

ARKELL, W. J., and TOMKEIEFF, S. I., *English Rock Terms*, Oxford, 1953.
The terminology of the quarryman and mason.

BLUEMEL, C., *Greek Sculptors at Work*, London, 1955.
A brief, but well-illustrated account of the equipment and working methods of Greek Sculptors.

MILLER, A., *Stone and Marble Carving*, London, 1948.
A clear, very readable account of modern sculptors' methods.

SMITH, G. F. H., *Gemstones*, London (10th edn.), 1949.
A very useful account of precious and semi-precious stones with a short description of cutting techniques.

SINKANKAS, J., *Gem Cutting*, Princeton, 1955.
This account of modern lapidary work includes much useful historical information.

HANSFORD, S. H., *Chinese Jade Carving*, London, 1949.
A valuable account of abrasion cutting and polishing with primitive tools.

WOODWORKING

EDLIN, H. L., *Woodland Crafts in Britain*, London, 1949.
A valuable general account of British timbers and their utilization with descriptions of working methods, many of them primitive.

GOODMAN, W. L., *A History of Wood-working Tools*, London, 1964.
A well illustrated and concise account of the development of the major types of wood-working tools.

WILDUNG, F. H., *Woodworking Tools at Shelburne Museum*, Riverdale (Md.), 1957.
MERCER, H. C., *Ancient Carpenters' Tools*, Doylestown (Penn.), 1960.
SLOANE, E., *A Museum of Early American Tools*, New York, 1964.
WELSH, P. C., *Woodworking Tools*, Washington, 1966.
BEALER, A. W., *Old Ways of Working Wood*, Barre (Mass.), 1972.
BLACKBURN, G., *An Illustrated Encyclopedia of Woodworking Handtools, Instruments and Devices*, New York, 1975.
These six books all cover very similar ground, although in very different ways, and are devoted almost entirely to a study of the woodworking tools in use in colonial and pioneer North America.

GREBER, J. M., *Die Geschichte des Hobels*, Zurich, 1956.
A detailed account of the development of the carpenter's plane.

KILBY, K., *The Cooper and his Trade*, London, 1971.
A comprehensive account of coopering in its many and diverse forms.

PINTO, E. H., *Treen and Other Wooden Bygones*, London, 1969.
An excellent description of turned wooden objects and other small carvings.

FIBRES AND TEXTILES

CROWFOOT, GRACE M., *Methods of Hand Spinning in Egypt and the Sudan*, Halifax, 1931.
Partly archaeological, partly ethnographic. A most useful introduction to hand spinning.

FANNIN, A., *Handspinning Art and Technique*, New York, 1970.
A comprehensive account of the history and techniques of spinning.

ROTH, L., *Primitive Looms*, Halifax, (3rd edn.), 1950.
A very valuable commentary on primitive looms from all parts of the world, with detailed accounts of their working.

HOFFMANN, MARTA, *The Warp-Weighted Loom*, Oslo, 1964.
A clearly illustrated study of surviving looms of this type from N. Europe, with valuable chapters on early looms.

BIRRELL, V., *The Textile Arts*, New York, 1973.
An excellent introduction to weaving, with and without a loom. Contains a concise history of weaving.

REGENSTEINER, E., *The Art of Weaving*, New York, 1970.
Written for the amateur weaver, this book gives a detailed account of how to set up most common looms and to weave on them.

EMERY, I., *The Primary Structures of Fabrics*, Washington, 1966.
A very systematic approach to the classification and description of textiles, essential to anyone working in this area.

MARKS, S. S. (Ed.), *Fairchild's Dictionary of Textiles*, London, 1959.
Based on the classic dictionary by Harmuth. An essential work of reference.

PRITCHARD, M. E., *A Short Dictionary of Weaving*, London, 1954.
A useful dictionary with a valuable section on vegetable dyes.

HARVEY, V., *Techniques of Basketry*, New York, 1974.
A very complete guide to all forms of basketry, both from the point of view of materials and of technique.

CRAMPTON, C., *Canework*, London, 1949.
One of a great number of books on basketry. Clear and concise. Brief chapter on history of basketry.

HUNTER, D., *Papermaking*, (2nd edn.), 1947.
The history of papermaking. A useful concise account.

BONE, HORN AND IVORY

PENNIMAN, T. K., *Pictures of Ivory and Other Animal Teeth, Bone and Antler*, Oxford, 1952.
A brief account of the distinguishing features of these materials.

WILLIAMSON, G. G., *The Book of Ivory*, London, 1938.
This book is not very useful from the present point of view, but it appears to be the only work of its kind.

PIGMENTS AND ADHESIVES

CHURCH, A. H., *The Chemistry of Paints and Painting*, London (2nd edn.), 1892.
Despite its age, a valuable source-book on the subject of media and pigments.

GETTENS, R. J. and STOUT, G. L., *Painting Materials: A Short Encyclopaedia*, New York, 1942.
A most valuable reference book.

THOMPSON, D. V., *The Materials of Medieval Painting*, London, 1956.
A useful, non-specialist, account of the subject.

BENTLEY, K. W., *The Natural Pigments*, London, 1960.
A useful general account of the natural pigments and dyes and their application.

MAIRET, ETHEL, *Vegetable Dyes*, London, 1939.
A very comprehensive account of vegetable dyes and dyeing.

HICKS, E., *Shellac: Its Origin and Applications*, London, 1961.
A useful account of Shellac, its preparation and use.

EXAMINATION: GENERAL

AITKEN, M. J., *Physics and Archaeology*, London, 1961.
The larger part of this book deals with methods of surveying and dating, but the final section gives a clear account of analytical methods.

BROTHWELL, D. R., and HIGGS, E. S. (Eds.), *Science in Archaeology*, London, 1963.
PYDOKE, E. (Ed.), *The Scientist and Archaeology*, London, 1963.
Both books cover in considerable detail various aspects of the material and technological examination of artifacts.

SEMENOV, S. A., *Prehistoric Technology*, London, 1964.
Despite the title, the book deals only with wear and fabrication marks on bone and stone tools viewed under the microscope. The methods of study are similar to those used in the police laboratory.

TITE, M. S., *Methods of Physical Examination in Archaeology*, London, 1972.
Although the first part of this book deals with methods of locating sites and the determination of age, the second part is most relevant giving a concise account of the methods used in the physical examination of artifacts.

BRILL, R. H. (Ed.), *Science and Archaeology*, Cambridge (Mass.), 1971.
LEVEY, M. (Ed.), *Archaeological Chemistry*, Philadelphia, 1967.
Both these books are the outcome of symposia and contain many valuable contributions that deal with the technological examination of a wide range of artifacts.

EXAMINATION OF ROCKS AND MINERALS

READ, H. H. (Ed.), *Rutley's Elements of Mineralogy*, London, 1948.
A most useful work of reference for the description of minerals, their properties and occurrence.

SMITH, H. G., *Minerals and the Microscope*, London (5th edn.), 1956.
A short but clear introduction to minerals in thin-section.

KEMP, J. F., *Handbook of Rocks*, New York (6th edn.), 1940.
A valuable account of the examination of rocks by macroscopic methods.

HARKER, A., *Petrology for Students*, Cambridge (8th edn.), 1954.
MOORHOUSE, W. W., *The Study of Rocks in Thin Section*, New York, 1959.
Two reasonably concise accounts of the thin-section examination of rocks. Both require of the reader a general knowledge of petrology.

EXAMINATION OF CERAMICS AND GLASSES

INSLEY, H., and FRECHETTE, V. D., *Microscopy of Ceramics and Cements*, New York, 1955.
RIGBY, G. R., *The Thin-Section Mineralogy of Ceramic Materials*, London, 1953.
Both books give a brief account of the use of the petrological microscope for the examination of ceramics. A knowledge of the mineralogy of ceramic materials is required of the reader.

CALEY, E. R., *Analyses of Ancient Glasses, 1790-1957*, New York, 1962.
A very valuable and clear account of the results of analyses of glasses.

EXAMINATION OF METALS

ALEXANDER, W., and STREET, A., *Metals in the Service of Man*, London, (3rd edn.), 1954.
The chapters on the structure of metals and metallography are a most useful simple introduction to the subject.

ROGERS, B. A., *The Nature of Metals*, Cambridge (Mass.), 1967.
SHRAGER, A. M., *Elementary Metallurgy and Metallography*, London, 1949.
Both books are written for students with little knowledge of the subject and give clear accounts of metallography.

SMITH, C. S., *A History of Metallography*, Chicago, 1960.
The early chapters dealing with pattern-welding and damascening are very valuable. Some knowledge of metallography is required of the reader.

CALEY, E. R., *Analysis of Ancient Metals*, London, 1964.
Discusses in detail the chemical, and in outline the spectroscopic analyses of metals. Much of the book requires a knowledge of chemistry in the reader, but there are valuable chapters of a more general nature.

GETTENS, R. J., *The Freer Chinese Bronzes, II*, Washington, 1969.
Although concerned only with the examination of early Chinese

bronzes, this book is a classic example of how to set about a technological study of this nature.

DOERINGER, S., MITTEN, D. G. and STEINBERG, A., *Art and Technology: A Symposium on Classical Bronzes*, New York, 1970.
An interesting group of essays many of which consider the problems of casting Greek and Roman bronzes.

EXAMINATION OF ORGANIC MATERIALS

TIEMANN, H. D., *Wood Technology*, London, 1947.
Contains useful clear chapters on the structure of woods and identification of timbers under the microscope.

SCHWANKL, A., *What Wood is That?* London 1956.
A useful, short introduction to the identification of timbers.

JANE, F. W., *The Structure of Wood*, London, 1956.
A detailed account requiring some knowledge of botany of the reader.

HEYN, A. N. J., *Fiber Microscopy*, New York, 1954.
STOVES, J. L., *Fibre Microscopy*, London, 1957.
LUNIAK, B., *Identification of Textile Fibres*, London, 1953.
All three books were written for the laboratory staffs of the textile and fur industries, and all give clear accounts of methods of examination.

GREEN, A. G., *The Analysis of Dyestuffs*, London, 1920.
Their identification in dyed and coloured materials. Requires a knowledge of chemistry of the reader.

INDEX